Hertfordshire
COUNTY COUNCIL
Community Information

2 8 AUG 2008

6/12

99

L32a

Please renew/return this item by the last date shown.

So that your telephone call is charged at local rate, please call the numbers as set out below:

	From Area codes 01923 or 0208:	From the rest of Herts:
Renewals:	01923 471373	01438 737373
Enquiries:	01923 471333	01438 737333
Minicom:	01923 471599	01438 737599

L32b

Zeile, 49,

D1327747

The Arctic Convoys

THE ARCTIC CONVOYS

Vice Admiral B. B. Schofield

MACDONALD AND JANE'S · LONDON

© 1977 Vice Admiral B.B. Schofield

First published in 1977 by
Macdonald and Jane's Publishers Limited
Paulton House, 8 Shepherdess Walk
London N1 7LW

ISBN 0354 01112 X

Maps and drawings by Ronald Nydegger Jr

Printed in Great Britain by
REDWOOD BURN LIMITED
Trowbridge & Esher

05.1.4P

Contents

APPENDIXES

LIST OF ILLUSTRATIONS
PHOTOGRAPHS

Between pages 38 and 39

The forecastle of HMS *Witch* almost unrecognisable under a thick coating of Arctic ice. *National Maritime Museum*

The German heavy cruiser *Admiral Hipper* in northern Norway where she formed part of the Northern Battle Group. *Imperial War Museum*

The triple 6in gun turrets of the cruiser HMS *Belfast* covered in ice. *Imperial War Museum*

Admiral Arseni Golovko, C-in-C Soviet Northern Fleet, and Rear Admiral D.B. Fisher, Senior British Naval Officer, North Russia. *Novosti Press*

Admiral Golovko, C-in-C Soviet Northern Fleet. *Novosti Press*

HMS *Onslow* and HMS *Ashanti* during operations in the Arctic. *Imperial War Museum*

HMS *Bulldog* one of the 1930 'B' class British destroyers converted for convoy escort operations. *Imperial War Museum*

HMS *Belfast* which rejoined the Home Fleet after repairs to extensive mine damage suffered early in the war. *Imperial War Museum*

The anti-aircraft ship HMS *Pozarica* – a converted merchantman. *Imperial War Museum*

A stick of bombs from German aircraft falls amongst ships of an Arctic convoy. *Imperial War Museum*

Russian naval choir entertains the officers and ship's company of the battleship HMS *Duke of York*. *Imperial War Museum*

An ammunition ship explodes during an air attack on convoy PQ 18 on 14 September 1942. *Imperial War Museum*

The Soviet submarine *K 21* in the Kola Inlet, showing the bleak nature of the surroundings. *Novosti Press*

Between pages 134 and 135

Swordfish IIIs of 813 Squadron (HMS *Campania*) at Murmansk early in 1945. *Imperial War Museum*

Swordfish aircraft on the flight deck of the Merchant Aircraft Carrier (MAC-ship) *Ancylus* in the Arctic. *Imperial War Museum*

The escort carrier HMS *Trumpeter* edges through the pack ice. *Admiralty*

Sweeping the decks of snow for the Swordfish of 842 Squadron aboard HMS *Fencer*. *Imperial War Museum*

The escort carrier *Nairana* seen from *Fencer*. *J.D. Brown*

A Swordfish of HMS *Activity*, in April 1944 covering Arctic convoys JW 58 and RA 59. *Imperial War Museum*

The German heavy cruiser *Admiral Hipper* and a destroyer in northern waters in July 1942. *J.D. Brown*

The Canadian corvette HMCS *Cobalt*, was typical of the small warships which escorted the Arctic convoys. *Imperial War Museum*

The crew of a cruiser's 6in gun turret try to snatch some sleep or read to pass the time. *National Maritime Museum*

Merchant ships of the Arctic convoy skirt the pack ice as they near the Kola Inlet. *National Maritime Museum*

Snow-covered Hellcats on board an escort carrier operating in pancake ice. *National Maritime Museum*

The German destroyer *Z28* was fitted out as a flotilla leader with extra accommodation in place of one 15cm gun on the after superstructure. *Foto Drüppel*

HMS *Anchusa*, another example of the 'Flower' Class corvette. *Admiralty*

MAPS AND DIAGRAMS

Acknowledgments

The author wishes to acknowledge with thanks the help of all those who, in one way or another, have assisted him with the writing of this book. In particular he would like to thank Rear Admiral Peter Buckley CB, DSO, and the Staff of the Admiralty Library, the Staff of the Ministry of Defence (RUSI) Library, Dr F. Forstmeier of the Militargeschichtles Forschungsamt, Freiburg, and Dr Jurgen Rohwer of the Bibliothek für Zeitgeschichte, Stuttgart. He also wishes to acknowledge the help of his wife who typed the manuscript.

The author and publishers wish to thank all those who have given permission for quotations to be made in this book from those of which they hold the copyright, viz. Messrs B. T. Batsford for whom the author had already written a book on *The Russian Convoys*, William Kimber and Company Ltd, Putnam & Co Ltd, Barrie & Jenkins Ltd, Cassell & Co Ltd, Hamish Hamilton, George Weidenfeld & Nicolson Ltd, Frederick Muller Ltd, Wehr und Wissen Verlagsgesellschaft, Athenäum Verlag, Bonn, and the Keeper of Stationery & Printing, Her Majesty's Stationery Office.

Diagram I

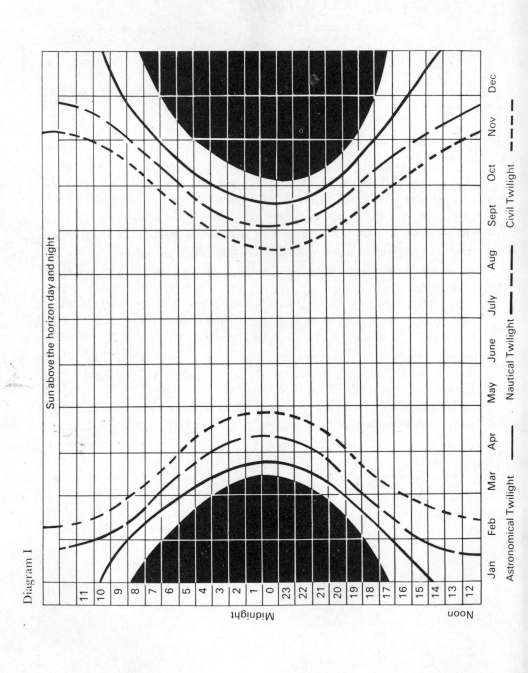

Sun above the horizon day and night

Astronomical Twilight ——— Nautical Twilight — — — Civil Twilight — · · —

Introduction

'They fought their way through, whatever the odds, during four years of war and so made a great contribution to the final victory.'
Admiral of the Fleet SIR RHODERICK McGRIGOR, GCB, DSO[1]

Convoy operations produced some of the hardest fought battles of the Second World War, notably in the Arctic and Atlantic Oceans and in the Mediterranean Sea. Because of the adverse climatic conditions and the enemy's favourable strategic situation, those which occurred round the Arctic convoys fighting their way to and from north Russia have a heroic character all of their own. They took place frequently under conditions bordering on the limits of human endurance, when the cold was so intense that no amount of clothing could keep it out. Spray froze on masts, rigging, and decks as it fell inboard, so that it was a constant struggle to keep guns in working order and, in the case of small ships like trawlers, to prevent the ship from becoming top heavy due to an accumulation of ice.

After assembly in a Scottish port or in the bleak harbour of Hvalfiord on the west coast of Iceland, the convoys were routed through the Norwegian and Barents Seas to Russia's only ice-free port Murmansk, at the head of the Kola Inlet. When ice conditions allowed, use was also made of the White Sea ports of Archangel and Molotovsk. The area through which the convoys sailed is notorious for blizzards, fog, and gales of great intensity, and the high northern latitudes produce a winter of perpetual night, changing gradually to a summer of continuous day (see Diagram I) – circumstances which had a profound effect on the operation of the convoys. The Northern Lights or Aurora Borealis, regarded in ancient times as portents of disaster, stretched their brilliantly coloured filaments of light across the night sky like the talons of some aerial monster clutching at the heavily laden merchants ships as they ploughed their way through the icy seas. The seasonal movements of the polar ice field which in winter sometimes approach to within 80 miles of the North Cape, whilst in summer recede as far as the north coast of Spitzbergen, also affected the operation of the convoys, the routes of which had to

---

[1] Vice Admiral Sir Ian Campbell and Captain Donald Macintyre, *The Kola Run* (Frederick Muller Ltd) Foreword, 1958

be adjusted accordingly. Even under the most favourable conditions, once east of the meridian of Greenwich, they could not avoid coming within range of the German aircraft stationed in north Norway and so they remained since the port of Murmansk lay only 90 miles from the nearest enemy airfield, and even Archangel 450 miles further east was not beyond their reach.

The warm water of the Gulf Stream which sweeps in a north-easterly direction across the Atlantic and up the Norwegian coast produces both fog and poor Sonar operating conditions when it mixes with the cold water of the Arctic, thus favouring the operation of submarines. Further, the deep water fiords with which the rugged Norwegian coast is indented provided the enemy with good anchorages from which ships could sally out and attack the convoys passing to the north of them.

These then were the circumstances in which Britain and the United States endeavoured to bring aid to Russia after that country had been invaded by Germany in June 1941. In the annals of maritime warfare no more difficult task has been attempted. 'In the light of previous strategical experience', wrote the late Professor Michael Lewis, 'we were undertaking the impossible task of passing convoys along hundreds of miles of enemy-held territory, where the air was completely dominated by the Luftwaffe, the sea patrolled by most of the surviving enemy surface fleet, and as many U-boats as Hitler cared to spare.'[1] How these difficulties were met and finally overcome are related within the pages of this book.

---

[1] Michael Lewis, *The History of the British Navy* (George Allen & Unwin Ltd, 1957), page 233

Chapter 1
OPERATION BARBAROSSA

Admiral Raeder's views

When on 1 March 1940 Hitler ordered planning to begin for the invasion of
Norway, the Commander-in-Chief of the German Navy, Grand Admiral
Erich Raeder fully supported the decision. It fitted in well with his plans for
the employment of both his surface ships and submarines which required
'that he must be firmly established in Norway in order to procure for the
German naval forces free and certain access to the Atlantic'.[1] It proved to be
a bold and successful stroke but it cost the German navy 1 heavy and 2 light
cruisers, 10 destroyers, 1 torpedo boat, 6 U-boats, and 15 minor craft. In
addition, both the battle-cruisers *Scharnhorst* and *Gneisenau* were damaged. Against this, Allied losses had amounted to 1 aircraft carrier, 1 cruiser,
1 anti-aircraft cruiser, 9 destroyers, and 6 submarines, but in proportion to
the size of their naval resources the German losses were the more severe
and, as events were to show, could be ill-afforded. However, as Raeder had
foreseen, the strategic gain was substantial, in fact even more so than he
realised at the time.

'I am not able to say when Hitler first began to consider seriously the
possibility of a campaign against Russia',[2] Raeder has written, but we now
know that in July 1940 Hitler had ordered his military advisers to start
planning for an attack on the Soviet Union without telling his naval
Commander-in-Chief who he knew was opposed to any action in the east so
long as Britain remained undefeated. The Russo-German Non-Aggression
Pact signed on 23 August 1939 suited Raeder very well as it meant that he
did not have to maintain ships in the Baltic with which to oppose the Russian
fleet and could concentrate all available forces in the North Sea and the
Atlantic. At a conference with Hitler on 26 September 1940, Raeder gave

---

[1] Carl Axel Gemsel, *Raeder, Hitler und Skandinavien* (Bernard und Graefe, 1965) page 235
[2] Grand Admiral Raeder, *Struggle for the Sea* (William Kimber and Company Ltd, 1959) page
193

his views on the future strategy of the war as he saw it. He favoured operations in the Mediterranean to include the capture of Gibraltar and Malta and the elimination of the British fleet from that sea, so freeing the Italian fleet for operations in the Atlantic. He advocated support for the Italian army in Libya to bring about the capture of the Suez Canal, followed by the occupation of Palestine and French mandated Syria. Thus Turkey and the Balkans would be cut off from British help and the way opened for an attack on the vital British oil supplies from the Middle East. It was an ambitious and on the whole, strategically sound plan, but Spanish co-operation was essential, and this was not forthcoming. Hitler gave the plan conditional approval and said he would confer with Mussolini and possibly General Franco as soon as the Japanese alliance was completed. France would need to be consulted about the proposed advance into Syria. Meanwhile, Britain strengthened her position in the Mediterranean despite the threat of invasion realising, as did Raeder, that as happened during the Napoleonic wars this would become the crucial theatre of the war.

Meanwhile other events conspired to reinforce Hitler's decision to attack Russia. That country's seizure of Lithuania, Estonia, and Latvia, and her ultimatum to Rumania demanding the return of Bessarabia and the surrender of northern Bukovina, had aroused Hitler's suspicions of her intentions and his anxiety about the Rumanian oil fields on which Germany depended for fuel. He came to believe that Britain's refusal to give in might be based on the hope of Russian intervention. On 18 December 1940, 'Führer Directive No 21[1], code-named *Barbarossa*, was issued. It envisaged an attack on the Soviet Union in May of the following year. Although the issue of such a Directive indicated that all further argument was useless, on 27 December Raeder made his final protest against it and pleaded once more for the adoption of his Mediterranean plan. 'It is absolutely necessary to recognise that the greatest task of the hour is the concentration of all our power against Britain', he said[1], but it was of no avail. Hitler tried to console him with the thought that the war against Russia would be over by the end of the year and that it was only a question of postponing operations in the Mediterranean for a few months. However, things did not work out that way. The launching of operation *Barbarossa* had to be delayed from the middle of May to the end of June as a result of Mussolini's inopportune and unsuccessful attempt to invade Greece which obliged Hitler to come to his rescue and ultimately seize control of the Balkans. Moreover, contrary to Hitler's expectations,

---

[1] Führer Naval Conference, 27 December 1940, para 3 *The Führer Naval Conferences* (Her Majesty's Stationery Office, 1948)

the campaign in Russia was to become the dominating factor of the war in Europe not for a few months, but for three long years.

Russia's attitude

Meanwhile, the Russian Premier Josef Stalin, having got what he wanted, was leaning over backwards in his attempts to placate his western neighbour. He ignored the warnings conveyed to him through British intelligence of the threat which Hitler was mounting against his country and which finally gave him two weeks' notice of the date when the German attack was to be launched.

If Stalin deliberately shut his eyes to the events going on around him, the Commander-in-Chief of the Russian Northern Fleet Admiral Arseni Golovko, one of the ablest of Soviet admirals, apparently did not. 'The operations of the Nazis did not catch us napping', he has written, 'for we were intensely alert to the situation on the other side of the frontier both at sea and ashore.'[1] In a broadcast on the evening of the day the German armies launched their assault, 22 June 1941, the British Prime Minister Winston Churchill pledged the support of his country to Russia and the Russian people, but the sudden volte-face of his erstwhile ally gave the Russian Premier a nervous breakdown and he was at a loss for words in which to reply to this generous offer. Also the memory of the Munich agreement and the abortive Anglo–French–Soviet discussions in the summer of 1939 had left a sour taste in his mouth. However, after recovering from the initial shock, on 18 July he replied to a personal message addressed to him by Churchill eleven days previously, with a request for the opening of a Second Front, a theme which as Churchill has recorded 'was to recur throughout our subsequent relations with monotonous disregard, except in the Far North, for physical facts.'[2] Churchill replied at length and informed Stalin that a sea-borne strike against German shipping in the north of Norway and Finland was being planned and that cruisers and destroyers were being sent to Spitzbergen as well as submarines to intercept German traffic along the Arctic coast. Further, the minelayer HMS *Adventure*, was being despatched to Archangel with various supplies which included an outfit of mines. These, according to Admiral Golovko 'were only suitable where the depth of water did not exceed 20–25m and were consequently quite valueless to us.'[3]

---

[1] Admiral Arseni Golovko, *With the Red Fleet* (Putnam & Co. Ltd, 1965), page 20
[2] W.S. Churchill, *The Second World War* (Cassell & Co. Ltd, 1948-53), Volume III, page 343
[3] Golovko, ibid, page 91

In pursuance of these arrangements a force under Rear Admiral W. F. Wake-Walker comprising the carriers *Furious* and *Victorious* with the cruisers *Devonshire* and *Suffolk* escorted by 6 destroyers sailed from Scapa Flow on 23 July to attack German shipping and installations in the Kirkenes–Petsamo area. The force was sighted by enemy reconnaissance aircraft on 30 July so the element of surprise was lost, the results achieved small, and the losses in aircraft heavy, the strength of the defences particularly in the Kirkenes area being stronger than had been expected. However, the operation reinforced Raeder's argument which he had repeated to Hitler two days after the force had sailed, that the capture of Murmansk was of the greatest importance. In the event the toughness of the Russian resistance aided by the difficult and roadless terrain prevented the German troops from fulfilling the Admiral's wish, though they did eventually manage to cut the railway between Murmansk and Leningrad. The Russians, however, overcame this inconvenience by constructing a link line between Belomorsk and Obozerskaya on the Archangel–Moscow line.

Murmansk

The city and port of Murmansk which was to play such an important part in the history of the Arctic Convoys, lies at the head of the Kola Inlet, the entrance to which is situated 200 miles east of the North Cape and 450 miles west of the White Sea entrance to the port of Archangel. As already mentioned, it is ice-free all the year round, and owed its origin to the First World War when it was used to supply the Russian armies. In 1939 it had a population of about 130,000 but large numbers were evacuated when war broke out in 1941. The anti-aircraft defences of the city were minimal and it was not until July 1942 that these were strengthened effectively, by which time most of the town in the words of Admiral Golovko 'had ceased to exist'.[1] The port facilities, though adequate for handling ordinary cargo in small quantities, were not geared to meet the heavy demands which were soon to be placed upon them. The heaviest crane lift was 11 tons, insufficient for unloading tanks, so eventually a crane ship had to be sent there for this purpose. Moreover, the stocks of coal and fuel oil were insufficient to supply a convoy of ships and their escorts.

The Kola Inlet

On the eastern shore of the Kola Inlet, a few miles south of Murmansk, is

---

[1] Golovko, ibid, page 91

Vaenga where a tanker was moored from which the convoy escorts refuelled. It was not a good anchorage, the water being deep and the holding ground poor. At the head of the bay was a pier alongside which two destroyers could berth and where a hutted camp for the accommodation of survivors from ships lost in transit was constructed later. Merchant ships waiting to berth at Murmansk anchored between Vaenga and the port and whilst there they were often exposed to air attacks. Near the entrance to the Inlet on its western side lay the Soviet naval base of Polyarnoe, a deep, narrow, well protected harbour with wooden jetties alongside which the ships of the Northern Fleet were berthed. Strangely enough there is no mention in Admiral Golovko's memoirs of the size of the fleet he had been appointed to command, but according to a reliable German source, it consisted of 3 old and 5 modern destroyers (1 of which was sunk during the initial air attack), 7 patrol vessels which included 3 torpedo boats, 15 submarines, 2 minesweepers, 2 motor torpedo boats, 15 patrol craft, and a number of auxiliaries as well as 116 aircraft. During the following weeks, the strength of the Northern fleet was increased by the requisitioning of fishing vessels for use as patrol craft and minesweepers and through the transfer of motor torpedo boats from the Baltic. The submarine force was augmented by 8 boats from the Baltic fleet, 6 of which were operational by the end of 1941. During the following year, additional submarines joined from the Far Eastern fleet and the Caspian.

A White Sea Flotilla was formed under Rear Admiral G. A. Stepanov composed of fishing vessels and merchant ships and at one time reached a strength of 100 ships. It was assigned to the protection of the Northern Sea Route and operated under Glasevmorput, the authority responsible for administering this route. The liaison between the Commander-in-Chief, Northern Fleet, and the Glasevmorput was far from satisfactory as Admiral Golovko is at pains to point out. Moreover, the slenderness of Russian resources combined with a low level of training prevented the Northern Fleet from rendering assistance to the operation of the Arctic Convoys on the scale which it was hoped would be possible.

The British Home Fleet

The British Home Fleet based at Scapa Flow in the Orkneys, on which the main burden of escorting supplies to north Russia was to fall, was commanded by the 56-year-old, but remarkably young-looking, Admiral Sir John Tovey who had been awarded the DSO for distinguished service in destroyers at the Battle of Jutland during the First World War. His fleet's strength varied with the demands constantly being made upon it to provide ships for operations in other areas, but in 1941 it comprised 2 aircraft carriers (1 of which, the *Furious* was almost at the end of her effective life), 2 battleships, 4 cruisers, and about 20 destroyers. An advantage possessed by the Commander-in-Chief, Home Fleet, was a direct telephone link with the Admiralty when his flagship was at her buoy in Scapa Flow, which allowed him to discuss operational matters with the First Sea Lord in person.

As regards air co-operation, which now played such a highly important part in the war at sea, Admiral Tovey could deal through the Admiralty with the Commander-in-Chief, Coastal Command at his Headquarters at Northwood, near London, and also for day-to-day requirements of reconnaissance and anti-submarine patrols with Combined Area Headquarters at Pitreavie, near Rosyth, which was manned by a mixed staff of naval and air force officers. Although by mid-1941 the strength of Coastal Command had noticeably increased, the numbers of aircraft available were still insufficient to meet all the demands upon them. Moreover, operating conditions for aircraft as well as ships in high northern latitudes were very unfavourable, especially during the winter months.

Anglo-Russian co-operation

With a view to establishing contact with the Russian Northern Fleet, in mid-July Tovey despatched Rear Admiral Philip Vian by air to Polyarnoe to confer with Golovko. He was accompanied by Rear Admiral G. Miles who was about to take up his appointment with the Military Mission which the Russians had agreed to accept in Moscow. The object of the meeting was to discover what facilities were available in the Kola Inlet and of what the Russians were in particular need. From entries in his diary it appears that Golovko took to Miles better than he did to Vian whom he accused of being brusque and 'speaking in a loud, peremptory tone of voice'. Vian reported that the anti-aircraft defences of the Kola Inlet were inadequate to permit its use as a base for British forces and soon after his return, in accordance with Admiralty instructions, Tovey sent him with the cruisers *Nigeria* and *Aurora* and two destroyers to make a reconnaissance of Spitzbergen, the group of islands situated 450 miles north of the North Cape which the Admiralty thought might be used as a base in lieu of the Kola Inlet.

Although an offshoot of the Gulf Stream keeps the bays on the west coast of the islands ice-free during the summer, there were absolutely no facilities there apart from a camp for the men who worked the coal mines. It would have called for an immense construction effort to convert these ice-covered islands into an operational base so, after Vian's report had been studied by the Admiralty, it was decided to evacuate the mining community who were mostly of Norwegian and Russian descent.

On 19 August Vian again left Scapa with his forces to carry out this task and to destroy the equipment. By 3 September it had been accomplished successfully and on his way back to Scapa he fell in with a German convoy to the east of the North Cape in heavy weather and poor visibility. In the action which followed, the German training ship *Bremse* (Commander von Brosy-Stein) was sunk, but the two troopships – carrying 1500 troops – she was escorting, managed to make good their escape. As will be related, the Spitzbergen islands were to prove useful as a refuelling rendezvous for convoy escort forces and at one time both Allied and German meteorological parties were operating there unknown to each other.

The first Arctic convoy

The Russians had lost a large number of aircraft during the initial stages of the German offensive and their need for fighter aircraft for the defence of Murmansk and the base at Polyarnoe was urgent. It was arranged therefore, that the veteran carrier HMS *Argus* should load 24 Hurrican fighters of No 151 Wing of the Royal Air Force and she sailed from Scapa on 21 August in company with six merchant ships loaded with raw materials of which our new ally was known to be especially short, such as wool, rubber, tin, etc. One of the ships also carried 15 crated Hurricanes, the balance of No 151 Wing. This was the first of many convoys which Admiral Tovey was called upon to organise. It was escorted by six destroyers and covered by the carrier HMS *Victorious* and the cruisers *Devonshire* and *Suffolk* under the command of Rear Admiral W. F. Wake-Walker. Then within range of Murmansk the *Argus* flew off her fighters but owing to German air activity over the Kola Inlet the six merchant ships were diverted to Archangel. Otherwise there was no interference on the part of the enemy with the operation.

The German navy was still suffering from the losses incurred during the invasion of Norway and according to Admiral Ruge[1] the only surface ships stationed in north Norway to support the left flank of General Dietl's troops were the Sixth flotilla comprising five 'T' class torpedo boats (see Appendix VII) together with some minesweepers and patrol craft. On 25 July, after reminding Hitler of the importance of capturing Murmansk and of the

---

[1] Vice Admiral Friedrich Ruge, *Sea Warfare* (Cassell & Co. Ltd, 1962), page 160

unpleasant fact that Dietl's troops had been brought to a standstill because they were unable to overcome Russian resistance in the Ribachi peninsula, Raeder went on to report 'it is possible for the destroyer (sic) flotilla to enter Mokovski Bay only if a motor minesweeping flotilla is provided and moreover if there is fighter protection, in view of the air situation'. [1] He went on to report that there were still U-boats operating in the area and two more were being sent. [2]

German forces in the Arctic

The German naval forces in northern waters were under Naval Group North, Admiral Boehm, with his headquarters at Kiel and he was responsible for all naval operations in his area. Under him, intitialiy, were the Flag Officer, Northern Waters, at Narvik, and the Naval Commander, Norway, at Oslo. The first named controlled the operation of fleet units in the area through the Flag Officer, Battle Group, whilst the Flag Officer, Northern Waters, was in charge of all matters concerning the use of Norway as a base for naval operations which included shore defences, minelaying, and minesweeping. This somewhat top heavy organisation existed until March 1943 when the post of Flag Officer, Northern Waters, was abolished, his duties being taken over by Naval Group North.

Admiral Ruge is critical of the failure of the German High Command to make better use of the Navy in support of the army operations, particularly in the Arctic. However, in 'Führer Directive No 21' it was stated that the naval effort was to remain concentrated against England. Thus when operation Barbarossa was launched the distribution of the German heavy ships was:

(a) Undergoing trials in the Baltic, the new battleship *Tirpitz*.
(b) At Brest the battle-cruisers *Scharnhorst* and *Gneisenau* and the heavy cruiser *Prinz Eugen*. The *Gneisenau* had been torpedoed on 6 April and hit by four bombs five days later so was unfit for sea. The *Prinz Eugen* had been hit by a bomb on 1/2 July and three weeks later the *Scharnhorst* suffered a similar fate.
(c) At Kiel the pocket battleship *Lützow* was being repaired after having been torpedoed by the British submarine *Spearfish* during the Norwegian operation.   *BEAUFORT A/C*

---

[1] According to Golovko there were also three Norwegian destroyers of the 'Steg' class, a minelayer, and an auxiliary cruiser
[2] Führer Naval Conference of 25 July 1941

(d) Also in the Baltic were the heavy cruiser *Hipper* and the light cruisers *Emden* and *Leipzig* together with all available destroyers minus the Sixth flotilla in the Arctic.

Although there were airfields at Petsamo, Kirkenes, Banak, Tromso, Bardufoss, and Narvik in northern Norway, from which some 230 aircraft of Flieger Korps V were operating in support of Dietl's troops, the pilots had not been trained in naval co-operation. However, they frequently raided the Kola Inlet and were a menace to the shipping anchored there. Compared with the titanic struggle being waged along the whole 1000-mile front to the south, the capture of Murmansk so ardently desired by Raeder must have seemed of comparatively little importance to the High Command whose eyes were fixed on Moscow. It was not until the pace of the offensive began to slacken and the activity of British forces along the Murman coast gave evidence of the Allies' increasing interest in the area, that Raeder felt bound to raise the matter again. At a conference with Hitler on 17 September 1941, he is reported as saying:

> 'The British realise the vital importance of the sea route off the Arctic coast for supplies of the German Armed Forces and they are operating in the northern area with several cruisers, destroyers, one or two aircraft carriers, and submarines'

and he went on to complain of the weakness of the German naval and air resources and the inability of the troop transports to proceed east of the North Cape. He pointed out that the approach of winter would reduce the effectiveness of the Luftwaffe and he pressed yet again for the capture of Murmansk. In a subsequent conversation with Hitler he raised the question of occupying Archangel. However, all that Hitler felt able to promise him was that the railway between that port and Moscow would be cut, a prophesy his army was unable to fulfill.

Aid to Russia

Russia's only ally during the crucial first six months of the German invasion was Britain and as soon as Stalin realised that that country was in no position to afford him the direct military help for which he clamoured, he concentrated on formulating demands for the maximum amount of armaments and raw materials which he trusted Churchill would make available to him in accordance with his offer of help. The United States, though still neutral, was also anxious to assist, but the main question uppermost in both British and American minds was: would Russia be able to withstand the onslaught of the German Wehrmacht?

In his meeting with President Roosevelt's special envoy. Mr Harry Hopkins, who had flown to Moscow in July, Stalin emphasised the Red Army's need of anti-aircraft guns in large quantity, of aluminium with which to manufacture aircraft, and of automatic guns and rifles. He recommended Archangel as the port of delivery since he mistakenly believed that it could be kept open during the winter with ice-breakers. However, it was not until the arrival of Mr Averell Harriman and Lord Beaverbrook, representing the American and British governments respectively, and their meeting with Stalin on 29 September that a full shopping list of Soviet requirements was drawn up. Unfortunately, the official protocol which specified the items which the two countries undertook to make available to Russia between October 1941 and June 1942, as Churchill has pointed out, ended with the words 'Great Britain and the United States will give aid to the transportation of these materials to the Soviet Union and will help with the delivery' but nothing was said about making good any losses which might be incurred during the process of delivery. This omission was to cause much misunderstanding, since the Russians regarded the failure to fulfil the expected quota as tantamount to sabotage on the part of their allies, not on that of the enemy!

The start of the PQ-QP convoys

Despite the somewhat chilly reception accorded to him in Moscow, Beaverbrook remained the established champion of the 'aid to Russia' programme, considering that it should have priority even over his own country's requirements. He so impressed Churchill with his views that the latter informed Stalin on 6 October: 'We intend to run a continuous cycle of convoys leaving every ten days' and 'In arranging this regular cycle of convoys we are counting on Archangel to handle the main bulk of deliveries'.[1] It was the Admiralty's intention to run convoys to north Russia on a 40-day cycle and the day the British and American delegates arrived in Moscow, 28 September, the first of the famous PQ series of convoys (the choice of the letters has been linked with a commander in the Operations Division of the Admiralty whose intitials were P.Q.R.) sailed from Iceland bound for Archangel, where it was due to arrive on 12 October. It comprised 10 merchant ships and was escorted by the cruiser *Suffolk* and two destroyers. Included in the cargo were 20 tanks and 193 fighter aircraft. It had an uneventful passage and arrived a day ahead of schedule.

---

[1] Churchill, ibid, Volume III, page 418

The shortened cycle on which the Prime Minister had promised Stalin the convoys would be run, and which had been made without working out the naval implications, placed the Commander-in-Chief Home Fleet, Admiral Sir John Tovey, in something of a predicament. Assuming a minimum escort of 1 cruiser and 2 destroyers, a total of 4 cruisers and 8 destroyers would have to be permanently allocated to this task. This took no account of weather damage, a very likely occurrence with the onset of winter, nor to the incidence of defects. He needed destroyers to screen his battleships and carriers should they be required to intercept German ships attempting to break out into the Atlantic, the Home Fleet's primary task, but he never had enough of these ships to meet requirements. Admiral Golovko records that during Admiral Vian's visit it had been agreed that the convoy route should be divided into two operational zones – 'One stretched from Britain to Bear Island via Iceland and the convoys along this route were provided with escorts by the British alone. The second zone covered the area between Bear Island and Archangel and the movements of convoys on this sector were covered by British ships and our own submarine, air and surface forces.' [1] But as events were to prove, the assistance of Soviet forces could not be counted upon so the British escort had to be strong enough to protect the convoys throughout the whole of the passage. From time to time Russian destroyers did sortie into the Barents Sea to meet an incoming convoy and they provided much appreciated and effective anti-aircraft gun support, but they were not designed for operating in such stormy waters.

Convoys PQ 2–5

A second convoy PQ 2, left Scapa Flow for Archangel on 17 October. It comprised 6 ships and all arrived safely. It was followed on 9 November by PQ 3 of 8 ships (one of which had to return), on 17 November by PQ 4 of 8 ships, and on 27 November by PQ 5 of 7 ships, all of which sailed from Hvalfiord in Iceland and reached Archangel without loss.

German reactions

On 13 November during a conference with Hitler, Admiral Raeder commented that enemy activity in the Arctic area had been less than expected, but he appreciated that the long winter nights were favourable for the passage of convoys. He reminded the Führer that air reconnaissance was

---

[1] Golovko, ibid, page 82

lacking – a fact which doubtless accounted for failure to locate the first PQ convoys mentioned above. He sought Hitler's permission to move the new battleship *Tirpitz* to Trondheim on completion of repairs and arcticisation and suggested an Atlantic sortie by the pocket battleship *Scheer* since the oil-fuel shortage would not permit such an operation by the former but there was plenty of diesel oil for the latter. However, after the loss of the *Bismarck* Atlantic sorties were out of favour with Hitler and all he would agree to was the movement of the *Scheer* to Trondheim or Narvik, but he promised to give further consideration to the deployment of the *Tirpitz*.

Shortly after this conference Raeder ordered the relief of the five 'T' class torpedo boats in north Norway by five of the *'Leberecht Mass'* class destroyers. These were larger and more powerfully armed ships mounting five 5-inch guns and eight 21-inch torpedoes. He also instructed the U-boat command to increase the number of submarines in the area so as to ensure that not less than three were always on patrol.

The Russian icebreakers managed to keep the Gourlo – the narrow neck of water giving access to the White Sea – open until 12 December and they cut a passage for seven ships of PQ 6 which had left Iceland on 8 December, but it was 23 December before they were berthed at the subsidiary port of Molotovsk and the icebreaker herself became fast in the ice together with the ships, which were obliged to remain there throughout the winter until the White Sea was again open to shipping the following June. The other two ships of the convoy berthed at Murmansk. In an entry in his diary for 10 December Admiral Golovko remarks: 'Matters are evidently moving in favour of Murmansk becoming the reception port for the convoys' and he goes on to say that he had raised this matter with the authorities in Moscow as far back as August and September, but no notice appears to have been taken of his representations. On Christmas Day, five days after the arrival of the two ships of PQ 6 he confides to his diary: 'The signs are that cargo vessels will sail into Murmansk. Now there is no end to our troubles.'[1]

Results to the end of 1941

By the end of 1941, 53 ships had been escorted to north Russia (50 to Archangel and 3 to Murmansk) and 34 had returned. None had been lost. A total of 750 tanks, 800 fighter aircraft, 1400 vehicles, and more than 100,000 tons of stores had been delivered to a hard-pressed ally and this despite the fact that the escorts of the convoys had been pitifully weak. A

---

[1] Golovko, ibid, page 86

cruiser accompanied each convoy all the way whilst a second one remained in support to the west of Bear Island and the anti-submarine escort normally amounted to 2 destroyers, a minesweeper, and 2 trawlers on the outward voyage and 1 destroyer and 2 minesweepers on the homeward one. Five minesweepers based on the Kola Inlet and two or three Russian destroyers reinforced the close escort as the convoy approached the Murman coast. Air coverage was provided by Numbers 269 and 330 squadrons of Coastal Command based on Iceland for the first 150 miles of the voyage only, thereafter there were only the few long-range patrols off the coast of Norway, the primary task of which was to search for U-boats.

Difficulties encountered

Admiral Tovey was well aware of the risks being run with the Arctic convoys and his anxiety was increased on receipt of intelligence of the strengthening of German surface forces and U-boats in north Norway. The general shortage of escort forces at that time and the shortness of the convoy cycle precluded any strengthening of the convoy escorts. In fact it was proving impossible to maintain the ten-day cycle which the Prime Minister had envisaged and the average interval worked out at fifteen days. This was in part due to a nine-day postponement of the sailing of PQ 3 due to intelligence reaching the Admiralty of preparations being made for a breakout into the Atlantic by the *Tirpitz* and the *Scheer*. It was also the result of weather damage sustained by the escort vessels and the impossibility of making it good in the short time available between voyages. To lessen the strain on the escorts and to take advantage of the long hours of darkness prevailing in the northern latitudes in which the Arctic convoys were operating, it was decided that after passing Bear Island, the convoy should disperse and ships should proceed independently and unescorted to the Kola Inlet. This enabled the escorts to proceed ahead and commence refuelling from the tanker which had been stationed there to relieve the Russians of responsibility for this duty.

The entry of the United States into the war against Germany following Japan's surprise attack on the American fleet in Pearl Harbour on 7 December 1941 was to have a profound effect on the volume of military supplies made available to Russia. What had begun as a trickle was soon to swell into a flood. It took some time for the German High Command to appreciate the increasing importance of the Arctic convoys. The German historian General Kurt von Tippelskirch comments:

'In the year 1941 the German High Command took little notice of the transport of

15

war material to the Russian harbours. Hitler was convinced of a quick ending to the campaign in Russia. . . . After the failure of the attack on Moscow, as the war against the Soviet Union took on a new and unexpected character, a systematic opposition to the convoy organisation was initiated, with the employment of German light naval forces, U-boats, and air units.'[1]

Given the position of strategic advantage conferred by the German occupation of Norway, a co-ordinated use of these three arms could well have made the running of these convoys so costly as to be unprofitable. However, except on one occasion as will be related, a failure by the enemy to make full use of his assets, coupled with a grim determination on the part of the defenders to succeed, enabled the Arctic convoys to be run at varying intervals throughout the rest of the war.

---

[1] Kurt von Tippelskirch, *Geschichte des Zweiten Welt-Krieges* (Athenäum Verlag, 1951), page 552

Chapter 2

THE THREAT FROM THE TIRPITZ

Raeder defines the Tirpitz's role

It will be remembered that at the last meeting between Hitler and his naval Commander-in-Chief Admiral Raeder, the former had promised to give further consideration to the movement of the *Tirpitz* from the Baltic to north Norway. At the next conference held on 29 December Raeder again raised the matter but two successful British raids in the Vestfiord and on Vaagso Island which had taken place a few days previously had brought the whole question of the defence of Norway to the fore, so he began by giving his views on the situation as it affected that country. He emphasised the vulnerability of German shipping on the route between Narvik and Bergen and the possibility that further raids might result in the destruction of coast batteries and even the establishment of bridgeheads which might lead to the loss of the whole country. Then, returning to the subject of the *Tirpitz*, he explained how her transfer to Trondheim would:

(a) strengthen Germany's position in the area and lessen the risk of enemy operations off the north Norwegian coast designed to turn the flank;

(b) oblige the British to maintain a strong force in home waters which would prevent the reinforcement of the Mediterranean, the Indian Ocean, and the Pacific; and

(c) provide strategic opportunities for attacks on the convoy routes between Britain and north Russia, as well as on enemy warships, and also the bombardment of military bases besides general interference with enemy operations in the area.

He well knew that the shortage of oil fuel, the stocks of which had fallen to 156,000 tons would limit the *Tirpitz*'s ability to carry out all these tasks, but he was quite right in gauging the effect which the presence of the ship in north Norway would have on British strategy. However, despite these powerful arguments, Hitler again deferred his decision on the battleship's movement and it was not until the next conference on 12 January that he gave his consent to Raeder's request. He was now convinced that the threat of an invasion of Norway by British forces was very real and that 'every surface ship not stationed in north Norway is wasting its time'.[1]

Effect of the Tirpitz's arrival in Norway

The *Tirpitz*, which had been moved to Wilhelmshaven in anticipation of Hitler's approval, made the passage from that port to Trondheim on the night of 14/15 January, but it was not until 17 January that British intelligence became aware of the fact and even then it was only reported that she had sailed and might, therefore, be attempting to break out into the Atlantic. As a result the sailing of PQ 9 from Iceland was postponed. The previous convoy which had sailed on 8 January was the first to suffer from enemy action, the *Harmatris*, the Commodore's ship being torpedoed by *U 454* (Lieutenant-Commander Hackländer) off the entrance to the Kola Inlet. She was towed into harbour, but Hackländer scored another success soon afterwards when he torpedoed the destroyer *Matabele* which was escorting the *Harmatris*, and she sank in two minutes. Only 2 men out of a complement of 200 were rescued alive although there were many bodies with life jackets floating about which the icy Arctic waters had quickly claimed. It was a grim foretaste of what sea warfare in these regions held in store.

U-boats off the Kola Inlet

The presence of U-boats close to the entrance to the Kola Inlet was, in Admiral Tovey's view, a reflection on the efficiency of the Soviet countermeasures and he ordered Rear Admiral H. M. Borough when he reached Murmansk in his flagship HMS *Nigeria* early in February to discuss the matter with Admiral Golovko. The Soviet Commander-in-Chief makes no mention of these discussions in his diary although he records the torpedoing of the two ships mentioned above with the comment: 'It appears that information about the dispatch of extra enemy submarines with experienced captains to the northern theatre was quite accurate'.[2]

Hitler fears an invasion of Norway

On 22 January Hitler held another naval conference at which the threat of

---

[1] Jochen Brennecke, *The Tirpitz* (Robert Hale & Company, 1963) page 36
[2] Golovko, ibid, page 87

an Allied invasion of Norway was again discussed. He now declared it to be the decisive theatre of the war and ordered Raeder to send reinforcements of surface ships and U-boats 'unquestioningly and without regard to any other considerations'. Two days later, after Hitler had countermanded an order that all available U-boats were to be transferred to Norway, Raeder gave orders that the number stationed there was to be increased from six to eight and that two were to be kept ready for sea at Trondheim and Bergen with eight on patrol in the Iceland–Hebrides area. These new dispositions were opposed by the chief of the U-boat command Rear Admiral Carl Dönitz, since at that time his U-boats were reaping a rich harvest off the east coast of the United States. Moreover, he did not share Hitler's belief in the threat of an Allied invasion of Norway, but nevertheless he had to make the dispositions which Raeder had ordered.

Churchill and the Tirpitz

On 23 January a reconnaissance aircraft of Coastal Command located the *Tirpitz* at anchor in Asafiord, 15 miles east of Trondheim, despite the camouflage with which she was covered. She was protected by buoyed anti-torpedo nets and was therefore a very difficult target to attack. The news of the discovery produced a strongly worded minute from the British Prime Minister to the Chiefs of Staff Committee.

> 'The destruction, or even the crippling of this ship is the greatest event at sea at the present time', he wrote. 'The whole strategy of the war turns at this period on this ship which is holding four times the number of British capital ships paralysed to say nothing of the two new American battleships retained in the Atlantic.' [1]

Raeder would have smiled with satisfaction had he been able to read this minute.

It was on the overstretched forces of Coastal Command that the strain of watching the *Tirpitz* was to fall most heavily. Unfortunately, most of its torpedo-carrying aircraft had been sent to the Mediterranean for the protection of Egypt against invasion, so that despite the grave view of the battleship's presence taken by Mr Churchill, the air forces available to attack her, should she make a sortie, were minimal since she was also at the extreme range of the Halifax and Stirling bomber aircraft then in service.

Convoys PQ 9, 10, and 11

On 1 February the delayed convoy PQ 9 sailed from Iceland in company

---

[1] Churchill, ibid, Volume IV, page 98

with the next scheduled convoy PQ 10 making a combined total of 10 ships. These and the 13 ships of PQ 11 which sailed from Loch Ewe five days later, all reached Murmansk without interference on the part of the enemy. For this the appalling weather and long hours of darkness were largely responsible.

'Ocean storms, prolonged snow squalls, thick vapours from the sea and dense fogs create unusually complicated navigational conditions and have become a second enemy to us', wrote Admiral Golovko in his diary at this time and, giving praise where it was certainly due he went on, 'The convoys naturally could not in any circumstances stop anywhere and await tolerable weather but had to go on regardless. And the convoys are going on.' [1]

All the same, with the approach of longer days and an improvement to be expected in the weather, together with the implementation of Hitler's orders to strengthen the forces in north Norway, the immunity from attack enjoyed by the Arctic convoys hitherto was about to end.

German reactions to the Arctic convoys

As news of the growing deliveries of war material and stores arriving at the port of Murmansk reached the German High Command, the suspicion was aroused that the Allies were preparing for a large landing operation in support of the Russian northern flank to take place in the spring. As part of the planned concentration of German surface forces in Norway the battle-cruisers *Scharnhorst* and *Gneisenau* with the heavy cruiser *Prinz Eugen* had successfully run the gauntlet of the English Channel from Brest to Wilhelmshaven and Brunsbuttel between 12 and 13 February. Both the battle-cruisers were mined off the Dutch coast and the *Gneisenau* was subsequently hit by bombs and took no further part in the war while the *Scharnhorst* was a long time repairing. This left only the *Prinz Eugen* which together with the pocket battleship *Scheer*, accompanied by three destroyers, sailed for Bergen on 20 February. They were sighted by a British reconnaissance aircraft the following forenoon but a squadron of torpedo carrying aircraft sent to attack them failed to find their target. On 22 February the two ships were located at anchor in Grimstad Fiord, south of Bergen, and the following day as they approached the channel leading to Trondheim the British submarine *Trident* torpedoed and severely damaged the *Prinz Eugen* but she managed to reach port; it was October before she was again operational.

---

[1] Golovko, ibid, page 88

Convoys PQ 12 and QP 8

Although the misadventures recounted above had thwarted Raeder's intention to effect a powerful concentration of ships with which to attack the Arctic convoys, Admiral Tovey still regarded the situation with misgiving. With the forces at his disposal he could not simultaneously guard against a breakout by the *Tirpitz* into the north Atlantic and at the same time assure the protection of the convoys to and from north Russia against surface ship attack. In order, therefore, to make the best use of his heavy ships and only aircraft carrier he arranged that the next pair of convoys PQ 12 outwards and QP 8 homewards should be sailed simultaneously from Hvalfiord (Iceland) and the Kola Inlet. They comprised 16 and 15 ships respectively and sailed on 1 March with augmented close escorts. Air patrols also were stepped up, a close watch being kept on the approaches to Trondheim.

On 5 March a German Focke Wulf 200 reconnaissance aircraft sighted PQ 12 seventy miles to the south-east of Jan Mayen island. At 13.15 hrs the following day the *Tirpitz*, wearing the flag of Vice Admiral Otto Ciliax and accompanied by the destroyers *Z 25, Hermann Schoemann,* and *Friedrich Ihn* put to sea to intercept it. Four U-boats on patrol to the west of Bear Island were deployed on a line at right angles to the expected line of the convoy's advance. Ciliax was not aware that his departure had been seen and reported by the submarine *Seawolf*, but the message did not reach Admiral Tovey until just after midnight on 7 March. Meanwhile he had ordered Vice Admiral A. T. B. Curteis in the battle-cruiser *Renown* with the battleship *Duke of York*, the cruiser *Kenya*, and six destroyers to sail from Hvalfiord on 3 March whilst he himself in the battleship *King George V* with the carrier *Victorious*, the 8-inch gun cruiser *Berwick*, and six destroyers sailed from Scapa the following day to rendezvous with the other force. It was his intention to patrol along a line between 50 and 100 miles south of the convoy route during the period when PQ 12 and QP 8 would be passing one another.

Blind man's buff

Apart from the one sighting report, Ciliax received no further information from air reconnaissance and so, unsuspecting, was heading straight towards a greatly superior British force. On receipt of the *Seawolf*'s report, Tovey, whose fleet was at the time 200 miles south of PQ 12, ordered all ships to raise steam for full speed and altered course to close the convoys. He told *Victorious* to be ready to carry out an air search to the south at dawn and, had not bad weather prevented flying operations, the *Tirpitz* would almost certainly have been located before she reached the vicinity of the convoys. During the night of 6/7 March PQ 12 had run into ice and one of the escorting destroyers had received serious damage, so the Escort Comman-der had altered the course of the convoy towards the south-east in search of open water. The snow squalls and poor visibility which prevented the *Victorious* from operating her aircraft also 'grounded' the seaplanes carried by the *Tirpitz*, so Ciliax had to rely on an estimated position of PQ 12 which he appreciated might be considerably in error.

At 10.00 hrs on 7 March he spread his three destroyers with orders to search towards the north-west across the expected course of the convoy, whilst he ordered the *Tirpitz* to steer in a westerly direction. At the time PQ 12 was some 75 miles to the north of him and the convoy having at 08.00 hrs resumed its north-easterly course, the destroyer search passed astern of it (see Diagram II).

At noon the two convoys passed each other and Admiral Tovey who had closed to a position 75 miles to the south-west of them, turned away in this direction, little knowing that the *Tirpitz* was at that moment 60 miles to the south-east of him and steering towards him at high speed. The German battleship passed some 60 miles astern of PQ 12 and 50 miles ahead of QP 8 and by 16.30 hrs was to the north of both convoys (see Diagram II). The three German destroyers had in fact, passed quite close to QP 8 but without sighting it. However, a Russian ship the *Izhora*, which was straggling to the north of the convoy was sighted by the *Friedrich Ihn* who sank her by gunfire at 16.30 hrs, but not before her victim managed to radio a distress message which was received by Tovey's flagship, the *King George V*. Unfortunately, the position given was incomplete but at 17.00 hrs direction-finding bearings of what could have been a German transmission were taken by the *King George V* and Admiral Tovey altered the course of his fleet towards the east in their direction. Shortly afterwards he hauled round to the north-east and was on the point of detaching six of his destroyers with orders to sweep south-eastward in search of the *Tirpitz* when the Admiralty informed him that intelligence indicated that the German ships intended to carry out prolonged operations in the area east of Bear Island and also that it appeared that Ciliax was unaware of the presence of the Home Fleet in his vicinity. Tovey thereupon changed his plan and, keeping his destroyers in company, he again steered to close the convoys.

At 19.40 hrs another bearing was taken of a transmission by the same ship as previously which indicated that, whoever she was, she was moving at high speed in a southerly direction, so 20 minutes later Tovey detached the six destroyers with orders to proceed to a position 150 miles to the south-east

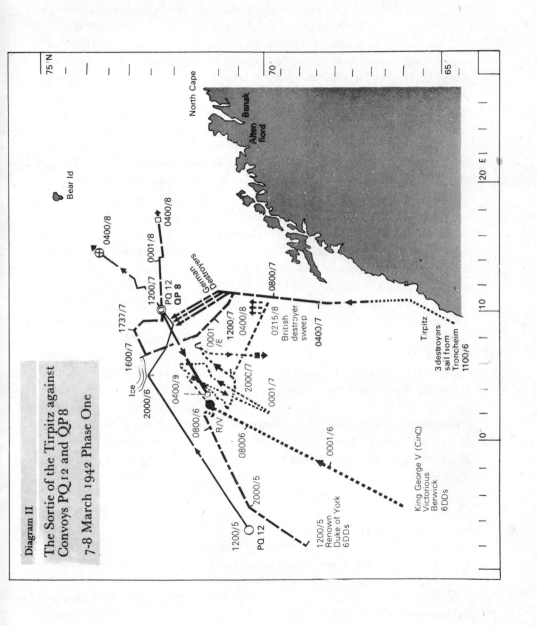

Diagram II

The Sortie of the Tirpitz against
Convoys PQ12 and QP8
7-8 March 1942 Phase One

75°N

Bear Id

North Cape

Banak

Alten fiord

70°

20° E

65°

0400/8

0001/8

0400/8

0400/8

1200/7

1737/7

1600/7

PQ 12
QP 8

German Destroyers

1200/7

0800/7

Ice

2000/6

0400/9

0001
/E

1200/7

0400/8

0215/8
British
destroyer
sweep

0400/7

0800/6

R/V

200C/7

0001/7

Tirpitz

3 destroyers
sail from
Troncheim
1100/6

08006

0001/6

2000/5

1200/5
Renown
Duke of York
6DDs

1200/5

PQ 12

King George V (CinC)
Victorious
Berwick
6DDs

10°

0°

and then sweep northward two miles apart until 06.00 hrs on the following day. If they failed to sight anything they were to return to Seidisfiord on the east coast of Iceland and refuel. At about the same time two more destroyers had to be sent back to Iceland to refuel and he was left with only one.

Ciliax's destroyers too were running short of fuel and after they had rejoined the *Tirpitz* he sent one into Tromso to refuel while with the other two he steered eastwards, intending to renew his search for the convoy at daylight the next day, 8 March. At 04.00 hrs he was obliged to detach the other two destroyers to refuel and at 07.00 hrs he took the *Tirpitz* northward across the estimated track of the convoy which at the time was 80 miles to the north-west of him, having been ordered by the Admiralty to pass north of Bear Island and in consequence was steering a northerly course. Having sighted nothing, at 10.45 hrs the *Tirpitz* altered course towards the west, assuming she had overrun her quarry. Soon after midday PQ 12 ran into ice and was obliged to haul round to the south-east, and subsequently to the south, and at one time during the afternoon watch it was only 60 miles from the *Tirpitz*. This was the second time that Ciliax had narrowly missed his prey, and on this occasion Tovey's battleship covering force was some 500 miles to the south-west and could not have intervened to protect the weakly escorted merchant ships if they had been attacked (see Diagram III).

Having heard nothing more since the second intercepted signal, Tovey had come to the conclusion that Ciliax must have abandoned the hunt and that the *Tirpitz* must be returning to base. He, therefore, steered for a position in the vicinity of the Lofoten Islands close to which he expected her to pass and from which the *Victorious*'s aircraft could reach her. However, at 17.30 hrs the Admiralty informed him that intelligence indicated that the enemy ship was still looking for the convoy in the area south of Bear Island, so at 18.20 hrs he hauled round to the north-east and headed in that direction. Although it is unusual for a force at sea in wartime to break radio silence there are occasions when the senior officer may consider it is desirable to do so. Tovey's heavy ships were still without a destroyer screen in U-boat infested waters and this was causing him some anxiety, but he also hoped that if he broke radio silence to acquaint the Admiralty of this fact and of his future intentions, the Germans would intercept the message and recall the *Tirpitz*. This would not only ensure the safety of the convoy but also bring her within range of *Victorious*'s aircraft.

At 20.00 hrs on 8 March Ciliax, not having sighted anything during his westerly sweep to the south of Bear Island, decided to abandon the operation and return to base. Once again Admiralty intelligence detected the battleship's movements and so informed Tovey who on the following day at

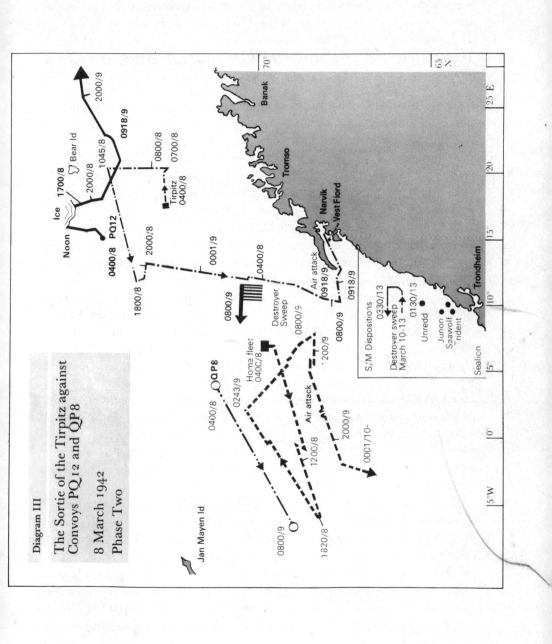

Diagram III

The Sortie of the Tirpitz against
Convoys PQ12 and QP8

8 March 1942
Phase Two

Jan Mayen Id

0800/9

1820/8

0001/10-

2000/9

1200/8

Air attack

QP8

0400/8

0243/9

Home fleet
040C/8

0800/9

Destroyer
Sweep

0800/9

0800/9

~200/9

0918/9

Air attack

0918/9

S/M Dispositions

Destroyer sweep
March 10-13

0130/13

0330/13

Unredd

Junon
Saawolf
ndent

Sealion

Trondheim

Narvik
Vest Fiord

Tromso

Banak

0400/8

0001/9

2000/8

1800/8

2000/8

PQ12

Noon

Ice   1700/8

2000/8

1045/8

0918/9

Bear Id

2000/9

0800/8

0700/8

Tirpitz
0400/8

70°

65°

5°W   0°   5°   10°   15°   20°   25° E

02.40 hrs altered course to the south-east in the hope of intercepting her. He warned the *Victorious* to be ready to fly off a search and striking force at dawn.

Victorious launches an air search and striking force

As the force closed the land, both the weather and the visibility steadily improved and at 06.40 hrs the *Victorious* launched a search force of six Albacore aircraft, followed an hour later by a striking force of twelve Albacores armed with torpedoes. The prospects for an attack seemed good provided they were lucky enough to locate the target. Just before they took off Tovey made them an encouraging signal 'A wonderful chance which may achieve most valuable results. God be with you.'

The *Tirpitz* was about 60 miles to the west of the entrance to the Vestfiord and steering towards Trondheim at high speed when at 08.00 hrs a look-out in the foretop sighted and reported a hostile aircraft which was identified as a carrier-borne type. This was an aircraft of the search force which had simultaneously seen and reported the battleship. The *Tirpitz* increased speed and altered course to the east at the same time launching two of her six Arado seaplanes and requesting fighter protection from the Luftwaffe stationed at Bodo. At 08.42 hrs the striking force coming up from astern sighted the *Tirpitz* 20 miles away in the direction of the rising sun. The wind was right ahead so that the Albacores were gaining on the battleship at only about 30 knots and it was clearly going to take time to reach a favourable position ahead of the target from which to attack. Although taking full advantage of the available cloud cover to avoid being seen, when the force was just about over the *Tirpitz* a break in the clouds exposed it to view and thereby prevented any hope of achieving surprise. The squadron commander thereupon gave the order to attack.

The sky was soon filled with bursting shell from the battleship's formidable anti-aircraft batteries but the attackers, with what Brennecke describes as 'that fanaticism of which every Briton is capable in the hour of greatest crisis'[1] pressed home their attacks whilst the great ship twisted and turned in an attempt to avoid the torpedoes aimed at her from both sides. In nine minutes the attack was over: two aircraft had been shot down and the remaining ten turned away and set course for the carrier, while the *Tirpitz* steamed on apparently unscathed. Ciliax believed that his flagship was in

---

[1] Brennecke, ibid, page 49

fact hit by one or possibly two torpedoes which failed to detonate. Although Captain Topp handled his ship with great skill, given her length and the way in which the attacks were pressed home, it appeared to him that it was impossible for her to have avoided them all. The German admiral may well have been right. The failure of torpedo pistols was a common enough occurrence at this time in both navies and, moreover, torpedoes dropped too close to the target would not have had time to run off the safety range or take up their proper depth setting, but the fact remained that the *Tirpitz* was undamaged.

Tovey's disappointment

From Tovey's point of view the failure of the torpedo attack was a singularly unfortunate ending to the long operation of blind man's buff which he had been obliged to play with his redoubtable opponent. As already mentioned, by her mere presence in north Norway the *Tirpitz* was able to exert a powerful influence on the running of the Arctic convoys which from now on had to be covered by a battleship-cum-carrier force.

German dissatisfaction

On the German side too there was dissatisfaction with the outcome of the sortie. Admiral Raeder complained to Hitler about the weakness of German naval forces in the northern area, the menace of the British aircraft carriers, and the inadequacy of the German Air Force which allowed enemy forces to enter Norwegian coastal waters with impunity. Lack of air reconnaissance was, in his view, largely responsible for the *Tirpitz*'s failure to locate the convoys. The Führer promised to confer with *Reichsmarschall* Goering about increasing the strength of the Luftwaffe in Norway and he approved the formation of a battle group to consist of the *Tirpitz*, *Scharnhorst*, the aircraft carrier *Graf Zeppelin* (when completed), two heavy cruisers, and a dozen or so destroyers. This ambitious project never materialised because the *Graf Zeppelin* was never finished, but on 19 March the 8-inch gun cruiser *Hipper* joined the *Tirpitz* and the *Scheer* at Trondheim and the build-up of German naval strength in Norway was thereby taken a stage further.

Chapter 3
OPPOSITION GROWS

Convoys PQ 13 and QP 9

On 20 and 21 March convoys PQ 13 and QP 9 left Iceland and the Kola Inlet respectively. Each consisted of nineteen ships and the distant covering forces comprised the battleship *King George V* (flagship of Vice Admiral A. T. B. Curteis), the battleship *Duke of York*, the battle-cruiser *Renown*, the carrier *Victorious*, the cruisers *Edinburgh* and *Kent*, and 11 destroyers. Before the convoys sailed Admiral Tovey instructed the escort forces that should either of the convoys be attacked by overwhelmingly superior forces their primary object was to shadow the enemy and ensure that he be brought to action by our own heavy ships or submarines. The close escorts of both convoys were weak and in the case of PQ 13 comprised the destroyers *Fury*, *Eclipse*, and *Lamerton*, 2 trawlers and 3 armed whalers, the last named being transferred to the Russian Navy. The cruiser *Trinidad* provided close cover. QP 9's escort consisted of the destroyer *Offa*, and the minesweepers *Sharpshooter* and *Britomart*, reinforced during the first two days of the voyage by five minesweepers based on Kola Inlet and a Russian destroyer which lost contact during the night of 22/23 March. The cruiser *Kenya* which sailed from the Kola Inlet on 22 March to provide close cover to QP 9, never made contact with the convoy which ran into a south-westerly gale force 8 to 9 on the following day.

During a snow squall on 24 March the *Sharpshooter*, catching sight of *U 655* on the surface, rammed and sank her, otherwise the voyage was without incident and all ships reached Iceland safely on 31 March. Not so, however, PQ 13. Four days after leaving Iceland it encountered a fierce north-easterly gale which scattered the ships over a distance of some 150 miles and when after four days of violence it blew itself out, the senior officer of the escort in HMS *Fury* scanned the horizon in vain for a sight of his charges. On 27 March, even though the gale had abated somewhat, the poor visibility made it difficult to locate the ships of the scattered convoy and at

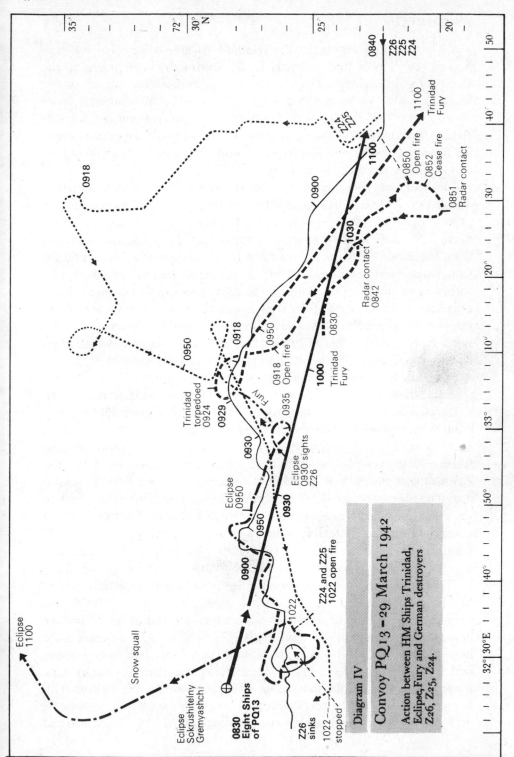

Stopped
1022

Diagram IV

Convoy PQ 13 – 29 March 1942

Action between HM Ships Trinidad,
Eclipse, Fury and German destroyers
Z26, Z25, Z24.

0840

Z26
Z25
Z24

1100
Trinidad
Fury

0850
Open fire

0852
Cease fire

0851
Radar contact

Radar contact
0842

1030

0830
Trinidad
Fury

1000
Trinidad
Fury

0900

0918
Open fire

0950

0918

0950

Trinidad
torpedoed
0924

0929

Fury

0935

0930

Eclipse
0930 sights
Z26

0930

0950

Eclipse
0950

0900

0950

1022

Z24 and Z25
1022 open fire

1022
stopped

Z26
sinks

0830
Eight Ships
of PQ13

Eclipse
Sokrushitelny
Gremyashchi

Snow squall

Eclipse
1100

0918

30° N

72°

35°

25°

20°

30°E

32°

40°

50°

10°

20°

30°

40°

50°

10.00 hrs on the following day the *Trinidad* which had been joined by the *Nigeria* (flagship of Rear Admiral H. M. Burrough) in rounding up the merchant ships, sighted a German BV 138 reconnaissance aircraft of the Second Coastal Air Wing 406 and rightly surmised that bombing attacks would soon follow. Beginning an hour later Ju88's of III Bomber Group 30 attacked intermittently throughout the day and as a result, 2 merchant ships, the *Raceland* and *Empire Ranger*, were sunk. The trawler *Blackfly* sent to look for survivors failed to find any.

Captain Pönitz with three German destroyers Z 24, 25, and 26 had been ordered to sail from Kirkenes to intercept the convoy and on reaching its expected line of advance he spread them three miles apart and swept north-westwards. That evening one of them sighted a boatload of survivors from the *Empire Ranger* and rescued them, and shortly after midnight Commander von Berger in Z 26 fell in with the SS *Bateau* and sank her by torpedo and gunfire after taking off the crew. From them information was obtained about the state of the convoy and the strength of its escort and Captain Pönitz concluded that the main body of the convoy must be to the south-east, so at 01.40 hrs on 29 March he ordered his ships to sweep in that direction at 25 knots. This action in fact took them to the south of PQ 13 and at 05.30 hrs, having sighted nothing, they ran north for three hours before resuming their westerly sweep in rapidly deteriorating weather conditions.

The convoy was split into two groups about 80 miles apart. The westerly group of eight ships was being escorted by the *Eclipse* and one trawler which at 06.45 hrs on 29th were joined by the British destroyer *Oribi* and the Russian destroyers *Sokrushitelny* and *Gremyashchi*. At 08.43 hrs the *Trinidad* with the *Fury* in company was steaming eastward at 20 knots to round up the easterly group of four merchant ships and bring them back to the other one when her radar operator detected an echo bearing 079°; 6½ miles and six minutes later one of the three German destroyers came in sight almost right ahead (see Diagram IV). Turning to starboard to open her A arcs the *Trinidad* opened fire at a range of 2900 yards. The target was the Z 26 which took violent avoiding action and although hit managed to maintain her speed and disappear into the mist. The *Trinidad* took action to avoid any torpedoes the destroyer might have aimed at her and at 09.22 hrs she herself, fired one at the retreating enemy ship which had once again come into view and was seen to be on fire. The torpedo appeared to be running correctly, although two others had failed to leave their tubes owing to being iced up, then suddenly it broke surface on the port bow and hit the cruiser on her port side, the resulting explosion damaging her severely. The ship took a list to port of 17° and her speed dropped to eight knots. The *Fury* which had been astern of the cruiser when contact was made with the enemy destroyers had turned in pursuit of the damaged *Z 26*.

The enemy ships were retiring on a course which took them towards the eight merchant ships and their escorts and in the poor visibility prevailing a melée ensued in which it was difficult to distinguish friend from foe. The *Fury*, having fired two salvoes at the *Eclipse* by mistake, now turned back to rejoin the damaged *Trinidad*, while the *Eclipse* continued the chase of the *Z 26*. At 09.50 hrs she sighted the enemy dimly through the snow and driving spray which, sweeping over the foremost gun and bridge froze as it fell, but despite these appalling conditions she continued to engage her opponent and inflict further damage which caused her to stop, with her stern awash and listing to port. The *Eclipse* was on the point of firing her last torpedo at her when the other two enemy destroyers suddenly appeared on her starboard beam about two miles distant. To make matters worse the snow suddenly ceased and visibility rapidly improved. The German ships immediately opened fire while the *Eclipse* made off at high speed to the north-west. However, before she was able to reach the shelter of a snow squall she had received two hits aft and had been holed above the waterline by two shells which burst close alongside. Being short of fuel and having nine seriously injured men she then hauled round to the east and proceeded independently to the Kola Inlet. The *Z 24* and *Z 25* now turned their attention to their sinking consort, rescuing 96 of her crew before setting course to return to Kirkenes. The damaged *Trinidad* escorted by the *Fury* limped slowly towards Kola Inlet. They were unsuccessfully attacked by *U 378*, but both ships reached harbour at 09.30 hrs on 30 March.

A group of four U-boats was lying in wait for the convoy off the entrance to the port and as the latter in two groups of eight and four ships with four still unaccounted for, approached Kildin Island it was attacked by *U 376* (Lieutenant-Commander Marks) and *U 435* (Lieutenant-Commander Strelow) which torpedoed and sank the freighter *Effingham*. The following day one of the missing ships, the *Induna*, which had run into ice and had subsequently taken the armed whaler *Silja* in tow – she having run out of fuel – was torpedoed by *U 436* (Lieutenant-Commander Seibicke) as she approached the harbour, but because of the stormy weather the incident went unobserved and it was three days before the survivors were rescued by a Russian minesweeper. The *Silja* was later towed in by the minesweeper *Harrier*. Out of the 19 ships of PQ 13, 5 had been lost, the heaviest casualties so far suffered by an Arctic convoy.

Reviewing the operations the German Naval Staff considered that the loss of a destroyer in exchange for one merchant ship was too high a price to pay and proposed that in future these should be given cover by the heavy ships. Admiral Schmundt, Flag Officer, Northern Waters, disagreed and favoured greater caution in their operation, but in any case the shortage of fuel prevented the implementation of the Naval Staff's proposals.

Increasing opposition met by convoys

From now on opposition to the passage of the Arctic convoys grew steadily and as a German historian has written 'the longer the days became the less the protecting night stood the convoys in good stead until finally in the summer months the enemy was no longer able to keep out of sight'.[1]

The change from winter to summer caused Admiral Tovey to review the conditions under which the convoys were being operated and he represented to the Admiralty the need to strengthen the escort forces in the face of the enemy's build-up of air, surface, and submarine forces with which to interdict their passage. The only source from which additional forces could be drawn was the Western Approaches Command and this meant depleting the already under-strength Atlantic convoy escorts. Moreover, in most of these ships the anti-aircraft armament was weak since priority had been given to anti-submarine weapons, the air threat in the Atlantic being negligible. The First Sea Lord, Admiral Sir Dudley Pound, well aware of the dilemma with which Admiral Tovey was faced, warned the Defence Committee that as the days lengthened heavy losses could be expected and the running of the Arctic convoys might become not worthwhile. The dominating factor, however, was the political one, and both the British and United States governments felt impelled to do everything possible to aid their Russian ally, cost what it may.

Convoys PQ 14 and QP 10

The next convoy for north Russia, PQ 14 of 24 ships sailed from Iceland on 8 April and two days later the homeward convoy QP 10 of 16 ships left the Kola Inlet. The close escort of PQ 14 consisted initially of the minesweepers *Hebe* and *Speedy* and 4 trawlers which were joined in a position 120 miles south-south-west of Jan Mayen Island by the cruiser *Edinburgh* (flagship of Rear Admiral S. S. Bonham-Carter), the destroyers *Bulldog* (Commander M. Richmond RN Senior Officer), *Beagle*, *Amazon*, and *Newmarket* and the corvettes *Oxlip*, *Saxifrage*, and *Snowflake*. The *Edinburgh* was carrying steel

---

[1] Tippelskirch, ibid, page 552

plating for the repair of the damaged *Trinidad* which the Russians were unable to provide. The ice edge was further south than usual and the convoy encountered it on the night of 10/11 April and as a result the *Hebe* and *Speedy* together with 16 merchant ships received damage which obliged them to return to Iceland. The eight remaining ships were sighted by an enemy reconnaissance aircraft on 15 April and thereafter were bombed intermittently for two days, fortunately without being hit. The U-boats which had also made contact were more successful and *U 403* (Lieutenant-Commander Clausen) torpedoed the Convoy Commodore's ship, the *Empire Howard* which blew up. The Commodore, E. Rees RNR was not amongst the few survivors rescued. A strong gale from the north-west was now encountered and enemy activity ceased, the seven surviving ships reaching Kola Inlet safely on 19 April.

The westbound convoy QP 10, escorted by 7 destroyers, 2 of which were Russian, 4 minesweepers, and 2 trawlers with the cruiser *Liverpool* providing close cover, was heavily attacked by aircraft and U-boats during the first three days of its voyage and as a result the *Empire Cooper* and *Harpalion* were sunk by Ju 88s of III Coastal Group 30 and *El Occidente* and *Kiev* by *U 435*. The enemy lost 6 aircraft with 1 damaged. On reaching longitude 30°E the two Russian destroyers and the three British minesweepers returned to the Kola Inlet. German destroyers were ordered out on two occasions to intercept this convoy but bad weather and poor visibility caused the operations to be cancelled.

Whilst the two convoys were on passage Hitler conferred with Raeder and stressed the need for torpedo-carrying aircraft to attack these convoys. Although the German Navy had 15 He 115 aircraft fitted with torpedoes their slow speed made them easy targets for anti-aircraft gunfire and it was obvious that some of the types used by the Luftwaffe would be more suitable. In Raeder's opinion, however, the torpedo was a naval weapon and the aircraft carrying it should be part of the navy. The Chief of the Luftwaffe, *Reichsmarschall* Hermann Göring, was unwilling to concede this point and so the fitting of torpedoes to the faster He 111 aircraft had been delayed. Eventually Raeder had given way and the first twelve crews to be trained for this type of attack reached Bardufoss airfield in north Norway on 1 May 1942, together with 60 Ju 88 bombers. During the month a formidable force of aircraft was assembled at this and adjacent airfields and by 1 June amounted to 103 Ju 88 long-range bombers, 30 Ju 87 dive bombers, 42 He 111 torpedo bombers, 15 He 115 torpedo-armed floatplanes, and a reconnaissance force comprising 8 FW Condors, 22 Ju 88s, and 44 BV 138s making a grand total of 264 aircraft.

During the conference referred to above, Hitler stressed the need to step up attacks on the Arctic convoys which he declared must be made the navy's principal target and he ordered plans to be prepared for a combined sea and air offensive to be launched against them in June.

The next pair of convoys PQ 15 of 25 merchant ships and QP 11 of 13 sailed from Iceland and the Kola Inlet on 26 and 28 April respectively. Admiral Tovey had protested about the size of PQ 15 which he wanted limited to 15 ships but political pressure and the large number of ships awaiting convoy led to his being overruled. However, the escort forces had been strengthened, those allocated to PQ 15 comprising 7 destroyers, the special anti-aircraft ship *Ulster Queen* (a former Irish Mail packet), and the submarine *Sturgeon* which was to accompany the convoy as far as longitude 5°E. Close cover was provided by the cruisers *Nigeria* (flagship of Rear Admiral H. M. Burrough) and *London*. The increasing hours of daylight had obliged the withdrawal of the submarine patrols off Trondheim which had been so successful and it had been decided to dispose these ships in moving patrol areas located 150 miles from the Norwegian coast, i.e. beyond the normal range of enemy reconnaissance aircraft. Also included in PQ 15 was the Catapult Aircraft Merchant (CAM) ship *Empire Morn* in which a catapult carrying a Hurricane fighter had been installed over the forecastle. It was intended to be used to shoot down enemy shadowing aircraft; on completion of his mission the pilot had to ditch alongside the nearest destroyer and hope for a speedy rescue from the icy water.

As a result of experience gained with previous convoys in which the short endurance of the escort vessels had severely restricted their ability to hunt and attack submarines, an oiler, the *Gray Ranger*, had been included in the convoy and this subsequently became standard practice.

Due to the depletion of the Home Fleet to meet the requirements of the forces needed for the capture of Madagascar, Admiral Tovey's command had been reinforced by the US battleship *Washington*, flagship of Rear Admiral R. C. Giffen USN, the heavy cruisers *Wichita* and *Tuscaloosa*, and a squadron of destroyers. These, together with his flagship the *King George V*, the carrier *Victorious*, the cruiser *Kenya*, and 10 destroyers (4 of which were American) left Scapa on 27/28 April to provide distant cover for the two convoys. Whilst this force was cruising to the south of the convoy routes, on 1 May the 'Tribal' class destroyer *Punjabi* was rammed by the *King George V* in poor visibility and cut in half. The stern half on which a number of depth charges were stowed sank rapidly and the charges exploded, increasing the damage the battleship had suffered from the collison. The forward half of the *Punjabi* stayed afloat long enough for five officers and 201 men to be rescued, after which the *King George V* had to return to Scapa prior to being docked at Liverpool. Vice Admiral Curteis in the *Duke of York* assumed command of the covering force.

Enemy aircraft located PQ 15 shortly before midnight on 30 April but poor visibility and frequent snow squalls saved it from attack until 20.00 hrs on the following day when six Ju 88s carried out what Admiral Burrough described as 'a ragged and poorly executed attack', losing one of their number without scoring a hit. At midnight on 1/2 May the *London* parted company with orders to cruise to the west of Bear Island and at 10.00 hrs on 2nd the *Nigeria* also left convoy PQ 15 and joined the *London*, the two cruisers now transferring their attention to QP 11. As the two convoys passed each other they exchanged information and the senior officer of PQ 15's escort was left in no doubt that the prospects for the rest of his voyage were anything but rosy. Attacks by enemy destroyers, aircraft, and U-boats could be expected and the ice-edge was uncomfortably far south. In the event the convoy was kept under constant observation by one or more aircraft and U-boats, but before any attacks developed an unfortunate mishap occurred.

On 2 May the Polish submarine *P 551* which had strayed 100 miles from her assigned patrol position was located and attacked by two of the convoy escorts and suffered damage which necessitated her being sunk after the crew had been taken off. At 01.27 hrs on 3rd in visibility of about four miles and often less a number of torpedo aircraft of I Coastal Group 26 attacked without being detected by radar. They torpedoed the Commodore's ship SS *Botavon* as well as the *Jutland* and *Cap Corso* all of which subsequently sank; Commodore Archer and 137 members of the ship's crew were rescued while two enemy aircraft were destroyed and another was damaged and subsequently crashed. However, the escorts managed to keep the shadowing U-boats at bay and no attacks took place. A bombing attack by Ju 88 aircraft occurred at 22.30 hrs on 3 May during which a trawler was damaged by a near miss and one aircraft was shot down, then nature took a hand and a south-easterly gale bringing a heavy snow storm and very reduced visibility saved PQ 15 from further attacks and it reached Kola Inlet at 21.00 hrs on 5th.

Although the passage of PQ 15 could not be called uneventful, it did not suffer the vicissitudes of the homeward bound convoy QP 11. Its through escort comprised the destroyers *Bulldog* (Commander M. Richmond RN) *Beverly*, *Beagle*, *Amazon*, *Foresight*, and *Forester* with 4 corvettes and a trawler. The escort was reinforced as far as longitude 30°E by the Russian destroyers *Kuibyshev* and *Sokrushitelny* and a British minesweeper. Enemy aircraft and U-boats made contact on 29 April and the following afternoon as the cruiser *Edinburgh* (flagship of Rear Admiral S. S. Bonham-Carter) was zig-zagging at high speed some fifteen miles ahead of the convoy to be in a good position to repulse any attempted attacks by enemy destroyers, she was struck by two torpedoes fired by *U 456* (Lieutenant-Commander Teichert) which blew off her stern and wrecked her steering gear. It was a brilliantly executed attack and Teichert tenaciously followed the damaged cruiser as she slowly made her way back to the Kola Inlet, but he was prevented from getting in another attack by the vigilance of the destroyers *Foresight* and *Forester* which together with two Russian destroyers, were screening her. However, Teichert transmitted a report of his success to the Flag Officer, Northern Waters, Rear Admiral Schmundt who, although for lack of heavy ship cover had not intended to order out his destroyers to attack these two convoys, changed his mind on receipt of the news. At 01.00 hrs on 1 May Captain Schulze-Hinrichs with the destroyers *Hermann Schoemann*, *Z 24*, and *Z 25* sailed from Kirkenes and sped north.

Meanwhile QP 11 which at 05.40 hrs on 1st was about 150 miles east-south-east of Bear Island, was unsuccessfully attacked by four He 115 torpedo-armed floatplanes. During the attack the *Amazon* forced a persistent surfaced U-boat shadower to dive, but it was evident from the number of high frequency/direction finding bearings being intercepted that the convoy was being shadowed by at least four submarines. The presence of ice ahead now obliged it to alter course to port to 275° and at 13.45 hrs the corvette *Snowflake* obtained three radar contacts on a bearing of 185°. The wind was north-north-east force 3 and visibility varied from 2 to 10 miles during intermittent snow storms, while there were heavy ice floes close on the starboard hand. Almost simultaneously with the *Snowflake*'s detection, the destroyer *Beverly* on the port bow of the convoy sighted three large destroyers bearing 210°. These were the German ships mentioned above and between them they mounted 10 5.9-inch and 5 5-inch guns as against the 6 4.7-inch and 3 4-inch guns of the 4 British destroyers now remaining with the convoy. However, Commander Richmond, employing aggressive tactics befitting to the name of his ship *Bulldog*, successfully thwarted five attempts by the enemy to get at the convoy. The German ships finally came upon a Russian straggler, the *Tsiolkovski* which they sank, the crew being rescued by a trawler and at 17.45 hrs on receipt of orders to go in search of the damaged *Edinburgh*, they withdrew. During the action the *Amazon* had received a hit in her steering gear and the *Bulldog* received minor splinter damage; the enemy ships, however, were undamaged.

The *Edinburgh*, now seven feet down by the bows, and with only two of her four shafts in action and no rudder, was making slow and very difficult progress eastward. At 06.00 hrs on 1 May the two Russian destroyers were obliged to part company with her as they were running short of fuel, so the *Foresight* which had been secured astern of the cruiser as a means of helping to keep her on a steady course, cast off in order to resume screening duties which in view of *U 456*'s persistence, was of greater importance. Left to her own devices, the *Edinburgh* yawed drunkenly from side to side, and Captain Faulkner found that the only way to keep her approximately on course was to go astern on one engine from time to time to correct the yaw. This reduced the rate of progress to around two knots. When Admiral Bonham-Carter received news of the attacks by the German destroyers on PQ 15 he fully expected that they would turn their attention to his damaged flagship, so he instructed the *Foresight* and *Forester* to act independently in the event of such an attack and while taking every opportunity to defeat the enemy's purpose, not to take undue risks in defence of the cruiser.

At 18.00 hrs on 1st the *Edinburgh* and her two escorts were joined by the Russian tug *Rubin* and six hours later by the British minesweepers *Hussar, Harrier, Gossamer,* and *Niger.* The tug unfortunately was not powerful enough to take a 10,000-ton cruiser in tow so she secured to the cruiser's port bow and, with the *Gossamer* acting as a drogue aft, a speed of three knots on a reasonably steady course was reached. The remainder of the escorts formed an endless chain patrol round them. The wind was blowing force 3 from the north-north-east and provided conditions did not deteriorate the chances of making the Kola Inlet were reasonably good.

At 06.27 hrs on 2nd the *Hussar* on the starboard quarter of the stricken ship suddenly found herself under fire from three ships, the silhouettes of which could be dimly discerned, so she turned away and fell back on the cruiser. The enemy destroyers had found their new target; using smoke and taking advantage of occasional snow storms, they tried hard to get within torpedo range of her but were successfuly prevented from doing so by the bold tactics of the *Foresight* and *Forester.* At the first report of the enemy's presence the *Edinburgh* had slipped both the tug and the *Gossamer* and, although slowly circling round not under control, she was able to engage the enemy ships with her B turret's 6-inch guns. Her second salvo hit the *Hermann Schoemann*, putting her engines out of action, destroying her armament control, and bringing her to a standstill. She took no further part in the action. The *Foresight* was now being engaged by the *Z 24* at a range of about 8000 yards and the *Forester* soon joined in the action, both ships playing a game of hide and seek with their more powerful opponents in the smoke screens and snow flurries. At 06.50 hrs just after the *Forester* had fired three torpedoes at the enemy ships, she was hit by three shells which killed the Commanding Officer, Lieutenant Commander G. P. Huddart RN, put Number 1 boiler and 'B' gun out of action and shattered the breech mechanism of 'X' gun. Three minutes later Z 24 fired four torpedoes which passed under the *Forester* and sped on in the direction of the *Edinburgh* which, being incapable of taking avoiding action, was struck by one of them on the port side amidships, almost exactly opposite to where the self-inflicted damage had occurred. She immediately listed to port and stopped and it was evident that at any moment she might break in two. The Admiral ordered the *Gossamer* alongside to take off the wounded and the passengers, but the cruiser meanwhile continued the action and by so doing prevented the Z 24 from going to the assistance of her damaged consort. However, the *Edinburgh*'s list steadily increased and when it had reached 17° and her guns would no longer bear on the enemy, Admiral Bonham-Carter ordered Captain Faulkner to abandon ship. About 440 officers and men were transferred to the *Gossamer* and 350, including the Admiral, to the *Harrier*, the operation being screened by smoke from the *Hussar*.

Meanwhile, the two undamaged enemy ships were engaging the *Forrester* which was being repeatedly straddled, but at 07.14 hrs the *Foresight,* seeing her predicament, boldly steamed between her and the enemy, drawing their fire. A salvo of torpedoes fired at the *Hermann Schoemann* missed but the *Foresight* soon found herself facing the concentrated fire of the Z 24 and Z 25 at a range of 4000 yards and after suffering four direct hits she was obliged to stop with only one gun remaining in action. It was a desperate situation but fortunately the enemy was deterred from pressing home his advantage by his concern to rescue the crew of the slowly sinking *Hermann Schoemann*. At 07.35 hrs the *Forrester* managed to get under way again and was able to repay her debt to her sister ship by interposing a smoke screen between her and the German destroyers who were still engaging the stricken *Foresight*. The Z 24 now went alongside the *Hermann Schoemann* and took off some 200 of her crew after which she was scuttled. Then, in company with Z 25, who had received a hit in her radio office, the two ships withdrew at high speed to the north-west and returned to Kirkenes.

As there was now no chance of saving the *Edinburgh* the Admiral ordered the *Foresight* to sink her with her one remaining torpedo and this done all ships headed for the Kola Inlet which they reached on 3 May.

Considering the circumstances the casualties suffered by the British forces were not heavy. In the *Edinburgh* 2 officers and 55 ratings had been killed and 23 wounded. The *Foresight* and *Forester* lost 2 officers and 19 ratings killed with 20 wounded. In addition 1 Merchant Navy officer on passage was

Above The forecastle of HMS *Witch* almost unrecognisable under a thick coating of Arctic ice. The hedgehog anti-submarine mortar is completely hidden and only the barrel of the superimposed 4.7in gun is showing. Destroyers were especially vulnerable to the effect of top weight caused by icing (*National Maritime Museum*). *Below* The German heavy cruiser *Admiral Hipper* in northern Norway where she formed part of the Northern Battle Group. She was armed with eight 20.3cm (8in) guns but her main machinery was unreliable (*Imperial War Museum*)

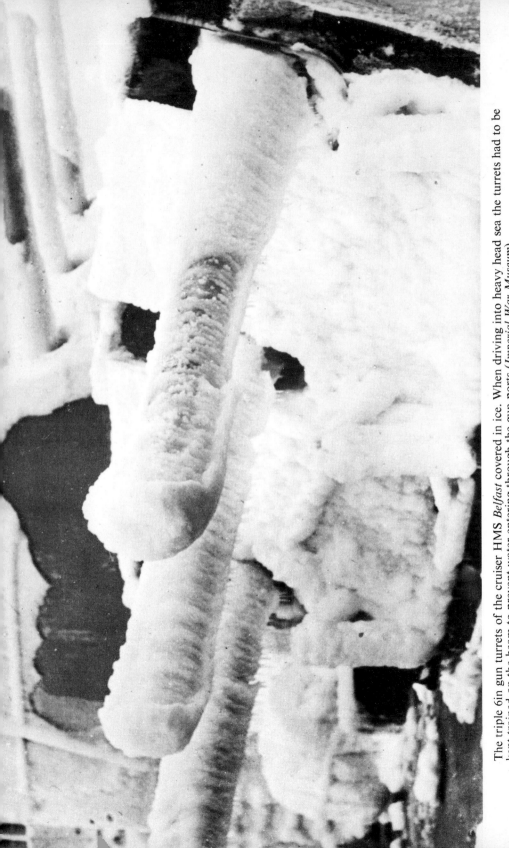

The triple 6in gun turrets of the cruiser HMS *Belfast* covered in ice. When driving into heavy head sea the turrets had to be kept trained on the beam to prevent water entering through the gun-ports (*Imperial War Museum*)

Above Admiral Arseni Golovko, C-in-C Soviet Northern Fleet and Rear Admiral D. B. Fisher, Senior British Naval Officer, North Russia, in conversation with officers of the British staff *(Novosti Press)*. *Below* Admiral Arseni Golovko with members of the crew of a submarine just returned from operations off enemy held territory *(Novosti Press)*

Above HMS *Onslow* and HMS *Ashanti* during operations in the Arctic. The latter has a light camouflage suitable for Arctic waters, whereas the former is painted a two-tone grey (*Imperial War Museum*). *Below* HMS *Bulldog* one of the 1930 'B' class British destroyers converted for convoy escort operations. The forward 4.7in gun was replaced by a hedgehog mounting and in place of the after 4.7in extra depth-charge throwers were fitted. An HF/DF aerial can be seen on the mainmast, an air-warning radar aerial on the fore topmast, and a surface warning radar 'lantern' above the bridge (*Imperial War Museum*).

HMS *Belfast* which rejoined the Home Fleet after repairs to extensive mine damage suffered early in the war. In 1943 she became flagship of Vice Admiral Burnett and played a leading role in the events leading up to the sinking of the German battle cruiser *Scharnhorst* (*Imperial War Museum*)

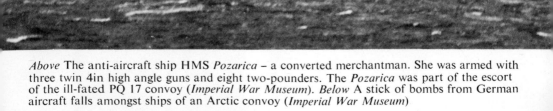

Above The anti-aircraft ship HMS *Pozarica* – a converted merchantman. She was armed with three twin 4in high angle guns and eight two-pounders. The *Pozarica* was part of the escort of the ill-fated PQ 17 convoy (*Imperial War Museum*). *Below* A stick of bombs from German aircraft falls amongst ships of an Arctic convoy (*Imperial War Museum*)

Above A Russian naval choir entertains the officers and ship's company of the battleship HMS *Duke of York* during a visit to Murmansk in 1943 (*Imperial War Museum*). *Below* An ammunition ship explodes during an air attack on convoy PQ 18, 14 September ,1942 (*Imperial War Museum*)

The Soviet submarine *K21* in the Kola Inlet, showing the bleak nature of the surroundings. Her captain Commander N. Lunin claimed a hit on the battleship *Tirpitz* during the PQ 17 operations but German records do not substantiate this claim (*Novosti Press*)

killed and 2 ratings wounded. Sixty men belonging to the *Hermann Schoemann* who had been left behind on a raft were later rescued by *U 88*.

The loss of the *Edinburgh* was only the beginning of the misfortunes which now began to overtake the Arctic convoys. With the help of the steel plating brought by that ship, the *Trinidad* had been patched up and made sea-worthy. On 5 May Admiral Bonham-Carter hoisted his flag on her preparatory to her return to Iceland and thence to the United States for permanent repair. Intelligence reports of possible movements by German heavy ships from Trondheim northwards, which turned out to be that of the pocket battleship *Admiral Scheer* to Narvik, delayed the *Trinidad*'s sailing until 13 May. Extensive precautions were taken to ensure her safe passage. As close escort she had the destroyers *Somali, Matchless, Foresight,* and *Forester,* whilst the cruisers *Nigeria* (flagship of Rear Admiral H. M. Burrough), *Kent, Norfolk,* and *Liverpool* screened by the destroyers *Inglefield, Escapade, Onslow,* and *Icarus* cruised to the west of Bear Island. Admiral Tovey in the *Duke of York* with the *Victorious,* USS *Washington,* and *Tuscaloosa* screened by 11 destroyers provided distant cover from a position further to the south-west. The Russians were asked to provide air cover for the first 200 miles of the voyage, but only three Hurricanes put in a brief appearance before returning to base. German reconnaissance aircraft quickly located the *Trinidad* and her escorts and by the evening of 14 May four of them had taken up shadowing positions and were reporting her movements at frequent intervals.

The first attack was delivered by a force of Ju 88 bombers at 22.00 hrs on 14 May. The wind was light, westerly, sea calm, visibility variable, and sky nine-tenths covered by low strato-cumulus clouds. The bombers failed to score any hits and at 22.37 hrs they were followed by about ten torpedo bombers. Whilst all eyes were watching their approach, at 22.45 hrs a single Ju 88 dived through the clouds towards the *Trinidad*'s starboard quarter and released a stick of bombs from a height of about 400 feet. One bomb hit the starboard side of the bridge structure and burst on reaching the lower deck where it started a fire which spread rapidly. A second bomb blew in a temporary patch abreast the Marines' mess deck and flooded 'B' turret magazine and adjacent compartments. The ship took on a list of 14° but managed to continue steaming at 20 knots and the torpedoes released by the distracting torpedo bombers were successfully avoided as were some more released during another attack fifteen minutes later. However, at 23.15 hrs it was necessary to stop the ship in order to reduce the draught of air reaching the fire and fanning the flames; soon after it was found to be out of control. As the ship was only about 170 miles from the enemy-held coast and in

U-boat infested waters it was evident that there was virtually no hope of saving her and abandon ship was ordered. The *Forester* had already taken off the wounded and passengers so now the ship's company were transferred to the other three destroyers. Admiral Bonham-Carter shifted his flag to the *Somali* and with the utmost reluctance at 01.20 hrs on 15 May he ordered the *Matchless* to sink the burning cruiser with torpedoes. On passage back to Iceland the four destroyers which had joined Admiral Burrough's cruiser force were attacked by 25 Ju 88 bombers when 350 miles from the nearest enemy airfield. Although no hits were obtained this was an indication of the extended threat which the Luftwaffe was now able to offer.

Commenting on the loss of the *Edinburgh* and *Trinidad*, Rear Admiral Bonham-Carter wrote:

> 'Until the aerodromes in north Norway are neutralised and there are some hours of darkness (that) the continuation of these convoys should be stopped. If they must continue for political reasons, very serious and heavy losses must be expected. The force of the German attacks will increase, not diminish.'

Admiral Tovey endorsed these views and reaffirmed his opinion that the convoys should be kept small, but as Mr Churchill has recorded in a minute which he addressed to the Chiefs of Staff Committee on 17 May 1942, 'Not only Premier Stalin but President Roosevelt will object very much to our desisting from running the convoys now. The Russians are in heavy action and will expect us to run the risk and pay the price entailed by our contribution . . . I share your misgivings but I feel it is a matter of duty.' [1]

Although with the lengthening days conditions were growing more unfavourable the next convoy to sail for north Russia was to be larger than any yet assembled.

---

[1] Churchill, ibid, Volume IV, page 233-4

Chapter 4

PRELUDE TO DISASTER

The German destroyer flotilla stationed in north Norway had lost two ships and it was believed that the remainder had suffered damage of one sort or another, and although there was the possibility of an attack by one or two of the pocket battleships, in making his dispositions for PQ 16 Admiral Tovey decided that the most serious threat to be guarded against was that of air attack. His cruisers with their heavier anti-aircraft armament were the best ships available for this purpose, but unfortunately he had only four of them, so he decided it was best to keep them concentrated and order them to give cover to the outward bound PQ 16 until it met the homeward bound QP 12 when they were to transfer to it. It was also arranged that all the merchant ships in PQ 16 should carry kite balloons and further to strengthen the anti-aircraft defence the anti-aircraft ship *Alynbank* and the CAM ship *Empire Lawrence* were included in the convoy. Five British and two Russian submarines patrolled to the south of the convoy route.

On 21 May convoy PQ 16 of 35 ships under Commodore N. H. Gale, RNR, in the SS *Ocean Voice* sailed from Hvalfiord escorted by the mine-sweeper *Hazard* and four trawlers, to be joined two days later by the *Alynbank*, the submarines *Trident* and *Sea-wolf*, the destroyers *Ashanti* (Senior Officer of the Escort Force, Commander R. G. Onslow RN), *Martin*, *Achates*, *Volunteer*, and ORP *Garland* with the corvettes *Honeysuckle*, *Starwort, Hyderabad*, and FS *Roselys*. The covering force comprised the cruisers *Nigeria* (flagship of Rear Admiral H. M. Burrough), *Norfolk*, *Kent*, and *Liverpool*, escorted by the destroyers *Onslow*, *Oribi*, and *Marne* which had sailed from Seidisfiord on 23 May. It steered to the north-east to reach a position from which it could cover both PQ 16 and QP 12, this convoy comprising 15 ships having sailed from the Kola Inlet on 21 May. The cruiser force was sighted and reported by enemy aircraft at 19.00 hrs on 23rd and about midnight it ran into dense fog.

The fog caused PQ 16 to split up into two sections and the destroyers had some difficulty in finding it. It was not until just after midnight on 24/25 May

41

that it was reassembled and at 05.35 hrs on 25th the cruiser force closed it and took station in pairs between the 4th and 5th and 5th and 6th columns, whilst the destroyers reinforced the screen. This formation had been designed to provide the best defence against air attack but it was not until fifteen hours later that it was put to the test.

Soon after the cruisers joined, a Focke Wulf reconnaissance aircraft began patrolling round the convoy, but to everyone's surprise the day passed quietly and the destroyers were able to replenish with fuel from the accompanying oiler *Black Ranger*. The first of a series of air attacks by III Coastal Groups 26 and 30 which were to last the greater part of five days, began at 20.35 hrs with the appearance of 7 He 111 torpedo aircraft and 8 Ju 88 bombers. 'It was a beautiful bright day, the sea calm and blue like the Mediterranean and the sky was now dotted with smoke from the flak shells', wrote Mr Alexander Werth, who was taking passage in SS *Empire Baffin* on his way to Moscow as a war correspondent.

'They went in a half circle round the front of the convoy, then after a few seconds of suspense they came right out of the sun. . . . They were after the cruisers in the middle of the convoy. The tracer bullets from our Oerlikons were rushing at the yellow belly of the Ju 88 as he swooped over us. A loud squeal, growing louder and louder, and then the explosion, as a stick of bombs landed between us and the destroyer on the port side.' [1]

The CAM ship *Empire Lawrence* flew off her solitary Hurricane aircraft which tore into the attackers shooting down one He 111 and damaging another. Unfortunately a trigger-happy gunner in one of the American ships opened fire on it as the pilot came into ditch, wounding him before he was picked up by the *Volunteer*. The SS *Carlton* suffered a fractured steam pipe from a near miss and was detached to return to Iceland in tow of the trawler *Northern Spray* but that was the only damage resulting from this attack.

Between 23.15 hrs and 23.30 hrs 12 Ju 88s delivered another but equally unsuccessful attack, then heavy grey clouds began to cover the sky and temporarily halted the air activity.

The presence of U-boats had been detected that afternoon when at 15.00 hrs the *Martin* sighted and attacked one seven miles on the convoy's starboard beam, but nearly twelve hours elapsed before an attack developed. At 03.05 hrs on 26th *U 703* (Lieutenant-Commander Bielfeld) torpedoed the SS *Syros*, 28 of her crew of 37 being rescued by the *Hazard* and the trawler *Lady Madeleine* before she sank.

PQ 16 and QP 12 had passed each other at 13.45 hrs on 25th but Admiral

---

[1] Alexander Werth, *The Year of Stalingrad* (Hamish Hamilton, 1946), page 31

Burrough, wishing to give the larger and more valuable convoy the support of his cruisers for as long as possible, an action which he considered to be in keeping with the spirit of his instructions, did not part company with PQ 16 until 04.00 hrs on 26th in a position 240 miles west-south-west of Bear Island. The low ceiling which persisted until the late afternoon saved the convoy from further air attack throughout the day but at 18.00 hrs eight He 111s and three Ju 88s made an abortive attack during which one of the escorting submarines was near-missed by a stick of bombs. The U-boats kept the escorts busy chasing them away as they tried to close the convoy, but direction-finding signals intercepted showed that they remained in company for another three days.

'I am not likely ever to forget this day', recorded Mr Werth in his diary for 27 May. It began with an ineffective air attack at 03.20 hrs shortly after which the convoy ran into heavy pack ice to the south of Bear Island and was obliged to alter course to the south-east for two hours to get clear of it. Disappointed by the lack of success so far achieved, the enemy now determined on an all out attack. It began with 111 Ju 88s and 7 He 111s at 11.15 hrs.

'For forty long minutes they attacked, usually in twos and threes, usually coming straight out of the sun, some diving low, others dropping their bombs from 200 feet. From their yellow, sharklike bellies one could see the obscene yellow eggs dropping, and after a moment of suspense one saw with relief the pillars of water leaping up.' [1]

The attacks continued intermittently for ten hours and as the sky began to cloud over with a ceiling of about 3000 feet the enemy aircraft were able to take up their attacking positions unseen.

At 13.10 hrs the SS *Alamar* was hit and set on fire by two bombs. This was their first success and it was followed five minutes later by another when the SS *Mormacsul* was damaged by two near misses. Both ships sank some 20 minutes later, their crews being rescued by the escorts. Between 14.05 hrs and 14.10 the Russian tanker *Stari Bolshevik* and the CAM ship *Empire Lawrence* were hit and set on fire. The trawler *Lady Madeleine* closed the last named and her Commanding Officer Lieutenant Commander Graeme Ogden RNVR asked her captain if she wanted any help.

'He shouted back something which I shall never know for at that moment I heard the cruel whine of bombers and looking aft saw three of them diving on us. I heard the swish of falling bombs but couldn't move our ship. The next thing I remember . . . the sky was full of strange shapes. We were covered with falling

---

[1] Werth, ibid, page 34.

wreckage and enveloped in suffocating brown smoke. I thought we must have been hit. When minutes later the smoke had cleared away there was no sign of the 12,000 ton *Empire Lawrence*.' [1]

Mr Werth watching from the *Empire Baffin* saw 'a flash which in the sun was not very bright and like a vomiting volcano a huge pillar of fire, smoke and wreckage shot two hundred feet into the air – and then slowly, terribly slowly, it went down to the sea.' [2] The explosion was caused by the TNT and ammunition in the ship's cargo and as most of the ships were similarly loaded, this incident had a profound effect on the crews of the remaining ships.

The crew of the *Stari Bolshevik* which included a number of women fought tenaciously to extinguish the fire and save their ship. She had fallen astern of the convoy and the destroyer *Martin* turned back during a lull to put the ship's doctor, Surgeon Lieutenant R. Ransome Wallis RNVR onboard. With some difficulty he and his sick berth attendant clambered up the side of the burning ship to be met by three women who led him to some bundles on deck which proved to be wounded men who were transferred to the *Martin*'s boat. After inspecting the damage to the tanker he returned to his ship and soon afterwards the *Lady Madeleine* came alongside and transferred five of the more seriously wounded survivors from the *Empire Lawrence*. 'One of these men, the second engineer, had a slightly depressed fracture of the outer layer of the skull which showed through a large scalp wound. As I was stitching him up we started to talk and I discovered he was one of my patients in peace time.' [3] A remarkable coincidence. With the help of the FS *Roselys* which went alongside and pumped water into the blazing forward hold, the crew of the *Stari Bolshevik* courageously fought and mastered the fire and she rejoined the convoy. For their devotion to duty the captain and first officer were made Heroes of the Soviet Union and the ship herself was awarded the Order of Lenin. The Board of Admiralty also sent their congratulations.

Near misses during the midday attacks had damaged the Polish destroyer *Garland*, the *Empire Baffin*, and the *City of Joliet*. The last named succumbed to her injuries and had to be sunk. When at 14.35 hrs the convoy reached a position about 80 miles south-east of Bear Island, ice conditions permitted a more northerly course to be followed, which enabled the distance from enemy airfields to be opened, and only one ineffective attack by

[1] Graeme Ogden, *My Sea Lady* (Hutchinson, 1963), page 121
[2] Werth, ibid, page 35
[3] R. Ransome Wallis, *Two Red Stripes* (Ian Allan Ltd, 1973), page 99

eight Ju 88s occurred during the afternoon. At 19.45 hrs, however, the enemy returned in strength and as before the attacks were delivered by a combination of Ju 88s and He 111s, the intention being that the former would so distract the defenders as to prevent them taking effective action to avoid the torpedoes of the latter. The *Empire Baffin* successfully avoided a torpedo which hit and sank the *Lowther Castle* whilst the *Empire Purcell* was hit by a stick of bombs and, like the *Empire Lawrence*, disintegrated with a loud explosion. The Commodore's ship *Ocean Voice* received a direct hit which tore away 20 feet of plating abreast Number 1 hold and started a fire, but she was able to maintain her station and reach port though by then she had only two feet freeboard forward.

Welcome clouds now began to gather overhead and no further attacks took place that evening, but with three days still to go and six ships lost the situation was anything but rosy.

> 'I felt far from optimistic', wrote Commander Onslow in his report, 'the question of ammunition began to worry me badly. . . . We were all inspired, however, by the parade ground rigidity of the convoy's station keeping including the *Ocean Voice* and the *Stari Bolshevik* who were both bellowing smoke from their foreholds.'

In the event the worst was over. During the forenoon three Russian destroyers, the *Grozny* (Senior Officer), *Sokrushitelny*, and *Kuibyshev* joined the escort and their anti-aircraft armament and no lack of ammunition provided most welcome reinforcement. At 21.30 hrs four Ju 88s carried out an unsuccessful attack and early the next morning two Ju 88s and six He 111s attacked also without success. Then in the evening further reinforcement arrived from the Kola Inlet in the shape of the minesweepers *Bramble*, *Leda*, *Seagull*, *Niger*, *Hussar*, and *Gossamer*. The convoy now split and six merchant ships escorted by the *Alynbank* and the *Martin* set course for Archangel. At 22.30 hrs this section was attacked by 15 and the Murmansk one by 18 Ju 88s but no hits were scored. On 30 May the Murmansk section suffered three more attacks during which two enemy aircraft were destroyed without loss or damage to the convoy. When 60 miles off the entrance to the Kola Inlet it received further protection from Russian manned Hurricane fighters. Whilst performing this duty the squadron leader, Lieutenant Colonel Boris Safonov, a most experienced pilot, was unfortunately shot down and lost.

At 16.00 hrs on 30 May the Murmansk section of PQ 16 'reduced in numbers, battered and tired but still keeping perfect station' passed Toros Island and entered the Kola Inlet, their hard-fought voyage completed.

While PQ 16 was fighting its way to north Russia the homeward convoy

QP 12 escorted by the destroyers *Inglefield* (Captain P. Todd RN), *Escapade*, *Venomous*, *St Albans*, *Boadicea*, and *Badsworth* with the anti-aircraft ship *Ulster Queen* and four trawlers was enjoying an uneventful passage, although shadowed by enemy aircraft from the forenoon of 25 May onwards. The CAM ship *Empire Morn* launched her Hurricane fighter which shot down one of the shadowers but the pilot was lost owing to the failure of his parachute to open when he baled out. Thick weather sheltered the convoy during the last part of its voyage and all ships reached port.

There were many lessons to be learned from the experiences of PQ 16. There was an obvious and urgent need for an aircraft carrier to accompany the Arctic convoys so that shadowing aircraft could be destroyed. More long-range radar sets were needed and also more anti-aircraft ships like the *Alynbank*. There was an evident need for rescue ships to prevent escort ships and trawlers from becoming overcrowded with survivors and to relieve the Escort Commander of anxiety for their recovery, whilst his ships counter-attacked the U-boats and fought off attacking aircraft. Finally it was essential to build up reserve stocks of ammunition at Murmansk.

Admiral Tovey was agreeably surprised by the comparatively small losses incurred by PQ 16 since four-fifths of the ships had arrived at their destinations. He attributed this to 'the gallantry, efficiency, and tireless zeal of the officers and men of the escorts and the remarkable courage and determination of those of the merchant ships. No praise can be too high for either.'

Although PQ 16 had not escaped without losses the German High Command was not satisfied with the result and especially the U-boat's lack of success. An entry in Admiral Dönitz's War Diary for 3 June 1942 reads:

'My opinion as to the small chances of success for U-boats against convoys during the northern summer . . . has been confirmed by experience with PQ 16. Owing to the difficult conditions for attack . . . the result, in spite of shadowing and a determined set-to by the boats, has been one steamer sunk and four probable hits. This must be accounted a *failure* when compared with the results of the anti-submarine activity for the boats operating. *U 436*, *U 703* have depthcharge damage, unfit to dive to greater depths. Three more boats have slight depthcharge damage, the effects of which . . . will probably mean some considerable time in dockyard.'

Dönitz reached the conclusion that during the northern summer the convoys could best be attacked by the Luftwaffe. In fact the claims made by the aircraft were greatly exaggerated and it was believed that the convoy had dispersed following the first attack on 25 May. They hoped the effect of the simultaneous dive-bombing and torpedo attacks would confuse the defence and this was believed to have been substantiated as also was that of the method of torpedo attack known as the Golden Comb. For this the aircraft approached the convoy in line abreast and released their torpedoes simultaneously. During the month which now elapsed before the next pair of convoys were ready to sail, these tactics were assiduously practised.

Calls made on the Home Fleet to provide ships to escort an urgently needed convoy for Malta prevented Admiral Tovey from assembling forces of sufficient strength to escort convoys PQ 17 and QP 13 until the latter part of June. When he learned that, like the previous convoy, PQ 17 was to consist of 35 ships, he proposed that it should be run in two sections and it was while discussing this point on the telephone with Admiral Pound that the latter suggested that in the event of an attack by German heavy surface ships after the convoy had entered the Barents Sea, he had it in mind to order the convoy to scatter. Such tactics had proved successful in the case of the convoy escorted by the armed merchant cruiser *Jervis Bay* when attacked in mid-Atlantic by the pocket battleship *Admiral Scheer*, but the lack of sea room in the Barents Sea with the ice to the north and the land to the south militated against their successful employment in that area unless ships were able to take cover in fog or snow. This last was a possibility but not a certainty on which Admiral Tovey for his part would not have been prepared to bank.

The Admiralty was aware that the German heavy ships *Tirpitz* and *Hipper* were at Trondheim and the *Scheer* and *Lützow* at Narvik and the indications were that the enemy intended to use these ships in conjunction with U-boats and aircraft in an attempt to annihilate the next convoy to Russia. As Admiral Tovey was to write in his despatch (*London Gazette*, 17 October 1950):

'The strategic situation was wholly favourable to the enemy. . . . His heavy ships would be operating close to their own coast, with the support of powerful shore-based air reconnaissance and striking forces and protected, if he so desired, by a screen of U-boats in the channels between Spitzbergen and Norway. Our covering forces on the other hand, if they entered these waters, would be without shore-based air support, one thousand miles from their base, with their destroyers too short of fuel to escort a damaged ship to harbour.'

If the German ships made a sortie he hoped that if he reversed the course of PQ 17 for 12 to 18 hours when it reached longitude 10°E, the German ships would be lured to the west and away from their shore-based air cover into waters where he could bring them to action under more favourable conditions. The Admiralty did not altogether agree with this strategy, but in the operational orders for the convoy a clause was included which envisaged the possibility of the convoy being turned back in certain circumstances of which the Admiralty would be the judge. West of Bear Island the safety of the convoy against surface ship attack was to be assured by Admiral Tovey's covering force but east of that meridian it would be the responsibility of the submarines, two of which were to accompany the convoy and the remainder disposed to intercept the German ships as they left port. The cruiser force accompanying the convoy was not to go east of Bear Island unless the convoy was threatened by enemy forces which did not include the *Tirpitz* but in any case it was not to go beyond longitude 25°E.

Admiral Tovey's views on the operation about to commence, as has been explained, did not accord with those of the Admiralty, especially with regard to the possibility of scattering the convoy. All experience to date had shown that ships should keep closed up for mutual support in the face of heavy air attack, but as will be seen, the matter was taken out of his hands.

Meanwhile, the German plan for an all-out attack on PQ 17, known as Operation *Rösselsprung* (see Appendix IX) had been drawn up. It was presented to Hitler on 1 June with an assurance that it would be executed only if adequate air cover were available and no superior enemy forces were within striking distance. After some consideration the Führer approved the plan with the proviso that the whereabouts of enemy aircraft carriers must be determined before the ships sailed so that the Luftwaffe could attack them. As it was impossible to guarantee fulfilment of this condition Raeder devised the expedient of executing the operation in two phases. On the location of the convoy the ships ordered to take part would be moved, the *Tirpitz* group to the Vestfiord and the *Scheer* group to Altenfiord, close to the North Cape, there to await Hitler's permission to proceed on phase two. When this was received the two groups would sail to meet at a rendezvous 100 miles north of the North Cape, and then proceed in company to attack the convoy in the Barents Sea between longitudes 20° and 30°E. U-boats and aircraft were to be responsible for giving early notice of the approach of the convoy.

On 27 June the long delayed convoy PQ 17 of 35 merchant ships under Commodore J. C. K. Dowding DSO, RNR sailed from Hvalfiord. One ship ran ashore on leaving harbour and another was damaged by ice in the Denmark Straits and returned for repair. The initial escort of the mine-sweepers *Halcyon*, *Britomart*, and *Salamander* with four trawlers was joined on 30 June by the close escort from Seidisfiord under Commander J. E. Broome RN Senior Officer, in the destroyer *Keppel* with the destroyers *Leamington*, *Wilton*, *Ledbury*, *Fury*, and *Offa*, the corvettes *Lotus*, *Poppy*, *Dianella*, FFS *La Malouine*, the anti-aircraft ships *Palomares* and *Pozarica*, and the submarines *P 613* and *P 615* in company. For the first time three specially equipped rescue ships the *Rathlin*, *Zaafaran*, and *Zamalek* were included in the escort. Attached to the convoy were the tankers *Gray Ranger* and *Aldersdale*, but the first, after damage from ice, had to be transferred to the homeward convoy QP 13.

As an additional protection against attack by German surface ships the British submarines *Sahib*, *Sturgeon*, *Unrivalled*, *Unshaken*, *Ursula*, *Tribune*, *Seawolf*, and *Trident* with the FFS *Minerve* and the Russian submarines *D3*, *K21*, *K22*, *Shch 402*, and *403* were stationed on two patrol lines off the north Norwegian coast (see Diagram V).

The ice had receded far enough for the convoy to be routed north of Bear Island and thus further from the enemy airfields in north Norway. Also, as Murmansk had, in the words of Admiral Golovko 'ceased to exist' as a result of heavy bombing attacks, all ships were routed to Archangel which was now free of ice.

The covering forces for the two convoys comprised the cruisers *London* (flagship of Rear Admiral L. K. Hamilton DSO) *Norfolk*, USS *Tuscaloosa* and *Wichita*, while Admiral Tovey in the battleship *Duke of York* with the battleship USS *Washington* (flagship of Rear Admiral R. C. Giffen USN) the carrier *Victorious* (flagship of Vice Admiral Sir Bruce Fraser), the cruisers *Nigeria* (flagship of Rear Admiral H. M. Burrough) and *Cumberland* and 14 destroyers. In an attempt to deceive the enemy into thinking that a raid on the Norwegian coast was intended, a dummy convoy consisting of the five ships of the First Minelaying Squadron and four colliers escorted by the cruisers *Sirius* and *Curacao*, some destroyers and trawlers, left Scapa on 29 June and steered to the east. If it had not been sighted by enemy reconnaissance on reaching longitude 1°E it was to turn back. To add to the deception a diversionary bombing attack on targets in southern Norway was laid on. Although the convoy made two advances eastward on 30 June and again on 1 July, the ruse failed as the enemy did not observe it.

The weather was fine on 1 July enabling the destroyers escorting PQ 17 to top up with fuel from the *Gray Ranger*. German radio intelligence had located the convoy during the forenoon and it was also sighted by *U 253* and *U 408* some 60 miles east of Jan Mayen Island. Two more U-boats *U 334* and *U 456* were ordered to close the convoy while the six boats of the 'Eisteufel' group (*U 251*, *U 335*, *U 657*, *U 88*, *U 457*, and *U 376*) were ordered to form a patrol line further to the east across the convoy's line of advance. During the afternoon, German air reconnaissance sighted PQ 17 and also what was thought to be the battleship covering force but which must have been Hamilton's cruiser force, though the latter was not aware of it.

Meanwhile, the two sections of QP 13 had sailed from Archangel and the

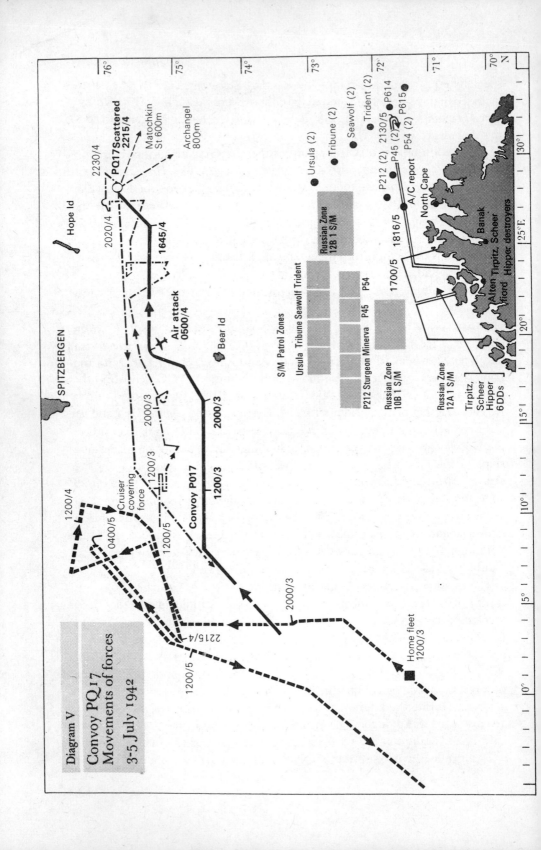

Diagram V

Convoy PQ17
Movements of forces
3–5 July 1942

N

SPITZBERGEN

Hope Id

Matochkin
St 600m

Archangel
800m

2230/4

PQ17 Scattered
2215/4

2020/4

1645/4

Air attack
0500/4

Bear Id

2000/3

2000/3

2000/3

2000/3

1200/3

1200/3

Convoy PQ17

1200/3

Cruiser
covering
force

1200/4

0400/5

1200/5

1200/5

1200/5

2215/4

2000/3

Home fleet
1200/3

Ursula (2)

Tribune (2)

Seawolf (2)

Trident (2)

P212 (2)   P614

2130/5   P45 (2)   P615

P54 (2)

A/C report

North Cape

1816/5

1700/5

Banak

Alten   Tirpitz, Scheer
fiord   Hipper destroyers

S/M Patrol Zones

Ursula Tribune Seawolf Trident

P212 Sturgeon Minerva   P45

Russian Zone
12B 1 S/M

P54

Russian Zone
10B 1 S/M

Russian Zone
12A 1 S/M

Tirpitz,
Scheer
Hipper
6DDs

Kola Inlet, comprising 12 and 23 ships respectively, and they joined up at sea on 28 June. This convoy was also located by enemy aircraft but as it was not the object of the operation no further action was taken against it. PQ 17 and QP 13 passed each other during the afternoon of 2 July in latitude 73°N longitude 3°E and the oiler *Gray Ranger* transferred to the homeward bound convoy. *U 456* managed to keep in close touch with PQ 17 but the other three boats were driven off temporarily by the aggressive tactics of the close escort.

At about 18.00 hrs, in visibility of ten miles, seven He 115s of I Coastal Air Wing 906 delivered an unsuccessful torpedo attack, one of them being shot down by the guns of the *Fury*. Its crew was rescued in a dramatic manner by one of the other seaplanes which landed alongside and picked them up.

Admiral Hamilton was hoping to keep the enemy guessing as to his whereabouts and so he cruised with his force some 40 miles to the north of PQ 17 thinking the enemy might be tempted to attack the convoy with his pocket battleships which he was quite willing to engage; the *Tirpitz* he thought might go for QP 13 which was closing the battleship covering force as it steamed south-west.

Thick fog developed during the night of 2/3 July and an opportunity was taken to alter the course of the convoy to the east at 07.00 hrs, the movement not being observed by the shadowing aircraft. However, Hamilton, unaware that his force had been sighted, decided that this was an opportune moment to disclose his presence to the enemy so he closed to within 20 miles of PQ 17 but due to the poor visibility the shadowing aircraft were temporarily out of touch. On receipt of information from the Admiralty that reconnaissance indicated that the ice edge lay further north than had been supposed, he sent the *London*'s Walrus aircraft to suggest to Commander Broome that he could now take the convoy 70 miles north of Bear Island. Clouds had prevented any of the ships from checking their dead-reckoning positions by observations of the sun, so not surprisingly there was a difference of some 20 miles between the cruiser flagship's estimated position and that of the senior officer of the escort, this caused Hamilton to suppose that the convoy was further to the south than in fact it was. On receipt of the message, Broome altered its course 30° to the north, but this did not satisfy Hamilton who, at 22.15 hrs sent the Walrus with a recommendation for a further alteration. Broome complied, albeit reluctantly, since he realised only too well that the northerly diversion, while opening the distance from the German airfields, would delay the convoy in reaching its destination and moreover, his instructions emphasised that 'the primary object is to get as much of the convoy through as possible and the best way to do this is to keep it moving eastwards

51

even though suffering damage'. At the same time as he launched the Walrus, Hamilton again closed the convoy with his cruisers and this time the shadowing aircraft sighted them, but being unfamiliar with the silhouettes of the refitted *London* and also those of the two US cruisers, the observer reported them as two carriers and a battleship. Having regard to the restrictions which Hitler had placed on the movements of his ships, this was an unfortunate error, which produced some confusion at Naval Group North.

Implementation of Phase 1 of Operation *Rösselsprung* started inauspiciously on the previous day 2 July when the *Tirpitz* (flagship of Admiral Schniewind) and *Hipper* with the destroyers *Hans Lody, Theodor Riedel, Karl Galster*, and *Friedrich Ihn* and torpedo boats *T 7* and *T 15* sailed from Trondheim for Altenfiord. The following day the *Scheer* (flagship of Vice Admiral Kummetz) and *Lützow* with the destroyers *Z 24, Z 27, Z 28, Z 29, Z 30*, and *Richard Beitzen* left Narvik for Altenfiord. The *Lody, Riedel*, and *Galster* grounded on Grimsöystraumen and had to return to Trondheim for repairs, and to make matters worse, the *Lützow* ran ashore on leaving Ofot fiord and could take no further part in the operation.

These mishaps were not known to the Admiralty which, after several days during which air reconnaissance of Trondheim had been prevented by cloud, received information on 3 July that the harbour was empty. Admiral Tovey and the forces escorting PQ 17 were at once informed and three hours later, at 22.22 hrs this information was supplemented by an appreciation that a move by enemy heavy units towards the north was in progress, that although this threatened the convoy, there was no immediate danger, and that, as the weather seemed to be favourable to the convoy's easterly progress, no action was being taken at present though developments were being awaited.

During the morning watch of 4 July, PQ 17 now steering east, passed some 60 miles north of Bear Island and at 05.00 hrs sustained its first loss when a single He 115 of I Coastal Air Wing 906, diving through a hole in the cloud, released a torpedo which hit the US freighter *Christopher Newport* amidships. Her crew were picked up by the rescue ships *Zaafaran* and *Zamalek* and the abandoned ship, unable to steam, was torpedoed by submarine *P 614* on the orders of Commander Broome and subsequently by *U 457*. The sea at the time was a glassy calm and fog patches produced by the sun shining on the ice-cold sea were being encountered.

From intelligence sources the Admiralty deduced that the German surface ships would attack PQ 17 between longitudes 15° and 30°E, i.e. sometime during 4 July, and so informed Admiral Tovey whose covering force at noon on that day was 100 miles west of the southern tip of Spitzbergen. At 12.30 hrs the Admiralty told Hamilton that he could take his cruiser force east of longitude 25°E unless Admiral Tovey ordered otherwise. The Commander-in-Chief, as he subsequently wrote in his report, regarded this signal as 'a reversal of the policy agreed between Their Lordships and myself' and having no information in his possession which justified the change, at 15.12 hrs he ordered Hamilton 'to leave the Barents Sea unless assured by the Admiralty that the *Tirpitz* cannot be met, once the convoy is eastward of 25°E or earlier at your discretion'. This message crossed one which Hamilton had made informing Tovey that he intended to remain in the vicinity of the convoy until the situation regarding the enemy surface ships' movements became clearer, but certainly not later than 14.00 hrs on 5 July. However, at 18.09 hrs he amended this and expressed his intention of withdrawing to the west at 22.00 hrs on 4th when the fuelling of his destroyers had been completed. At 18.58 hrs the Admiralty told Hamilton that 'Further information may be available shortly. Remain with convoy pending further instructions.'

Meanwhile at 16.45 hrs, in order to open the range from Banak airfield, he suggested to Broome that the convoy alter course from east to north-east. The fog had now lifted, although patches still remained here and there, and the sky was overcast, but the ceiling sufficiently high to favour the enemy's aircraft. The latter were not long in taking advantage of these conditions and at 19.30 hrs a force of Ju 88s from Coastal Group 30 and He 115 torpedo aircraft attacked but were prevented from achieving any success by the aggressive tactics of the US destroyer *Wainwright* (Commander D. Moon USN) which had just closed the *Aldersdale* to refuel when the attack came in. Casting off immediately, Moon sailed into the low-flying Heinkels with his guns blazing, and all their torpedoes missed. The bombers likewise had no success.

However, at 20.20 hrs a more serious attack developed when a force of some 30 He 111s of Coastal Group 26, boldly led by Captain Eicke, carried out a Golden Comb attack, letting go their torpedoes right in the middle of the convoy. Four aircraft were shot down but three ships were hit. The *Navarino* was struck by two torpedoes amidships and at once started to settle. The US freighter *William Hooper* managed to avoid one torpedo but was struck by another on the starboard side which exploded in her engine room. The Russian tanker *Azerbaijan* was hit just forward of her engine room but was able to continue steaming and a fire caused by the explosion was fought and eventually mastered. The rescue ship *Zaafaran* rescued 8 men who had been blown overboard from the *Azerbaijan*, 30 survivors from the *Navarino*, and 11 from the *William Hooper*, while the *Rathlin* picked up 44 from the *William Hooper* and 19 from the *Navarino*. The abandoned

William Hooper was eventually sunk by *U 334*, one of four U-boats still trailing the convoy.

Admiral Hamilton, who had watched the air attack from his flagship then ten miles north of the convoy was surprised that some of the enemy aircraft had not attempted to attack his cruisers, but the destruction of PQ 17 was uppermost in the enemy's mind. By 21.00 hrs the attack was over and Commander Broome, having steamed through the convoy, resumed his position at its head, well satisfied with its performance in the face of a determined, but not very successful attack. His only anxiety, like that of Commander Onslow in PQ 16, was whether the ammunition would hold out. Provided it did, he was convinced that PQ 17 'could get anywhere'. However, at this juncture fate intervened in a way which took everyone concerned with the safety of the 30 surviving ships of the convoy by surprise.

Chapter 5
DISASTER

It was with considerable misgivings that the Admiralty agreed to the sailing of PQ 17. From a naval point of view it was a most unsound operation of war, but political considerations were paramount. The Russians were fighting desperately to stem the German onslaught and American ships loaded with war materials of all kinds were arriving daily in Iceland for onward transit to north Russia. British and American transport experts favoured the longer but safer route into Russia via the Persian Gulf but Lord Beaverbrook had agreed with Stalin, neither of them understanding the difficulties to be overcome, that aid to Russia would be channelled through the northern ports and both Churchill and Roosevelt had accepted this decision.

As on the evening of 4 July the escorts of PQ 17 were successfully resisting the heavy air attack to which the convoy was being subjected, 1800 miles away in the office of the First Sea Lord in London, Admiral Sir Dudley Pound was conferring with officers from the Intelligence Division regarding the possible disposition of the German surface ships in general, and the *Tirpitz* in particular, relative to the convoys PQ 17 and QP 13. Commander (now Vice Admiral Sir Norman) Denning whose particular task this was and whose knowledge of German radio traffic had enabled him to predict the Channel dash of the enemy battle-cruisers *Scharnhorst* and *Gneisenau*, told him that he was 'tolerably certain' that the Narvik force had moved north and was now at Altenfiord, hard by the North Cape, and that the *Tirpitz* force had joined it. In reply to the First Sea Lord's query whether the last named was still in harbour, Denning told him that he could give no firm assurance but, knowing the customary radio conversation accompanying the sailing of the destroyers preceding that of a heavy ship, he was confident he would know as soon as such a move took place. This reply did not altogether satisfy Admiral Pound and after a visit to the Submarine Tracking Room, he returned to his office and called a meeting of the senior officers of the naval staff concerned with the operation of the Arctic Convoys. Time was obviously running out and a decision regarding PQ 17 was becoming urgent.

After outlining the situation in the light of the information he had just gathered from the Intelligence Division, he invited opinions from all those present. A chart lay on the table showing the estimated positions of the convoys and their covering forces and it was evident that if the German ships were about to leave or had left Altenford, they could intercept PQ 17 any time after 02.00 hrs on 5 July. The possibility of turning the convoy back and ordering Admiral Tovey with his battleship covering force to steam towards it at high speed was discussed. While such action might well have prevented the execution of the German plan, having regard to Hitler's proviso about attacking the aircraft carrier, it would not have given the Russians the promised supplies and there was a possibility that the ships in convoy might not have sufficient fuel to make the return voyage to Iceland.

An alternative course was for the battleship covering force to accompany the convoy right through to Archangel, but with only one carrier equipped with aircraft much inferior in number and performance to those deployed on the German airfields in north Norway, such action had nothing to recommend it. If the carriers were put out of action and the battleships damaged, the door to the Atlantic would be wide open for the *Tirpitz* to escape and far heavier losses in merchant ships would result than if the whole of PQ 17 were destroyed.

Yet another suggestion was to withdraw Hamilton's cruiser force as intended, and allow the convoy to continue its course with the destroyer escort. Whilst this certainly had the merit of keeping the merchant ships concentrated for mutual protection against air and U-boat attack, it would make the task of the *Tirpitz* and her consorts that much easier. If they did the job properly, not a single ship would survive.

After two hours of deliberation and having heard the views of everyone present it fell to Admiral Pound to make what must have been the most difficult decision of his long career. After a few minutes thought he turned to the Director of the Signal Division and said, 'Tell the cruisers to withdraw to the westward at high speed and the convoy to disperse'. In the event two signals were made. The first one timed 21.11 hrs on 4th to the cruisers and a second one twelve minutes later told the escorts of PQ 17: 'Owing to the threat from surface ships convoy is to disperse and proceed to Russian ports'. This was amended 23 minutes later to, 'Convoy is to scatter'.

The receipt of these two signals, both of which were prefixed *most immediate* produced similar reactions from both Admiral Hamilton and Commander Broome. To both these officers they conveyed the impression that an attack on the convoy by enemy surface ships was imminent and they acted accordingly. One of the cruisers, the *Norfolk*, had flown off her aircraft just before the signals were received, so Hamilton held on towards the east for half an hour whilst unsuccessful attempts were made to recall it. The visibility was extreme except for fog patches and there were numerous growlers around. At 22.30 hrs Hamilton led his cruisers round passing south of the convoy to get between it and the expected enemy force and steadied on a westerly course at a speed of 25 knots. Broome closed the Commodore's ship the *River Afton* to have a few words with Commodore Dowding who was ignorant of the instructions which both the cruisers and destroyers had received. When he saw the *Keppel* approaching, flying the signal to scatter from her masthead, Dowding could hardly believe his eyes. Broome put him in the picture and has recorded, 'When I sheered *Keppel* away from the *River Afton* I left an angry and, I still believe, unconvinced Commodore'.[1] However, when the message had been passed to the equally astonished masters of the merchant ships they carried out the instructions for scattering with naval precision. The ships in the centre column continued their course whilst those to starboard and port turned outwards until they were separating like the ribs of a fan. All ships increased to full speed and from now on they would navigate independently but obeying a natural instinct some ships tended to keep together for mutual support.

After clearing the convoy Broome ordered the other destroyers of the escort force to join him. He had not received the Admiralty's signal ordering the cruisers to withdraw to the west but he could see that this was what they were doing and, being convinced that an action with the enemy was imminent, he proposed to Hamilton that he should join him and this the Admiral approved, so expecting any moment to see the enemy ships appearing over the horizon, the four cruisers and six destroyers headed west.

The anti-aircraft ships *Palomares* and *Pozarica*, together with the four corvettes, three minesweepers, four trawlers, and three rescue ships were without a convoy to protect and, like the merchant ships, were now on their own. Broome, on leaving, had told the two submarines to act independently and they took up patrol positions in the path of the supposedly approaching enemy. The *Pozarica*, screened by the corvettes *Poppy*, *Lotus*, and *La Malouine*, steered north-east towards the ice barrier and was joined by the *Rathlin* carrying some 60 survivors. The *Palomares* and the *Dianella*, *Salamander*, and *Britomart* headed south-east. The trawlers *Lord Middleton*, *Lord Austin*, and *Northern Gem* also headed north-east while the trawler *Ayrshire* (Lieutenant J. S. Gradwell RNVR) took the freighters *Silver Sword*, *Troubador*, and *Ironclad* under his wing and steered north. The

---

[1] Captain Jack Broome RN (ret'd), *Convoy is to scatter* (William Kimber, 1972), page 193

rescue ships *Zaafaran* and *Zamalek* with the tanker *Aldersdale* started off in company but by the following morning had separated. The remaining ships of the convoy steered in an easterly direction at their best speed.

The enemy soon realised what had happened to PQ 17 and the air was full of radio chatter as they made plans for its destruction. Three wings of Air Wing 30 under Captains Kahl, Stoffregen, and Herrman began a series of round-the-clock attacks on the hapless merchant ships in which the U-boats formerly shadowing the convoy, joined. *U 88* claimed the first victim when she torpedoed the *Carlton* in the early hours of 5 July. An hour later *U 703* sank the *Empire Byron* with a torpedo amidships and followed up this success by sinking the Commodore's ship, *River Afton* around midday. *U 456* put a torpedo into the *Honomu* and aircraft accounted for the *Washington*, *Bolton Castle*, *Peter Kerr*, and *Pankraft* as well as damaging the *Paulus Potter* and *Earlston*, the last being sunk subsequently by *U 334*. The *Paulus Potter* however, remained afloat until 13 July when she was torpedoed by *U 255* which salvaged secret documents from the wreck providing the Germans with detailed information about the convoy operation. Later that afternoon the *Fairfield City* and *Daniel Morgan*, emerging from a protecting fog bank, were set upon by three Ju 88s which sank the former and damaged the latter which was given a *coup de grâce* by *U 88*. A group comprising the tanker *Aldersdale*, the freighter *Ocean Freedom*, the rescue ship *Zaafaran*, and the minesweeper *Salamander* fought off the attacking aircraft with some success but ultimately the *Aldersdale* and *Zaafaran* were hit, their crews being taken off by the *Salamander* and rescue ship *Zamalek* which was coming up astern. In the first 24 hours of the onslaught 13 freighters and one rescue ship had been sunk.

Although by the following day the surviving ships had put some 400 miles between themselves and the enemy airfield at Banak and were, therefore, approaching the supposed range limit of the enemy bombers, these managed to reach out and on 6 July sank the *Pan Atlantic*. The same day *U 255* sank the *John Witherspoon*, and the following day the *Alcoa Ranger*. That day *U 355* found and sank the *Hartlepool*, while *U 457* despatched the hull of the *Aldersdale*. On 8 July the *Olopana* which had reached the coast of Novaya Zemla and was heading south for the White Sea was caught by *U 255* which, after torpedoing her, surfaced and finished her off with gunfire. There were, however, three ships which in spite of being attacked, managed to reach Archangel. They were the Russian tanker *Donbass*, the freighter *Bellingham*, the rescue ship *Rathlin*, this last packed with 240 survivors from the sunken ships.

At 02.30 hrs on 6th the Admiralty informed the escorts of PQ 17 that an attack by German surface ships was probable during the next few hours and instructed them to avoid destruction so that they could return to the scene of the attack to pick up survivors after the enemy had retired. This information was based on a number of sightings of the German ships after they sailed from Altenfiord. Hitler's permission to execute Phase 2 of Operation *Rösselsprung* was given during the forenoon of 5 July and at 11.37 hrs the *Tirpitz*, *Scheer*, *Hipper*, and seven destroyers were authorised to proceed. The force was sighted and unsuccessfully attacked by the Russian submarine *K 21* at about 17.00 hrs and an hour later a Catalina flying boat of Number 210 squadron of the RAF operating from a Russian base, reported 11 strange ships steering 065° at 10 knots. Next the British submarine *Unshaken*, which was moving to take up a new patrol position further east, reported the *Tirpitz* and *Hipper* with at least 6 destroyers in company with 8 aircraft steering 060° at 22 knots, but she was unable to get into position for an attack. Finally, the British submarine *Trident* made a sighting report at 20.29 hrs on 5th but she, too, was unable to make an attack.

Captain N. A. Lunin of the *K 21* had fired a salvo of four torpedoes at the *Tirpitz* and claimed to have hit her, though post-war enquiries have established that this was not the case. However, the Admiralty, hoping that the report was correct, suggested to Admiral Tovey on three occasions during the night of 5/6 July that *Victorious*'s aircraft might now be able to get in an attack on the supposedly damaged battleship. The battleship covering force was at the time some 450 miles away to the south-west and so could not get within range of the *Tirpitz* under some ten hours' steaming, but the Admiralty hoped that if the force were seen to be steering in an easterly direction the *Tirpitz* might be reluctant to go too far east in search of the ships of the convoy for fear of being cut off. At 06.45 hrs on 6th, on hearing the approach of an enemy reconnaissance aircraft, Admiral Tovey altered the course of his force to the east and endeavoured to attract its attention, but without success, so he resumed his previous south-westerly course. At 10.40 hrs on the same day he was joined by Hamilton with his cruisers and destroyers and the weather having deteriorated so that it was unsuitable for operating aircraft, the force set course for Scapa Flow which was reached on 8 July.

Meanwhile news of the success of the U-boats and aircraft in disposing of the ships of PQ 17 made it evident to the German Naval Command that the *Tirpitz* force was no longer needed and at 21.30 hrs on 5th, much to Admiral Schniewind's disappointment, Operation *Rösselsprung* was called off, the force entering Kaafiord the following day.

To return to the scattered remnants of PQ 17, the anti-aircraft ships *Palomares* and *Pozarica* with the minesweepers *Halcyon*, *Salamander*, and

Britomart, the corvettes *Poppy* and *La Malouine*, the rescue ship *Zamalek* and the freighters *Ocean Freedom*, *Samuel Chase*, *Hoosier*, *El Capitan*, and *Benjamin Harrison* had managed to reach an anchorage in the Matochkin Strait which separates the two halves of Novaya Zemlya. Here they were joined by the trawlers *Lord Austin*, *Lord Middleton*, and *Northern Gem*, and later by the corvette *Lotus* carrying the gallant Commodore Dowding whom she had found floating on a raft with two other members of the *River Afton*'s crew. She had subsequently picked up a further 78 survivors from the crews of the *River Afton* and *Pankraft*. It seemed to all who had reached this bleak and desolate bay that they were probably the sole survivors of the convoy and the mood onboard all ships was grim. Captain J. H. Jauncey RN of the *Palomares*, being the senior officer, called a meeting of commanding officers and masters of all ships present at which it was decided that no time must be lost in vacating the exposed and undefended anchorage in which they found themselves.

The seventeen ships left the anchorage on the evening of 7 July and headed south for the entrance to the White Sea. On clearing the Strait they ran into dense fog which persisted until midnight and the *Benjamin Harrison* losing touch, returned to the anchorage. In the afternoon of 8 July the fog again thickened, but hugging the coast and hoping to pass east to Kolguev island, the little convoy steamed on. Suddenly, without warning, it ran into ice and in a moment all was confusion as engines were reversed, sirens hooted, and ships manoeuvred to avoid collision with each other. The *Ocean Freedom* nevertheless severely damaged her bows when she hit the ice. With the help of radio telephony the convoy re-formed on a westerly course which was maintained until clear water was reached on the morning of 9 July. All of a sudden the fog lifted and two boatloads of survivors from the *Pan Atlantic* were sighted and recovered. All eyes now scanned the southern horizon for signs of the Russian aircraft which had been requested, the convoy being now only 60 miles from the mainland, but instead the unwelcome silhouette of a Blohm and Voss reconnaissance aircraft appeared, a certain warning that air attack would follow.

During the pseudo night of 9/10 July 40 Ju 88s of II Coastal Group 30 carried out a series of attacks over a period of four hours during which the freighters *Hoosier* and *El Capitan* were damaged, abandoned, and subsequently sunk by *U 376* and *U 251* respectively. Their crews were picked up by the corvette *Poppy* and the trawler *Lord Austin* as the rescue ship *Zamalek* with 240 survivors onboard could not take any more. This ship had, in fact, had a very narrow escape from destruction being at one time surrounded by near misses which caused damage to her engines and she had to stop for repairs. When she rejoined the convoy the gallant little ship which had been given up for lost was cheered by her consorts. Another freighter, the *Samuel Chase*, had also been damaged during the bombing and was taken in tow by the *Halcyon*. On 11 July Commodore Dowding led the remnants of his convoy through the White Sea and so to Archangel. His sadness at the loss of so many fine ships and their valuable cargoes was mitigated slightly when he found the freighter *Bellingham*, the tanker *Donbass*, and the rescue ship *Rathlin* safely in harbour, nevertheless it appeared to him that only 5 ships (including the missing *Benjamin Harrison*) had survived out of 30, and that his convoy had met with disaster.

However, on this same day 11 July, three more ships which owed their survival to the initiative of Lieutenant J. A. Gradwell RNVR commanding the trawler *Ayrshire* dropped anchor in Matochkin Strait. They were last heard of heading north for the ice-edge after the convoy had scattered. Using the *Troubadour* with her stiffened bows as an ice-breaker, Gradwell shepherded his charges some 20 miles into the icefield, and when they could make no further progress they hove to. Immediately all hands were set to painting white the masts, funnels, and ships' sides facing south in the hope that by so doing they would escape being sighted by prowling enemy reconnaissance aircraft. Fires were banked so that smoke should not betray them and here they remained for two days during which they listened with tense feelings to the distress calls of their consorts as, one after another, they fell victims to the enemy U-boats and aircraft. When at last these agonising radio calls ceased, Gradwell decided to continue the voyage. A southerly wind had packed the ice against the ships and it took some time to free them, but eventually they reached open water and, skirting the ice edge as close as possible, on 10 July they made a landfall on the north island of Novaya Zemlya. After laying up in a bay for twenty-four hours they got underway and steamed south, reaching Matochkin Strait the following day. Here they found the *Benjamin Harrison* which had been joined by the damaged Russian ship *Azerbaijan*. Gradwell went ashore and with some difficulty persuaded a Russian signal station to report their arrival to the authorities at Archangel.

When Commodore Dowding heard that five more ships of his convoy had reached the anchorage in Matochkin Strait he began organising an escort force to go out and bring them in. He sailed on 16 July in the corvette *Poppy* with the *Lotus* and *La Malouine* and after a stormy passage reached Byelusha Bay in southern Novaya Zemlya where he rescued twelve survivors from the *Olopana* who were encamped ashore. A little further up the coast he came across the *Winston Salem*, which, having escaped the attentions of the enemy, had had the misfortune to run aground south-east of North Guisini Nos. She proved a welcome and hospitable rallying point for survivors from the *Hartlebury* and *Washington* but as she was hard and fast on a reef, refloating her would require powerful tugs and take time, so Dowding pressed on northward. In Moller Bay he found the CAM ship *Empire Tide*. She, too, had grounded but luckily had managed to get off and had become host ship to a large number of survivors who had made serious inroads into her stock of provisions. Dowding therefore distributed the survivors amongst the three corvettes and left for Matochkin Strait, telling the master to be ready to sail with him as soon as he returned.

Reaching his destination on 20 July he transferred to the Russian tug *Murman* which had arrived at the anchorage and which, because her bows were strengthened against ice, he decided would be the best ship to lead the mini-convoy of five freighters, three corvettes, and a trawler. After picking up the *Empire Tide*, but having to leave the *Winston Salem* aground, he hastened south. On 22 July the convoy was joined by the anti-aircraft ship *Pozarica*, the Russian destroyers *Gremyaschi* and *Grozny*, the corvette *Dianella*, and the minesweepers *Bramble*, *Hazard*, and *Leda*, and all ships reached Archangel safely on the evening of 24 July. Four days later the *Winston Salem* which, with the help of two Russian tugs, had been refloated also arrived bringing the total number of ships of PQ 17 to escape destruction to 11 (see Diagram VI). Of the 35 ships of the original convoy, 2 had turned back, 8 had been sunk by air attack, 9 by U-boats and 7, damaged by air attack and abandoned, had been sunk by U-boats. The Germans had achieved all this with the loss of only five aircraft.

The stores and equipment lost with the ships amounted to 430 tanks, 210 aircraft, 3350 vehicles, and 99,316 tons of cargo. Although many of the survivors of the sunken ships endured terrible hardships adrift in open boats in the inhospitable Arctic Ocean, happily the loss of life was not as great as it might have been had the convoy been shelled by the powerful German surface ships appointed to encompass its destruction. In all 153 merchant seamen were lost. The 1300 survivors landed at Archangel presented the Soviet authorities with a difficult problem since accommodation, food, and clothing were all in very short supply in war-torn Russia. There were a number of medical cases amongst them suffering from frost bite, immersion foot, and other injuries and for these the Russians did their best with the limited and somewhat primitive hospital facilities available.

Although the decision of Admiral Pound to order convoy PQ 17 to scatter may have been premature, as Admiral Tovey subsequently maintained,[1] it is

---

[1] Commander-in-Chief, Home Fleet's despatch on PQ 17

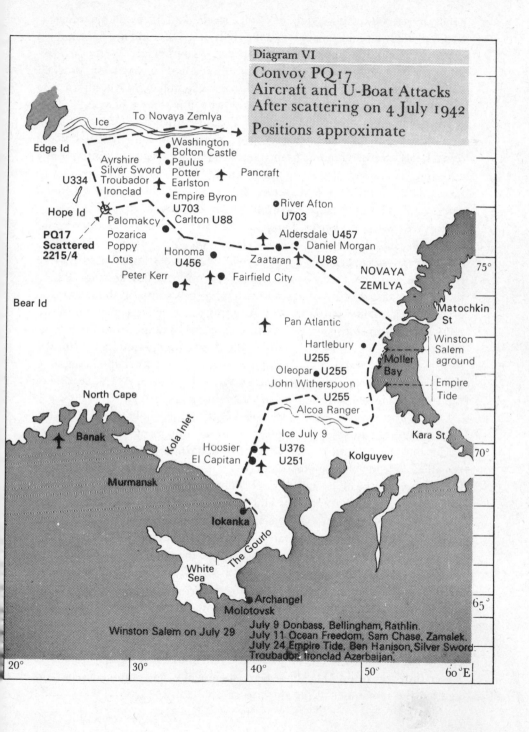

Diagram VI

Convoy PQ17
Aircraft and U-Boat Attacks
After scattering on 4 July 1942

Positions approximate

To Novaya Zemlya

Ice

Edge Id

Washington
Bolton Castle
Ayrshire
Silver Sword   Paulus
Potter   Pancraft
Troubador   Earlston
Ironclad

U334

Empire Byron
U703

Hope Id

PQ17
Scattered
2215/4

Palomakcy
Pozarica
Poppy
Lotus

Carlton U88

River Afton
U703

Aldersdale U457
Daniel Morgan

Honoma
U456

Zaataran U88

Peter Kerr

Fairfield City

Bear Id

NOVAYA
ZEMLYA   75°

Matochkin
St

Pan Atlantic

Winston
Salem
aground

Hartlebury
U255

Moller
Bay

Oleopar U255
John Witherspoon
U255

Empire
Tide

Alcoa Ranger

North Cape

Ice July 9

Kara St

Kola Inlet

Hoosier   U376
El Capitan U251

Banak

Kolguyev   70°

Murmansk

Iokanka

The Gourlo

White
Sea

Archangel
Molotovsk   65°

Winston Salem on July 29

July 9 Donbass, Bellingham, Rathlin.
July 11 Ocean Freedom, Sam Chase, Zamalek.
July 24 Empire Tide, Ben Hanison, Silver Sword
Troubador, Ironclad Azerbaijan.

20°   30°   40°   50°   60°E

generally agreed by those who have since studied all the available information that in the circumstances it was the right one. He could not have known that Hitler's interference would delay the execution of Operation *Rösselsprung* by twenty-four hours and had the formed convoy been attacked with determination by the German forces assembled in Altenfiord, the casualties in ships and personnel might well have been heavier. In the opinion of the German naval historian, Dr Jurgen Rohwer, 'Pound's decisions leading to the scatter order were reasonable and in fact quite a remarkably accurate reading of the German Naval Command's intentions'.

Before closing the chapter on the ill-fated convoy PQ 17 it is necessary to record a further incident in this series of tragic events. The homeward bound convoy QP 13 of 35 ships escorted by the destroyers *Inglefield* (Senior Officer), *Achates*, *Volunteer*, *Intrepid*, and ORP *Garland*, the anti-aircraft ship *Alynbank*, the corvettes *Starwort*, *Honeysuckle*, *Hyderabad*, FFS *Roselys*, the minesweepers *Niger* and *Hussar* with two trawlers had had an uneventful passage, the enemy as already mentioned, having made PQ 17 the primary target of his attack. On reaching the vicinity of the north-east point of Iceland, in accordance with Admiralty instructions, it split into two sections. Sixteen ships steered to pass east of Iceland and so to Loch Ewe, whilst the remaining 19 escorted by the *Niger* (Senior Officer), *Hussar*, *Roselys*, and the trawlers *Lady Madeleine* and *St Elstan* shaped course to pass along the north coast of Iceland and so to Hvalfiord. As this section of the convoy approached the land the visibility deteriorated.

Off the north-west corner of Iceland a British mine-field had been laid to catch any German ships attempting to break out through the Denmark Straits into the Atlantic to attack shipping. A narrow channel of clear water ten miles wide lay between the southern edge of the mine-field and the land through which the ships had to pass. The existence of the mine-field was unknown to the merchant ships and bad weather had prevented all ships from checking their positions by astronomical observations before making the land. The *Niger* went on ahead in order to try to obtain a fix, but mistook the loom of an iceberg for the land and altered the course of the convoy in a way which took it right into the mine-field. The *Niger* blew up and sank with heavy loss of life and the freighters *Hybert*, *Heffron*, *Marramar*, *Rodina*, and *Exterminator* also struck mines and foundered. A sixth ship *John Randolph* was damaged but reached port. Gallant rescue work was performed by the *Roselys* and the two trawlers which remained in the dangerous waters regardless of their own safety for six and a half hours, picking up survivors of whom they recovered 211. The *Hussar*, meanwhile, had obtained a shore fix and led the remainder of the ships to safety.

Thus ended the worst period in the history of the Arctic convoys. 'When sorrows come, they come not single spies, but in battalions.'

Chapter 6
THE COMEBACK

The heavy losses suffered by PQ 17 which were not unexpected led the Admiralty to press for a suspension of the Arctic convoys until the season of continuous daylight had passed and the ice-edge had receded further north. Mr Churchill, however, did not agree with this suggestion. In a minute to the First Sea Lord dated 15 July he said,

> 'Suspend the sailing of PQ 18 as now proposed from 18th inst. See what happens to our Malta operation. If all goes well, bring the carriers *Indomitable*, *Victorious*, *Argus*, and *Eagle* north to Scapa Flow and collect with them at least five auxiliary aircraft carriers together with all available '*Didos*' (small new cruisers with a powerful anti-aircraft armament) and at least 25 destroyers. Let two 16-inch battleships go right through under this air umbrella and destroyer screen, keeping southward, not hugging the ice, but seeking the clearest weather, and thus fight it out with the enemy. If we can move our armada in convoy under an umbrella of at least a hundred fighter aircraft we ought to be able to fight our way through and out again, and if a fleet action results, so much the better.' [1]

The reference to Malta was to an operation already agreed upon to relieve that hard pressed island and which, in any case, obliged a postponement of the next Arctic convoy.

At first sight the Prime Minister's suggestion appeared to have much to commend it. It accorded with one of his favourite sayings 'In defeat – defiance' but the Admiralty had to consider the war at sea as a whole and the shortage of aircraft carriers was so acute they could not afford the risk of damage to these ships which such an operation would entail. Further, the lack of facilities in the Russian ports for the repair of a damaged ship, as the Trinidad incident had shown, meant a voyage of 1500 miles, much of which under the threat of air and U-boat attack, to bring a damaged ship home. As Captain Roskill has commented, 'this meant hazarding our entire carrier strength for a purpose which could not justify taking such risks with irreplaceable ships'. [2]

---

[1] Churchill, ibid, Volume III, page 238.
[2] Captain S. W. Roskill, *The War at Sea* (HMSO, 1954–61), Volume II, page 278

When, after accepting the Admiralty's unwillingness to fall in with his suggestion, Mr Churchill informed Premier Stalin of the reasons for a temporary cessation of the Arctic Convoys, he received a very brusque reply.

'Our naval experts consider the reasons put forward to justify the cessation of convoys to the northern ports of the USSR wholly unconvincing . . . I never expected that the British Government would stop dispatch of war materials to us just at the very moment when the Soviet Union, in view of the serious situation on the Soviet German front, requires materials more than ever.' [1]

How badly the Russians were in need of British and American help at that time is discussed later. A postwar German investigation into the effect of Allied help to Russia states:

'It is, however, a fact that deliveries of American goods up to the *beginning of the year 1942* (my italics) were of the greatest importance to the Russian army. The American trucks, the delivery of telephone equipment, and boots met its critical needs.' [2]

After the success of the operations against PQ 17 the German High Command was most anxious to repeat it and on 21 July steps were taken to locate PQ 18 on the assumption that it would sail towards the end of the month. There were several false alarms resulting from reports of ship movements in the area and these cost the enemy a large quantity of aviation fuel, but eventually it became clear that the sailing of the next convoy had been postponed and routine reconnaissance patrols were resumed. The enemy forces, however, were not inactive during the interval between convoys. An operation code-named *Wunderland* was undertaken against Russian shipping in the Kara Sea. Air reconnaissance showed that the passage north of Novaya Zemlya was free of ice and on 16 August the *Admiral Scheer* accompanied by *U 251* and *U 601* left Narvik and, rounding Cape Zhelania three days later, entered the Kara Sea. The Soviet icebreaker *Sibiryalov* was encountered and sunk after very stout resistance on the part of her crew. On 27 August Port Dickson was bombarded for about two hours and considerable damage was done to the port installations, then the *Scheer* returned by the same route reaching Narvik on 30 August. Much to Admiral Golovko's indignation Glasevmorput delayed 36 hours before informing him of the presence of the enemy raider in its area. Meanwhile prowling U-boats sank a steamer, five tugs, and a lighter as well as bombarding the radio stations on Capes Zhelania and Khodovarikha. On 28 August

---

[1] Churchill, ibid, Volume III, page 242
[2] Wolfgang Schlauch, *Rüstungshilfe der USA an die Verbündeten im Zweiten Weltkrieg* (Darmstadt, 1967), page 118

U 591 laid mines off the Yugor Strait which later claimed the Soviet patrol ship *Murman*, and between 4 and 8 September the destroyers *Richard Beitzen*, *Z 29*, and *Z 30* laid mines in the Kara Strait.

It was necessary to replenish with ammunition the British ships which had reached north Russia, and on 20 July the destroyers *Marne*, *Martin*, *Middleton*, and *Blankeney* left Scapa and although sighted by an enemy aircraft *en route*, reached Archangel without incident. They were followed on 13 August by the US cruiser *Tuscaloosa* escorted by the US destroyers *Rodman* and *Eamons* and the British destroyer *Onslaught*. The cruiser carried 300 tons of stores and 167 members of the ground staff of two Hampden squadrons which it had been decided to send to operate in north Russia during the passage of the next convoy. In addition she embarked a medical unit and stores which it was hoped would be able to alleviate the conditions under which the sick and injured Allied seamen were existing. The Russians, however, while accepting the medical stores, would not allow the personnel to land and the issue had to await resolution on the Churchill–Stalin level. The *Tuscaloosa* and her three destroyers together with the *Marne* and *Martin* left Murmansk on 24 August unaware of the activities of the *Scheer*. The *Marne*, *Martin*, and *Onslaught* were detached to sweep along the north Norway coast and on the following day encountered the German mine-sweeper *Ulm* (Lieutenant-Commander Biet) which was on her way to lay mines off Cape Zhelania as soon as the *Scheer* had rounded it on her return journey. She was quickly sunk.

Admiral Tovey, meanwhile, was planning new tactics to combat the triple threat to which the Arctic Convoys were now subject. He was convinced that the convoy escort must be strong enough to counter an attack by surface ships, but for this he did not consider it necessary to risk his battleships in the Barents Sea. He intended to form what he termed a Fighting Destroyer Escort (FDE) of some 12 to 16 destroyers which would reinforce the close escort of corvettes and trawlers. In the event of a surface ship attack the destroyer force would be manoeuvred to attack the enemy, otherwise it would reinforce the screen providing anti-submarine and anti-aircraft protection. He was confident that such a force would prevent the enemy from pressing home his attack on the convoy. His only carrier *Victorious* had had to be taken in hand for a refit on completion of the Malta convoy operation, but to give the convoy additional anti-aircraft protection he decided to include in its escort one of the new escort carriers just coming into service. They had a complement of twelve Sea Hurricane fighters and three Swordfish anti-submarine aircraft, a small number compared with the strength of the Luftwaffe in north Norway, but he felt sure that even so few would be able to break up enemy bomber and torpedo aircraft formations seeking to attack the convoy.

A further and most important measure taken to give protection to the convoy and one which had been advocated prior to PQ 17 by the Commander-in-Chief, Coastal Command, Air Chief Marshal Sir Philip Joubert de la Ferté, was to transfer some of his search and strike aircraft to north Russia. In his view had such a force been available during the passage of that disastrous convoy it might not have been considered necessary to give the order to scatter. This time his advice was taken, and a force consisting of four photographic reconnaissance Spitfires, No. 210 Catalina Reconnaissance Squadron and Nos. 144 and 255 Hampden torpedo/bomber squadrons under the command of Group Captain F. L. Hopps RAF was sent to Russia. Unfortunately, one of the Hampdens was hit by anti-aircraft fire and crashed near Vardsoe, Norway, on 5 September and from secret papers recovered from the wreck the Germans learned valuable information about the measures being taken for the protection of PQ 18 and QP 14. However, so confident were they that it was the threat of air attack which had brought about the scattering of PQ 17 that they did not alter their plans. These provided for the Luftwaffe and the U-boats to attack PQ 18 whilst the southbound convoy QP 14 was to be the target of the *Scheer*, *Hipper*, and *Köln* during its passage through the Barents Sea. In the event these ships accompanied by destroyers after being ordered to Altenfiord on 10 September took no part in the operation as will be seen.

By the beginning of September the ships detached from the Home Fleet to take part in Operation Pedestal for the relief of Malta, with the exception of the *Victorious*, had returned to Admiral Tovey's command and preparations were made to sail another convoy to north Russia. After the experience of PQ 17 Admiral Tovey decided to direct the next convoy operation from his flagship HMS *King George V* in Scapa Flow, where he would be in direct contact by telephone with the Admiralty. This was to prove a wise decision. His plan provided for the battleships *Anson* (flagship of Vice Admiral Sir Bruce Fraser) and *Duke of York* with the cruiser *Jamaica* and five destroyers to cruise for short periods to the north-west of Jan Mayen Island to give distant cover to the convoys, while the cruisers *Norfolk* (flagship of Vice Admiral Bonham-Carter), *Suffolk*, and *London* with two destroyers cruised to the west of Spitzbergen in support of an operation involving the landing of reinforcements and stores for the Norwegian weather station at Barentsburg (Spitzbergen). It seemed to be an opportune moment to effect this, the probability being that the Luftwaffe would be too busy with the convoys to observe what was taking place.

69

Under the new arrangements for the protection of convoys PQ 18 and QP 14 it was no longer desirable for them to sail simultaneously since the plan allowed for the FDE to transfer from the northbound to the southbound convoy in the Barents Sea, and in order to fox the U-boats which waited off Iceland to obtain a first sight of the convoy after it had sailed, the greater part of the ships were assembled in Loch Ewe whence they sailed on 2 September.

PQ 18 comprised 39 ships and the tanker *Atheltemplar*, together with three motor minesweepers being transferred to Russia and the rescue ship *Copeland*. As the destroyers of the FDE would be making the double passage without entering harbour, and would need to refuel at sea, two extra tankers, the *Gray Ranger* and *Black Ranger* designated as Force Q accompanied the convoy. The close escort comprised the destroyers *Malcolm* (Senior Officer) and *Achates*, the anti-aircraft ships *Ulster Queen* and *Alynbank*, the corvettes *Bryony*, *Bergamot*, *Bluebell*, and *Camelia*, the minesweepers *Harrier*, *Gleaner*, and *Sharpshooter*, submarines *P 614* and *P 615* and four trawlers. The FDE under Rear Admiral R. Burnett in the cruiser *Scylla* was organised as follows;

> Force A: *Onslow* (Senior Officer), *Onslaught*, *Opportune*, *Offa*, *Eskimo*, *Somali*, *Ashanti*, and *Tartar*.
> Force B: *Milne* (Senior Officer), *Marne*, *Martin*, *Meteor*, *Faulknor*, *Intrepid*, *Impulsive*, *Fury*.
> Force P: RFAs *Oligarch*, and *Blue Ranger*, destroyers *Oakley*, *Cowdray*, *Worcester*, *Windsor*.

The escort carrier *Avenger*, the first of such ships to be assigned to an Arctic convoy, had her own escort of the destroyers *Wheatland* and *Wilton*, the three ships being designated the Carrier Force.

Admiral Burnett with Force B and the Carrier Force joined the convoy south-west of Jan Mayen Island on 9 September. Force P, meanwhile, went on ahead to Lowe Sound, Spitzbergen, being followed by Force A which topped up with fuel prior to joining the convoy. On 11 September the *Scylla* and five destroyers from Force B temporarily left the convoy to fuel from Force P, the other three destroyers replenishing from Force Q. During the forenoon of 13 September Force A joined the convoy and that afternoon the *Scylla* and the five ships of Force B returned to complete the FDE which was disposed as shown in Diagram VII.

To cover the movements of enemy surface ships the submarines *Tribune*, *Tigress*, and *P 34* were stationed off the Norwegian coast in areas to the north of Narvik until 10 September when they moved to new patrol positions 100 miles north of the North Cape and were joined by the submarines

Above A convoy entering the Kola Inlet seen over the stern of an escorting destroyer (*Imperial War Museum*). *Below* The Soviet destroyer *Bezposhchadny* belonging to the Black Sea Fleet but several of her sister ships were attached to the Northern Fleet. Known as Type VII, they had been designed with technical assistance from the Italian Navy and proved too lightly built for operations in the Arctic (*Imperial War Museum*)

As PQ 18 fights its way to north Russia a torpedoed tanker goes up in flames after being struck by a torpedo launched by a German aircraft. A 'Tribal' class and a 'Hunt' class destroyer can be seen in the foreground (*Imperial War Museum*)

The battleship *Tirpitz*, a sister ship of the *Bismarck*, which posed a constant threat to the Arctic convoys until destroyed by the Royal Air Force on 12 November 1944 (*Imperial War Museum*)

The battleship HMS *King George V* flagship of the Commander-in-Chief, Home Fleet but later relieved by her sister ship HMS *Duke of York*. They were armed with ten 14in guns of a new design (*Imperial War Museum*)

Above The cruiser HMS *Sheffield* which took part in most of the important naval actions in support of the Arctic convoys. Although only armed with 6in guns, in company with HMS *Jamaica* carrying a similar armament, they successfully drove off the much more heavily armed enemy ships *Lützow* and *Hipper* during the battle of the Barents Sea on 31 December 1942 (*Imperial War Museum*)

Right Admiral Otto Schniewind who held the post of Flag Officer Battle Group with his flag in the *Tirpitz* (*Imperial War Museum*)

Above HMS *Edinburgh*, a sister ship of HMS *Belfast*. As flagship of Rear Admiral S. Bonham-Carter she sank in the Barents Sea after being twice torpedoed in action with the enemy in May 1942 (*Imperial War Museum*). *Below* The escort carrier HMS *Nabob* after being torpedoed aft by *U 354* during an air strike against the *Tirpitz*. She was manned by the Royal Canadian Navy and despite the damage she continued to operate aircraft and returned to base (*Imperial War Museum*)

Above The A/A cruiser HMS *Scylla*. With her sister ship HMS *Charybdis* they carried an armament of eight twin 4.5in guns instead of the ten 5.25in guns for which they were designed. The former was Rear Admiral Burnett's flagship during the PQ 18 operation (*Imperial War Museum*). *Below* HM Trawler *Northern Gem* one of a large number of fishing trawlers requisitioned by the Admiralty on the outbreak of war for minesweeping and patrol duties. They rendered outstanding service in support of the Arctic convoys (*Imperial War Museum*)

Above HMS *Campania* one of
four uncompleted merchant ships
converted to escort carriers in
British shipyards. Unlike those
built in the United States these
were diesel engined, twin screw,
and were better able to maintain
their speed in bad weather. They
operated 16 Swordfish and
Wildcat aircraft (*Imperial War
Museum*). *Left* Grand Admiral
Karl Dönitz, who commanded
the U-Boat arm of the German
Navy with great distinction and
in 1943 succeeded to the
command of the *Kriegsmarine*
and ultimately as head of the
government (*Imperial War
Museum*)

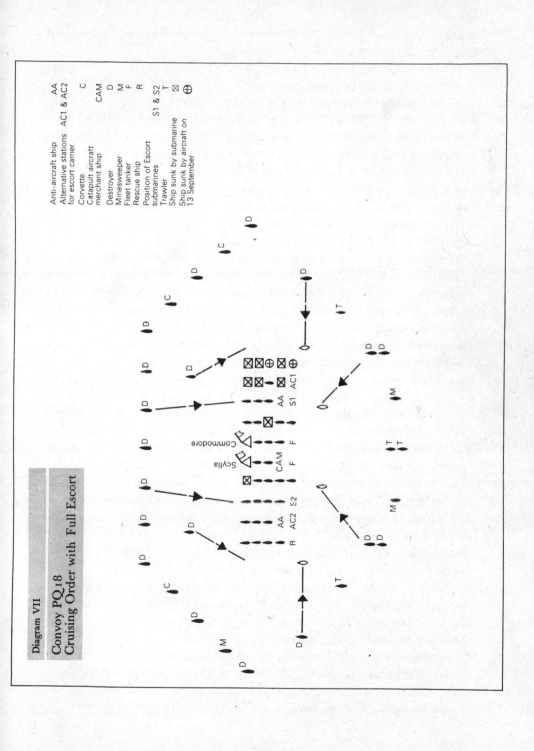

Diagram VII

Convoy PQ.18
Cruising Order with Full Escort

Anti-aircraft ship   AA
Alternative stations   AC1 & AC2
for escort carrier
Corvette   C
Catapult aircraft   CAM
merchant ship
Destroyer   D
Minesweeper   M
Fleet tanker   F
Rescue ship   R
Position of Escort
submarines   S1 & S2
Trawler   T
Ship sunk by submarine   ⊠
Ship sunk by aircraft on   ⊕
13 September

Unique, *Unreal*, *P 456*, *P 2210*, and *P 540*. Mines were laid by the FF submarine *Rubis* off Senja on 19 September.

PQ 18 was located by enemy aircraft on 8 September but they lost it again due to low cloud and did not regain contact until 13.20 hrs on 12th. The U-boats which were disposed – three on a line 120 miles long running north from position 74° 30′N, 3° 00′W, four between Spitzbergen and Bear Island and five more with orders to close the area – did not gain contact with the convoy until 12 September. The *Avenger*'s anti-submarine aircraft, in co-operation with the escorts, kept them at bay and at 21.00 hrs on 12th *U 88* was sunk by the *Faulknor* ahead of the convoy. The following day at 08.55 hrs *U 405* and *U 589* managed to penetrate the screen and torpedo the freighters *Stalingrad* and *Oliver Elsworth*, both of which subsequently foundered. At 15.00 hrs on 13th, just as the *Scylla* and five destroyers were rejoining the screen and while the convoy was still 450 miles from the nearest German airfield, the Luftwaffe delivered its first attack when six Ju 88s bombed it from a height of 4000 feet without damage to any ship or loss to themselves. Half an hour later, some 30 torpedo-armed Ju 88s and 55 He 111s from Coastal Group 30, I Bomber Group 26 and III Bomber Group 26 made a determined attack using the Golden Comb technique previously described. The Commodore ordered an emergency turn of 45° together to starboard to comb the tracks of the torpedoes, but the signal was either not seen or was misunderstood by the ships of the two starboard columns which turned in succession and six of the seven ships were hit.[1] A further two ships in the centre of the convoy – *Macbeth* and *Sukhona* – were also struck and all of them subsequently sank. The *Avenger*'s fighters shot down five enemy aircraft but four Hurricanes were lost. At 16.15 hrs a handful of He 115 seaplanes made an unsuccessful low level torpedo attack, being foiled by the intense barrage fire of the escort ships. The rescue ship *Copeland* recovered 163 survivors from the stricken ships and whilst doing so was herself attacked by two torpedo bombers, but managed to avoid the torpedoes aimed at her. The last attack of the day came in at 20.35 hrs when it was nearly dark, but it, too, was unsuccessful.

Taking stock of the situation after these attacks the captain of the *Avenger*, Commander A. P. Colthurst, decided that it was unwise to send his obsolete fighters to shoot down the better armed shadowing aircraft, sometimes as many as nine, circling the convoy. They would be better employed, he considered, as a combat air patrol over the convoy ready to break up formations of enemy aircraft as they came in. The correctness of his appreci-

---

[1] *Empire Beaumont*, *John Penn*, *Empire Stevenson*, *Wacosta*, *Africander*, *Oregonian*.

ation was proved the following day. In the meantime *U 457* had managed to penetrate the screen and at 02.26 hrs on 14th torpedoed the tanker *Athel-templar* in the engine room. Owing to the presence of several U-boats in the vicinity and the inability to spare escorts to tow and escort her to Spitz-bergen, 120 miles away, it was decided to sink her. Seven hours later the escort force hit back when *U 589* reported by a Swordfish aircraft was attacked by the *Onslow* and, after a hunt lasting three hours, finally sunk.

The air attacks were renewed at 12.35 hrs on 14th when some 20 torpedo-armed aircraft of Bomber Group 30 came in low on the convoy's starboard bow. This time they concentrated their attacks on the *Avenger* which launched her fighters whilst steaming head to wind ahead of the convoy. The *Ulster Queen* drew out of the convoy to support the carrier. 'It was a fine sight', commented Admiral Burnett, 'to see the *Avenger* peeling off Hurricanes whilst streaking across the front of the convoy from port to starboard inside the screen with her destroyer escort blazing away'. No ships were hit as a result of the attack and a high level bombing attack which followed at 13.00 hrs was equally unsuccessful though the *Avenger* had a narrow escape. Another torpedo attack by 25 aircraft came in soon after-wards, the *Avenger* again being the chief target. Her fighters and the ship's guns accounted for several for the attackers but the freighter *Mary Lucken-back* in the starboard wing column was hit and blew up. The last attack of the day came in at 14.30 hrs. It was delivered by about 20 bombers from a height of between 6000 and 4000 feet, though a few attempted shallow-dive bombing. No hits were scored. On the following day the convoy was again attacked by high level bombers when at a distance of 400 miles from Banak airfield and, although some ships were near missed, none was hit. The U-boats, however, remained in contact and at about 03.00 hrs on 16th *U 457* was sunk by the *Impulsive*.

Later that day Group North ordered the U-boats operating around PQ 18 to transfer their attention to QP 14. This convoy comprising 15 freighters under Commodore Dowding with the rescue ships *Rathlin* and *Zamalek*, escorted by the destroyers *Blankney* and *Middleton*, the anti-aircraft ships *Palomares* and *Pozarica*, the corvettes *Poppy*, *Dianella*, FFS *La Malouine*, the minesweepers *Bramble*, *Leda*, and *Seagull* and four trawlers, all veterans of the PQ 17 débâcle, had left Archangel on 13 September and three days later Admiral Burnett began the transfer of the FDE and the Carrier Force from PQ 18 to QP 14. The movement took place in three groups in the hope that the enemy might not notice the withdrawal of so many ships from PQ 18. During the next two days the Soviet destroyers *Gremyashchi*, *Kuibyshev*, *Sokrushitelny*, and *Uritski* joined the escort and the anti-aircraft capability of the two larger ships was to prove most welcome. Whilst rounding Kanin Nos at the entrance to the White Sea on 18 September the convoy was attacked in poor visibility by aircraft from Bomber Groups 26 and 30. At 08.20 hrs during the first attack, twelve He 111s came in from astern flying low over the water and dropped their torpedoes. All ships except the freighter *Kentucky* managed to avoid them. An hour later the attack was repeated and this time there were no casualties but some Ju 88 bombers, synchronising their attacks with those of the torpedo/bomber aircraft, scored a hit on the disabled *Kentucky* which sealed her fate. The CAM ship *Empire Morn* catapulted her Hurricane fighter during the first attack and it shot down two He 115 float planes. The following day, although by now the convoy was crossing the Dvina bar, twelve Ju 88s bombed the ships for an hour, but no hits were obtained. A gale sprang up as the ships were entering harbour and three which had run aground and were being guarded by the *Ulster Queen* were also attacked, but they were all refloated without being hit. One Ju 88 failed to return.

The German attacks on PQ 18 carried out with remarkable persistence, though not as crippling as those on PQ 17, nevertheless were severe. Thirteen ships had been lost, three to U-boats and ten from air attack. The cost to the enemy, however, had been far higher, amounting to three U-boats and 22 aircraft.[1] Admiral Golovko, whose bitter comments on the misfortunes of PQ 17 showed a lack of understanding of the risks involved, was more realistic regarding its successor. 'Such then are the results of the September convoy PQ 18', he wrote in his diary. 'They confirm once more that given resolute action by covering forces and adequate preliminary combat measures, the enemy's surface ships can be neutralised while the attacks of U-boats and aircraft can be repulsed.'[2]

Meanwhile the homeward bound convoy QP 14 which, on 17 September in position 75°N 48°E had been joined by Admiral Burnett in the *Scylla* with the FDE, the anti-aircraft ship *Alynbank*, the submarines *P 614* and *P 615*, the Carrier Force and Force Q. For its size – 15 freighters – it was the most heavily defended convoy to make the return passage. As has been mentioned, it was Group North's intention to use the ships assembled in Altenfiord to attack this convoy and they were under orders to sail on 13 September. However, on that day Hitler reminded Admiral Raeder of their importance to the defence of Norway and of the undesirability of risking them unduly, so Raeder cancelled the operation. Admiral Tovey thought it

---

[1] This is the official German figure
[2] Golovko, ibid, page 130

probable that the strength of the FDE, the presence of the RAF torpedo aircraft in north Russia, and that of the Allied submarines were factors which contributed to this decision.

So it was with the U-boats and the Luftwaffe only that QP 14 had to contend. During the convoy's passage through the Barents Sea the weather was thick with patches of fog and intermittent snow squalls. Intense cold hampered the operation of the *Avenger*'s anti-submarine aircraft, but they had the help of a Catalina aircraft operating from the Kola Inlet. During the forenoon of 18 September, an enemy shadower sighted the convoy but lost touch; later that day two U-boats were spotted by the Catalina some distance north-east of the convoy and another 20 miles astern, but no attacks developed. As Force Q had exhausted its stock of oil fuel the two destroyers were sent into Lowe Sound to fetch the tanker *Oligarch* and one of the destroyers of Force P. After rounding the south cape of Spitzbergen on the morning of 19 September Admiral Burnett ordered aircraft and destroyers to carry out a special search for U-boats, three of which were sighted at distances of 7, 12, and 20 miles from the convoy but all dived before they could be attacked, and were not seen again that day. However, the next day the U-boats closed in and a series of incidents destroyed the calm of the hitherto uneventful voyage. There were, in fact, seven U-boats operating against QP 14 and at 05.20 hrs on 20th *U 435* torpedoed and sank the minesweeper *Leda* in the rear of the screen, but aggressive action by the patrolling Swordfish aircraft and the escorts prevented them from achieving any further success until later in the day.

At 08.20 hrs a shadowing aircraft appeared and was just in time to observe the convoy's alteration of course to the south-west, but the forenoon and afternoon brought no further incidents until 15.30 hrs when *P 614* unsuccessfully attacked *U 408* of which she caught a glimpse in a snow squall. Shortly afterwards Burnett ordered the two British submarines to patrol astern of the convoy before returning to base. But the U-boats had not given up and at 17.20 hrs *U 255* torpedoed the freighter *Silver Sword* (a survivor from PQ 17) and she had to be sunk.

As by now the danger of air attack appeared to be past and the hard-worked crews of the *Avenger*'s aircraft were badly in need of rest, Burnett transferred his flag to the destroyer *Milne* (Captain I. M. R. Campbell RN) and at 18.30 hrs detached the *Scylla* and *Avenger* with an escort of three destroyers, to return to Scapa. At the same time he requested coastal command to provide anti-submarine air patrols. No sooner had the carrier and her escort parted company than *U 703* torpedoed the 'Tribal' class destroyer *Somali* on the port wing of the screen. She was taken in tow by the

Ashanti which also provided her with electric power. On 22 September the tanker *Blue Ranger* of Force P was encountered and as the *Ashanti* was running low on fuel, by a fine display of seamanship, without slipping the tow, her captain Commander R. G. Onslow RN succeeded in topping up with fuel from the tanker. After a successful tow of 420 miles the weather, unfortunately, deteriorated and early on 24 September, after the wind had reached gale force, the *Somali* broke in two and sank. Most of the crew had been transferred to the *Ashanti* so that there were only 80 onboard when disaster struck, but only 35 including the Captain, Lieutenant-Commander C. Maud RN were rescued.

Early on 22 September Admiral Burnett, having satisfied himself that all was well with the tow and the convoy had turned over command of the escort force to Captain A. Scott-Moncrieff RN in the *Faulknor* and parted company. The convoy now had an escort of 11 destroyers and 9 smaller vessels and a Catalina aircraft had arrived in response to the Admiral's request. Unfortunately, in making an attack on a U-boat a few hours later, the Catalina was damaged by the U-boat's gunfire and obliged to ditch and there were no more aircraft available to relieve it. At 06.30 hrs on 22nd, about an hour after Burnett had taken his departure, *U 435* penetrated the screen and in quick succession torpedoed the freighters *Bellingham* (a survivor of PQ 17), *Ocean Voice* (Commodore Dowding's ship), and the tanker *Gray Ranger*. The rescue ships *Rathlin* and *Zamalek* were quickly on the scene and between them picked up 144 survivors from the three ships. Commodore Dowding and his staff were rescued by one of the escorts. This was the final assault on QP 14, the surviving ships reaching Loch Ewe on 26 September.

Taking the two convoy operations together in which 15 ships out of a total of 55 convoyed had been lost together with a 'Tribal' class destroyer, a minesweeper, a fleet tanker, and 4 aircraft (3 pilots were rescued), and having regard to the strength of the opposition, Admiral Tovey did not consider these losses to be excessive. The advantage of having a carrier with the convoy had been amply confirmed. Nevertheless, risks had been run, particularly with regard to the tankers on the survival of which the success of the operation depended. The two in Lowe Sound were lucky to escape observation. One factor, though, was highly satisfactory and that was the way in which the officers and men of the Carrier Force and FDE had stood up to eighteen days of continuous operations under Arctic conditions and the strain of U-boat and air attacks. The crew of the *Avenger*'s aircraft had proved that they were capable of operating under the most arduous conditions and they were singled out by the Commander-in-Chief for special praise.

To the enemy, the results of the operations were disappointing. They had lost 33 torpedo-armed aircraft, 6 Ju 88 bombers, and two Blohm and Voss long range aircraft and the official German comment bore witness to the efficiency of the defence: 'It was found that not only was it impossible to approach the carrier to launch an effective attack on account of fighters', said the Luftwaffe report, 'but that a wide screen of warships made the launching of torpedoes against the inner merchant vessels an extremely hazardous undertaking'. There was no doubt, too, that by failing to use his surface ships as originally planned, Admiral Raeder missed a chance of success which was not to recur under such favourable conditions. As regards the U-boats, these had paid dearly for their successes. Three had been lost and five damaged and on 23 September *U 253,* waiting off Iceland for QP 14, was sunk by a patrolling Catalina aircraft.

Chapter 7

THE ATTACK ON CONVOY JW 51B

The interrelation of the various theatres of the war was now to be demonstrated in a way which greatly eased the difficulties of running the Arctic convoys. The Allies had finally agreed on a large scale landing in North Africa, to take place in October or early November, code-named Torch. The operation inevitably made heavy demands on the Home Fleet so that a temporary cessation of the Arctic convoys was necessary. The immediate problem was now to break the news to the Russian Premier. He had been told of the impending assault by Churchill during his August visit to Moscow, but he had not appreciated that it would involve a suspension of the convoys. After an exchange of telegrams with President Roosevelt, it was agreed to delay informing Stalin until arrangements had been finalised regarding the sailing of a number of ships independently to north Russia as an experiment, and also the provision of air support for the Russian armies defending the Caucasus. The information was transmitted in telegrams dated 9 October from Roosevelt and Churchill. They were not well received.

Single ship sailing

At the end of October thirteen ships were sailed singly from Iceland unescorted and at intervals to space them 200 miles apart, but the experiment was not a success. Five ships arrived, four were sunk by a combination of air and U-boat attacks, one ran ashore on Spitzbergen, and three turned back. Eight ships were also sailed in the reverse direction and seven arrived safely, one being intercepted and sunk by the German destroyer *Z 29* on 7 November.

German mining activities

Meanwhile, permission having been received from the Russian authorities for the hospital unit to land at Vaenga, it left Scapa in the cruiser *Argonaut* escorted by the destroyers *Intrepid* and *Obdurate* on 13 October and reached Kola Inlet without enemy interference on 21 October. For the return journey the crews of the two Hampden squadrons who had turned over their aircraft to the Russians, were embarked as well as survivors from the ships lost in PQ 18. Whilst this operation was in progress the enemy was busy laying mines: the destroyers *Richard Beitzen*, *Friedrich Eckholdt*, *Z 29*, and *Z 30* off Kanin Noss at the entrance to the White Sea, which later claimed the Soviet icebreaker *Mikoyan*, and *U 592* off the Yugor Straits a little further to the east. Unaware of the presence of a Norwegian meteorological party on Spitzbergen, *U 212* and *U 586* disembarked a German one there at this time and the two stations operated unknown to each other for several months.

Air threat reduced

On 23 October General Montgomery's Eighth Army launched its famous offensive against Field Marshal Rommel's Afrika Korps at Alamein and two weeks later the Allies landed at Casablanca, Oran, and Algiers. As a result the German High Command felt obliged to redeploy the Luftwaffe squadrons from north Norway to airfields in Sicily where they could be used to repel the new threat. Thus one of the greatest obstacles to the operation of the Arctic convoys was removed.

Convoy QP 15

A large number of unloaded merchants ships by now had accumulated in White Sea ports and, unless extracted before the onset of winter, would become frozen in. The Admiralty had received intelligence of the reduction of the enemy's air strength in north Norway and decided that these ships could be brought back with a comparatively weak escort without great risk. Admiral Tovey suggested that the convoy be limited to twenty ships, but the shortage of shipping at that time was acute and the Admiralty insisted that all available ships must sail. In all 30 ships were nominated for convoy QP 15 due to sail on 17 November, but one failed to sail, and one ran aground, so only 28 put to sea. The close escort consisted of the corvettes *Bryony*, *Bergamot*, *Bluebell*, and *Camelia*, the minesweepers *Halcyon*, *Britomart*, *Hazard*, *Sharpshooter*, and *Salamander*, the anti-aircraft ship *Ulster Queen*, and one trawler. The Soviet destroyers *Baku* and *Sokrushitelny* were detailed to accompany the convoy during the first part of the voyage. It was also planned further to reinforce the escort in the Barents Sea with the destroyers *Faulknor* (Captain A. Scott-Moncrieff), *Impulsive*, *Intrepid*,

Icarus, and *Echo* which would be relieved later by the destroyers *Musketeer*, *Oakley*, *Orwell*, *Ledbury*, and *Middleton*. Cover to the west of Bear Island was to be provided by the cruisers London (flagship of Rear Admiral L. K. Hamilton), and *Suffolk* escorted by the destroyers *Forester* and *Onslaught*. The submarines *Uredd* (Norwegian), *Juron* (Free French), *P 312*, and *P 216* were ordered to patrol off the entrance to Altenfiord in case any of the enemy surface ships should emerge.

When three days out the convoy encountered the first of a series of gales which virtually blew it apart and with the almost negligible amount of daylight at that time of the year it was impossible to reassemble it. Both the Soviet destroyers were damaged, the *Baku* suffering numerous cracks in her hull plating, while the *Sokrushitelny* lost her stern and subsequently foundered. Admiral Golovko ordered the rest of the flotilla to sea to assist, and 187 officers and men of the *Sokrushitelny* were rescued with very great difficulty, and of these a quarter subsequently died from exposure. The two British destroyer groups failed to make contact with the convoy which had broken up into a number of small groups by the time it reached Bear Island. The enemy had decyphered a signal giving information about the sailing of QP 15 and eight U-boats had been ordered to patrol to the east of Bear Island to intercept it. The Admiralty believed that they were waiting north of the island and diverted the convoy to the south of it, but on 23 November *U 625* torpedoed the freighter *Goolistan* and *U 601* the *Kuznetz Lesov*, both of which were lost. Group North had intended to sail the *Hipper* and a squadron of destroyers to intercept the convoy but the weather was considered too bad for both the cruiser and the destroyers to operate effectively, especially as air reconnaissance was lacking. In due course the 26 surviving ships of QP 15 reached Iceland. This was the last of the PQ–QP series of convoys as, for reasons of security, it had been decided to rename the Arctic convoys JW outwards and RA homewards, both beginning with the number 51.

Raeder confers with Hitler

On 19 November whilst QP 15 was making its stormy passage across the Barents Sea, Admiral Raeder made one of his periodic visits to Hitler during which he repeated the views he had expressed previously that operations against the Arctic Convoys should be undertaken only when the object to be attained was worthwhile. He instanced the QP convoys because they were usually lightly protected and so good results could be expected. The shortage of oil fuel, he told Hitler, was hampering fleet movements while British aerial mining was severely taxing the available minesweeper forces.

The pocket battleship *Lützow* and the cruiser *Prinz Eugen*, he announced, were ready to move from the Baltic to Norway, but the *Tirpitz* had engine trouble and was in need of a refit. Because of the fuel shortage Hitler would only agree to the transfer of the diesel driven *Lützow*, but he repeated his fear of an invasion of Norway during the long winter nights and the need to strengthen the light forces there. Raeder pointed out that the withdrawal of the Luftwaffe squadrons had exposed the weakness of the coast defences and Hitler then ordered that a minimum of 23 U-boats was to be maintained in Arctic waters. He also ordered consideration of the invasion of Iceland and the construction of special submarines for the purpose.

British convoy policy revised

It was not until mid-December that the forces could be assembled to escort another convoy to north Russia, but in the meantime considerable discussion had taken place between the Admiralty and Admiral Tovey as to the best method of doing so. The season of almost perpetual darkness and severe gales which settles over the Arctic about mid-November placed great restrictions on the use of air reconnaissance by both sides and Admiral Tovey was in favour of running a number of small, lightly escorted convoys. The Admiralty, however, did not agree and insisted that the next convoy should be delayed until sufficient escorts were available for a large convoy to be sailed. This meant waiting until 22 December, by which time the first half of the favourable 'dark' period would have passed. Finally, the Admiralty agreed to the convoy being sailed in two sections, with an interval of a week between them. Each section would consist of about sixteen ships escorted by destroyers. Two additional 6-inch gun cruisers were to be attached to the Home Fleet and these the Admiralty insisted, against Admiral Tovey's advice, must give the convoys cover well into the Barents Sea. This insistence was justified.

Convoys JW 51A and B

Convoy JW 51A of sixteen ships including an RFA tanker, sailed from Loch Ewe on 15 December escorted by the corvettes *Honeysuckle* and *Oxlip*, the minesweeper *Seagull*, and two trawlers. The destroyers *Faulknor* (Captain A. Scott-Moncrieff RN Senior Officer), *Echo*, *Ingelfield*, *Fury*, *Eclipse*, *Beagle*, and *Boadicea* joined to the north-east of Iceland after topping up with fuel at Seidisfiord. Four submarines were deployed to watch the entrance to Altenfiord. The cruisers *Sheffield* (flagship of Rear Admiral R.

Burnett) and *Jamaica* with the destroyers *Opportune* and *Matchless*, designated Force R, cruised to the west of the convoy in the same general area as
the battleship *King George V* (flagship of Admiral Sir John Tovey), the
cruiser *Berwick*, and three destroyers until the convoy had passed south of
Bear Island on 22 December. Burnett then sent his two destroyers to fuel
from the tanker and join the convoy escort whilst his two cruisers followed a
route 60 miles south of the convoy to Kola Inlet which was reached on 24
December, a day ahead of the convoy. The enemy did not detect the passage
of the convoy and some of the ships went on to the White Sea, arriving at
Molotovsk on 27 December.

Five days before convoy JW 51A sailed, the *Lützow* left Gotenhafen in
the Baltic and a week later reached Altenfiord where she relieved the *Scheer*
which was due for refit. The movements were not detected by the Admiralty.

Convoy JW 51B consisting of fourteen freighters sailed from Loch Ewe
on 22 December as planned, with a close escort comprising the corvettes
Rhododendron and *Hyderabad*, the mine-sweeper *Bramble*, and two trawlers
and was joined off Iceland on 24 December by the destroyers *Onslow*
(Captain R. St. V. Sherbrooke DSO, RN, Senior Officer) *Oribi*, *Obedient*,
Orwell, *Obdurate*, and *Achates*. Distant cover was provided by the battleship
Anson (flagship of Vice Admiral Sir Bruce Fraser), the cruiser *Cumberland*
with the destroyers *Forester*, *Icarus*, and *Impulsive* which sailed from Iceland
on 26 December to relieve Admiral Tovey's force.

The convoy's route was the same as that followed by JW 51A but this time
it was located by German reconnaissance aircraft and also by *U 354* on 24
December and tentative arrangements were made for the ships at Altenfiord
to intercept it, the operation being known as *Regenbogen* (Rainbow). The
sortie was to be combined with one already planned for the *Lützow* by way
of a shakedown cruise after her recent refit and this fact may have had some
influence on subsequent events.

The first five days of the convoy's passage were uneventful but on the
evening of the sixth day when the convoy was between Jan Mayen and Bear
Islands, a fierce gale was encountered which reduced the visibility considerably. During the night of the 28/29th the destroyer *Oribi* had a gyro compass
failure and lost touch, and so did the trawler *Vizalma* and five freighters, so
the following afternoon Captain Sherbrooke detached the *Bramble* to
search for the missing ships. Admiral Burnett timed his departure from the
Kola Inlet on 27 December to cover convoy JW 51B when it reached
longitude 11°E, which he estimated would be about noon on 29 December.
His instructions forebade him to close within 50 miles of it unless surface
craft attacked it, since the U-boats were usually clustered round the convoy.

As before, he kept well south of the convoy route, but on reaching the longitude of the Kola Inlet (33½° E) he turned north-west across its route with the intention of passing to the north of it and of covering it from a position between 40 and 50 miles astern, this being the most likely direction from which enemy forces might be expected. His reason for moving to the north of the convoy was to gain the advantage of the light over an enemy approaching from the south and also to avoid being detected by air reconnaissance. He considered these advantages outweighed the disadvantage of accepting a less favourable position from which to cut the enemy off from his base and he was to be proved right. However, his plan was upset by the convoy being 20 miles to the south and 60 miles to the west of the position expected, so instead of taking up a position astern of the convoy he found himself some 30 miles north-west of it on 31 December, the day which he suspected was the most likely one for an attack.

Operation Regenbogen

Despite the bad weather *U 354* (Lieutenant-Commander Herbschleb) had shadowed the convoy successfully since he first sighted it six days previously and at noon on 30 December he reported it as being 'weakly protected'. This was just the information needed to allow Operation *Regenbogen* to be executed. At 18.00 hrs on 30 December the cruiser *Hipper* (flagship of Vice Admiral Oscar Kummetz) with the pocket battleship *Lützow* (Captain Stänge) accompanied by the 5th Destroyer Division comprising the *Friedrich Eckholdt*, *Richard Beitzen*, *Theodor Riedel*, *Z 29*, *Z 30*, and *Z 31*, put to sea. Kummetz's orders were to destroy the convoy, to avoid action with superior forces, not to waste time rescuing crews, and to prevent the enemy from doing so, to capture a few captains for questioning and even a single ship, if possible.

By making a slant to the north-west on leaving Altenfiord, the German squadron avoided the Allied submarines on patrol off the entrance and no report of its departure was received by the Admiralty. Shortly after sailing Kummetz received a message from Admiral Kluber (Group North) which read, 'In spite of operational orders, exercise restraint if you contact enemy of comparable strength since it is undesirable to run excessive risk to the cruisers'. This was not a very encouraging signal and, as will be related, it exerted a sinister influence on the outcome of the operation. At midnight on 30/31 December he was informed that the convoy was within a rectangle drawn 240 miles north and 120 miles east of position 71° 30'N, 36° 00'E steering east at between 7 and 12 knots and that *U 354* and *U 626* were in

83

contact with it. A warning was included that two British cruisers with their destroyer escort had sailed from Kola Inlet on 27 December and might be with the convoy and that there were three to four enemy submarines at sea. Despite the crippling restrictions placed upon him, Kummetz evolved a plan of attack which, had it been executed boldly, might have achieved a resounding success.

At that time of the year the sun never rose to less than 6° below the horizon so that nautical twilight began about 08.00 hrs and ended round about 14.50 hrs local time (see Diagram I). This meant that there would be about two and a half hours during the forenoon when it would be light enough to distinguish ships at a distance of up to ten miles, depending on the visibility, and this he selected as the most suitable time to attack the convoy. He ruled out night attack on account of the danger from the escorting destroyers' torpedo fire and decided to approach the convoy from astern in view of the uncertainty regarding its position and speed of advance. He decided to spread his destroyers fifteen miles apart to cover a broad front and that the *Hipper* and *Lützow* would attack from different directions to confuse the defence. He hoped that the escorts would close whichever ship first made contact, leaving the field clear for the other one. To this end, during the night the *Hipper* and the *Lützow* opened out to 75 miles from each other, the former to the north and the latter to the south. The destroyers remained with the *Hipper*, the intention being that they should start spreading at 08.00 hrs if the light allowed. During the attack the *Eckholdt*, *Beitzen*, and *Z 29* were to work with the *Hipper* and the *Riedel*, *Z 30*, and *Z 31* with the *Lützow*.

At 07.15 hrs on 31st the *Hipper*, steering to the north-east at high speed passed about 20 miles astern of the convoy and a few minutes later the silhouettes of two ships were sighted so Kummetz ordered the *Eckholdt* to investigate, the *Hipper* meanwhile turning bows on to reduce her own silhouette. After a few minutes, no report having been received from the destroyer, at 07.42 hrs the cruiser resumed her easterly course and reduced speed to 10 knots as it was too early to put the plan into execution. As the light improved, more silhouettes of ships began appearing against the eastern horizon, leaving Kummetz in no doubt that he had fallen in with the convoy earlier than he had expected, so he ordered the course of his flagship to be reversed until the light should improve still further, but in making this turn he lost contact with his destroyers. When detached, the *Eckholdt* set off on a south-easterly course and she was followed by the rest of the division. The order to spread was now unnecessary and in anticipation of one to join their respective ships, the *Riedel* group began to move towards the *Lützow* whilst the *Eckholdt* group started to shadow the convoy in accordance with orders now received from the Admiral. So far, Kummetz's plan was working out exactly as he had intended.

The situation at 08.30 hrs on 31 December
(see Diagrams VIII and IX)

At 08.30 hrs on that bitterly cold morning of 31 December with 16° of frost registered and all the ships engaged covered with a mantle of snow and ice, conditions were about as unfavourable for fighting a naval action as could be imagined. The weather, however, was clear with visibility of about seven miles to the north and ten to the south, except when snow squalls occurred when it shut down suddenly as if a curtain had been drawn. The convoy steering east with its escort of five destroyers, two corvettes, and a trawler, now consisted of twelve ships and it had reached a position about 220 miles north-west of the Kola Inlet. Abour 45 miles to the north the trawler *Vizalma* was escorting the freighter *Chester Valley*, one of the two stragglers, while the *Bramble* was on her own five miles north-east of the convoy, still searching for the other one. Admiral Burnett with the *Sheffield* and *Jamaica* was some 30 miles north of the convoy, between it and the *Vizalma*. None of these four groups was aware of its position relative to the others.

The *Hipper* had just crossed 20 miles astern of the convoy while the *Lützow* from a position 50 miles to the south-east of it was just starting to close in. At this moment the *Odburate* (Lieutenant-Commander C. E. D. Sclater) on the convoy's starboard bow sighted and reported two of the *Eckholdt* group destroyers bearing south-west from her and apparently crossing the convoy's wake on a northerly course. Captain Sherbrooke told her to investigate and as she turned to do so the third ship of the group came in sight. The enemy destroyers turned away to the north-west, shadowed by the *Obdurate* and nothing further happened until 09.30 hrs when they opened fire on her. This time it was *Obdurate*'s turn to withdraw towards the convoy but the enemy made no move to follow her. On seeing the gun flashes Captain Sherbrooke headed in their direction, telling *Orwell*, *Obedient*, and *Obdurate* to join him and leaving *Achates* and the other escorts to lay a smoke screen between the enemy and the convoy.

Kummetz had now decided to delay no longer in launching his attack on the convoy and he ordered the two destroyer groups to join their respective ships. However, as it grew lighter and more and more ships could be seen, he was faced with the difficulty of distinguishing friend from foe, the penalty of having lost touch with his destroyers. At 09.39 hrs the *Hipper* swung round

85

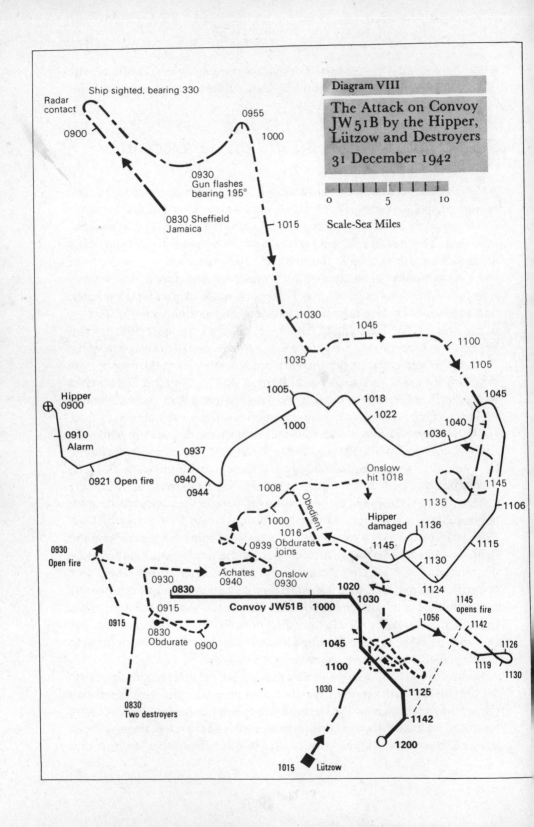

Ship sighted, bearing 330

Radar contact

0900

0955
1000

0930
Gun flashes
bearing 195°

0830 Sheffield
Jamaica

1015

Diagram VIII

The Attack on Convoy JW 51 B by the Hipper, Lützow and Destroyers

31 December 1942

0   5   10

Scale–Sea Miles

1030

1045   1100

1035   1105

1045

Hipper
0900

0910
Alarm

0921 Open fire

0937

0940

0944

1005

1000

1018

1022

1040

1036

1145

1106

Onslow
hit 1018

Hipper
damaged

1135

1136

1145

1130

1124

1115

1008

1000

Obedient

1016
Obdurate
joins

0939

0930
Open fire

0930

Achates
0940

Onslow
0930

0915

0830
Obdurate   0900

0830

Convoy JW51B   **1000**

1020

1030

1145
opens fire

1056

1142

1126

1119

1130

1045

1100

1030

1125

1142

1200

0830
Two destroyers

1015   Lützow

to an easterly course and as she did so, Sherbrooke identified her from her beam silhouette and her four symmetrically sited turrets. The sighting was mutual and the *Hipper* challenged, but even though the British ships made no reply Captain Hartmann dared not open fire for fear they were ships of the *Eckholdt* group. However, at 09.42 hrs he could see the *Achates* laying smoke and there being no doubt about her identity he fired a few salvos in her direction, but without effect. The *Onslow* which had been joined by the *Orwell* now engaged the *Hipper* at a range of about 5½ miles and Captain Hartmann, suspecting a torpedo attack, turned away. For the next half hour the big cruiser and her much smaller opponents conducted a running fight during which shots were exchanged from time to time, the destroyers firing by radar and the *Hipper* using the convoy as an aiming point but every now and then taking cover in smoke. All the time the enemy ship was making ground to the north-east, but Sherbrooke appreciated that in the threat of torpedo attack he had a weapon which gave him the initiative though he could not afford to use it unless he could be certain of crippling his more powerful opponent who, having complete freedom of action, was a very difficult target.

At 09.55 hrs Sherbrooke was joined by *Obedient* whilst *Obdurate* was still approaching from the south-west, but having lost track of the *Eckholdt* group and fearing lest they had reached a position from which they could attack the convoy, he told the two destroyers to close it while with the *Orwell* he continued to prevent the *Hipper* from doing so. The convoy, meanwhile, had altered course to south-east and was making good progress at nine knots under cover of the smoke screen laid by the *Achates*, *Rhododendron*, and trawler *Northern Gem* and reinforced by *Obedient* and *Obdurate* as they approached.

At 10.08 hrs it appeared as if the *Hipper* had given up the attempt to close the convoy and was retiring to the north but in fact this was part of Kummetz's plan to lure the escorts away from the convoy and give the *Lützow* a clear run. At 10.13 hrs he signalled to his forces '*Hipper* to north of convoy and there are four enemy destroyers between us and the convoy' and at the same time he evidently decided to try to drive off Sherbrooke and his two destroyers for he ordered Captain Hartmann to turn and re-engage them. After a few inaccurate opening salvos the *Hipper* scored four hits on the *Onslow* which put her two forward guns out of action, shot away her main aerials, and started a fire in the forward superstructure and in the messdeck below it, as well as destroying both radar sets and holing the engine-room. Amongst the casualties was Captain Sherbrooke, severely wounded in the face and unable to see, but he refused to leave the bridge and have his wound

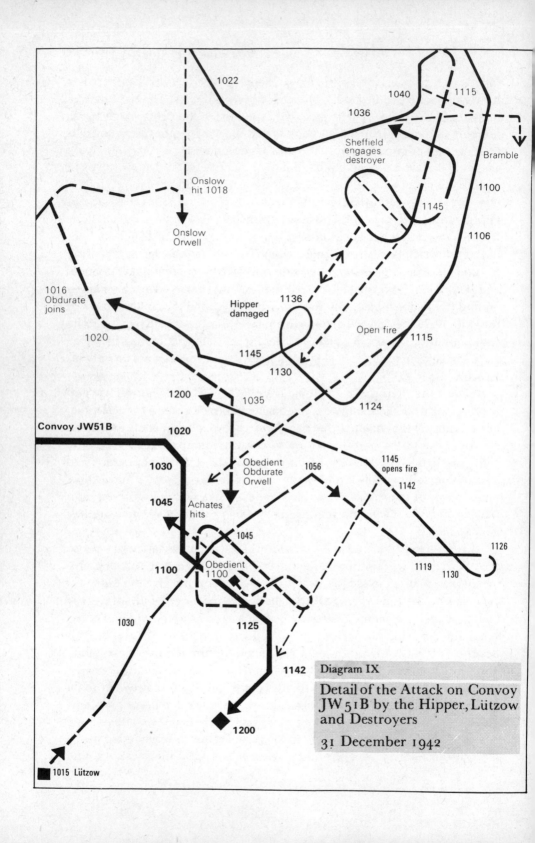

1022

1040 1115

1036

Sheffield
engages
destroyer

Bramble

Onslow
hit 1018

1100

1145

Onslow
Orwell

1106

1016
Obdurate
joins

Hipper
damaged

1136

Open fire

1145

1020

1145

1115

1130

1124

1200

1035

Convoy JW51B   1020

Obedient
Obdurate
Orwell

1056

1145
opens fire

1030

1142

Achates
hits

1045

1045

1100

Obedient
1100

1126

1030

1119   1130

1125

1142

Diagram IX

**Detail of the Attack on Convoy
JW 51 B by the Hipper, Lützow
and Destroyers**

1200

31 December 1942

1015 Lützow

dressed and continued to direct his destroyers and his ship until assured that Commander Kinloch in the *Obedient* had taken charge. Fortunately, at this critical stage in the action a snow storm descended, reducing visibility to about 2 miles and the *Hipper* was lost to view. How successful he had been in protecting the convoy can be seen from an entry made in the *Hipper*'s log:

'The (British) destroyers conducted themselves very skilfully. They placed themselves between *Hipper* and the convoy (so) that it was impossible to get near the ships.'

The covering force closes in

Away to the north Admiral Burnett was in a quandary. He was uncertain of the exact position of the convoy which he believed to be to the east of him, but at 08.58 hrs *Sheffield*'s radar had registered a contact bearing north-west 7½ miles which the plot indicated was steering east at 25 knots. The dim outline of a ship was momentarily seen on this bearing and *Sheffield* altered course away. At 09.32 hrs gun flashes were seen against the southern horizon but these were thought to be anti-aircraft fire so he turned to port to close the unknown ship which was, in fact, the *Chester Valley* escorted by the *Vizalma*. Then at 09.41 hrs heavy gunfire was heard, the flashes of which could be seen to the south and a few minutes later Sherbrooke's report of sighting three enemy destroyers was received.

The indications now were that the convoy was further to the south than expected but the unknown ship still puzzled him for stragglers are usually found astern of a convoy, so he held on to the northward while he discussed the situation with his flag captain (Captain A. W. Clarke RN) and his staff. He soon reached a decision to act on the well-known naval axiom 'When in doubt steer for the sound of the guns' and at 09.55 hrs the cruisers turned south and increased speed to 25 knots, working up gradually to 31 knots. At 10.30 hrs radar contacts indicated ships bearing 140° 15 miles and 180° 12 miles, both apparently steering east at high speed, so at 10.35 hrs he altered course parallel to them and a minute later he observed a burst of fire on his starboard bow. This was the *Hipper* engaging the unfortunate minesweeper *Bramble* which had been caught up in the battle. A few salvos from the German cruiser at close range brought her to a standstill and Kummetz ordered the *Eckholdt* group to finish her off. The *Bramble* managed to send off an enemy report before she was overwhelmed but only the *Hyderabad* received it. At 10.54 hrs the easterly of the two contacts obtained by the *Sheffield*, which was in fact the *Hipper*, appeared to have altered course towards the south so Burnett conformed and set off in pursuit.

89

The Lützow closes in

At 10.30 the commodore of the convoy had signalled a further alteration of course to south as the *Obedient* and *Obdurate* were closing in on the port quarter with the *Orwell* joining some ten minutes later. The *Achates* continued to lay smoke astern while the damaged *Onslow* was moving up to take station ahead and endeavouring to home the cruiser force on to the scene of the action. About this time the corvette *Rhododendron* on the convoy's port quarter reported smoke bearing south-west and ten minutes later she sighted a large ship bearing 160° distant two miles and steering north-east. This was the *Lützow* with the *Riedel* group of destroyers closing in to attack the convoy. Captain Stänge had observed the gun flashes of the action between the *Hipper* and the destroyers and receiver the *Hipper*'s confirmatory signal, but like all the participants in this confused, twilight battle, he was experiencing difficulty in distinguishing friend from foe. When, therefore, at 10.50 hrs he sighted an unknown ship on his port hand, probably the *Rhododendron*, he turned to a south-easterly course and reduced speed, waiting for a snow squall which had temporarily reduced the visibility, to clear. The convoy, meanwhile, had altered back to a south-easterly course and was about five miles on the *Lützow*'s starboard beam and well within the range of her guns.

Commander Kinloch, with his three destroyers was coming up the convoy's port side and at 11.00 hrs as the visibility improved he sighted a large enemy ship and two destroyers bearing 060° which he mistook for the *Hipper*, so he led round and made smoke to shield the convoy. It was in fact the *Lützow* he had sighted but behind her on the same bearing was the *Hipper* approaching at 31 knots and engaging an unidentified target to the east, probably the *Bramble*. At 11.15 hrs, however, the cruiser transferred her fire to the *Achates* which had been ordered to join the *Onslow* ahead of the convoy and which emerged from behind a smoke-screen she had been laying into full view of the *Hipper*. In a few minutes the *Achates* was crippled, her captain Lieutenant-Commander A. H. T. Johns RN killed, together with 40 of his ship's company. Her first lieutenant, Lieutenant Peyton-Jones RN took command and the ship's speed being now so reduced that she could no longer overtake the convoy, he recommenced making smoke and continued to do so until the action was over, then the damage his ship had received caused her to capsize. The trawler *Northern Gem* rescued 81 members of the crew. Having knocked out the *Achates*, at 11.20 hrs the *Hipper* shifted her fire to the *Obedient* at a range of 8500 yards, straddling her and shooting away her radio aerials, but to avoid the possibility of being torpedoed at

11.25 hrs Captain Hartmann swung round to the north and three minutes later into the sights of the guns of Burnett's cruisers.

British cruisers engage the Hipper

The British ships, as Burnett had hoped, had the advantage of the light and could see the *Hipper* plainly whereas the enemy was unaware of their presence until they opened fire. Burnett led his cruisers round to a course roughly parallel to that of the *Hipper*, the *Sheffield* opening fire at 11.30 hrs while still under helm at a range of about 13,000 yards. The *Jamaica* followed and the *Hipper*, taken by surprise, did not reply until her opponents had fired four salvos and scored three hits. One shell burst in Number 3 boiler room which reduced her speed to 28 knots, and another set the hangar on fire. Turning to starboard through 270°, the German cruiser steadied on a westerly course and disappeared in a pall of smoke. With destroyers to the south and cruisers to the north and bearing in mind the instructions he had received on sailing, Kummetz decided to cancel the operation and at 11.37 hrs he ordered all ships to break off the action and retire in a westerly direction.

The British cruisers conformed to the *Hipper*'s turn and at one time the range dropped to 8000 yards, but unfortunately at that moment fire had to be checked because the target was obscured. At 11.43 hrs the *Eckholdt* group of destroyers were sighted at a range of 4000 yards and in an ideal position to fire torpedoes so *Sheffield* put her helm hard over and steered for the leading ship with the intention of ramming. The *Eckholdt* which had mistaken the British cruisers for the *Hipper* and *Lützow*, suddenly found herself enveloped in a hail of fire from the former at a range which fell at one time to 1000 yards and in a few minutes she was a blazing shambles. The *Jamaica* engaged the *Beitzen* but she promptly turned away under smoke and escaped damage.

The Lützow's missed opportunity

It will be remembered that the *Lützow* was marking time to the north-east of the convoy waiting for the light to improve and at 11.27 hrs Captain Stänge decided that the moment had come to close in and attack so he turned to starboard and steadied on a north-westerly course. This enabled him to maintain touch with the *Hipper* with which he had exchanged recognition signals a few minutes previously. At 11.42 hrs some ships of the convoy could be distinguished to the south-west so he opened fire on them at a range of about 9 miles but only one ship, the *Calibre*, was hit, most of the shots falling short. The Commodore immediately executed an emergency turn of 45° to starboard and Commander Kinloch in the *Obedient* some four miles astern of the convoy led his destroyers round to the east and began to lay a smoke screen between the merchant ships and the enemy. This became effective after a few minutes and obliged the *Lützow* to cease fire.

Kinloch now sighted the *Hipper* and two destroyers some seven miles to the north steering a westerly course so he ordered his three destroyers to turn together to north-west which made the *Obdurate* the leading ship and this was an advantage as her radio, unlike the *Obedient*'s, was still in action. On receipt of Kummetz's order to withdraw, the *Lützow* had increased speed to 24 knots and was endeavouring to join the *Hipper* when at 11.55 hrs she sighted Kinloch's three destroyers 7500 yards on her starboard beam and opened an accurate fire on them which the destroyers returned. At 12.02 hrs the *Obdurate* was damaged by a near miss and the three ships turned away to port keeping between the enemy and the convoy but the *Lützow* continued on her westerly course and the action ceased.

Enemy ships withdraw

Meanwhile, having dealt with the *Eckholdt* group of destroyers, Burnett resumed the chase of the *Hipper* which was now 12½ miles to the south-west. She came into sight briefly at 12.15 hrs, but soon afterwards the threat of torpedo attack by the *Beitzen* and *Z 29* obliged him to turn towards them and the *Sheffield* was just about to open fire on them when the *Lützow* appeared on the same bearing and at 12.29 hrs both cruisers opened fire on the pocket battleship at a range of 14,500 yards. The *Lützow* replied and the *Hipper* from a position somewhat further ahead, joined in. The *Lützow*'s shots fell short but those of the *Hipper* were dangerously accurate so Burnett turned away to disengage and also to avoid any torpedoes which the destroyers might have fired. At 12.45 hrs when he resumed his westerly course the enemy ships had disappeared from view and although they were tracked by radar until 14.00 hrs no opportunity occurred of renewing the engagement. Not wishing to be drawn too far away from the convoy – the position of which he was still in doubt – Burnett abandoned the chase and swept towards the south in case the German cruiser *Nürnberg*, which had also been reported in Altenfiord, should be lurking in the vicinity. She was, in fact, not considered sufficiently seaworthy for winter operations in those stormy waters.

Effect of U 354's signal

U 354 which had originated the report which triggered off Operation *Regenbogen* and which, although a spectator of the action, could not have had any very clear idea of what had taken place, now initiated a signal which was to have serious repercussions. At 11.45 hrs Lieutenant-Commander Herbschleb signalled Group North 'According to our observations, the battle has reached its climax. I see nothing but red.' The message was taken as indicating that the operation had gone according to plan and that a victory was in the making, and it was passed to Hitler at his headquarters.

As she approached Altenfiord, the *Hipper* was sighted by the former U-boat *Graph*, but she was travelling too fast for an attack to be mounted. However, three hours later the *Graph* saw a destroyer approaching in tow of another and attacked but her torpedoes missed.

Convoy JW 51B arrives and RA 51 sails

Convoy JW 51B which had been so stoutly and successfully defended, escaped further attention from the enemy and having been joined by two minesweepers and two Russian destroyers on the afternoon of 2 January, reached the Kola Inlet the next day. A detachment with the Russian escorts went on to Archangel, arriving there on 6 January. Admiral Burnett's task was not yet finished; he had to cover the westbound convoy RA 51 of 14 freighters which had sailed from the Kola Inlet in a north-casterly gale on 30 December, escorted by the destroyers *Faulknor, Fury, Echo, Eclipse, Inglefield*, and *Beagle*, the minesweeper *Gleaner*, and four trawlers. Its route took it 150 miles south of JW 51B and well clear of the scene of the action. Three U-boats lying in wait for it, the positions of which were known, were avoided and RA 51 had an uneventful voyage, reaching Loch Ewe on 11 January. The *Sheffield* and *Jamaica* were relieved during the last half of the voyage by the cruisers *Kent* (flagship of Rear Admiral L. K. Hamilton) and *Berwick* and reached Seidisfiord on 2 January.

On receipt of news of the action Admiral Tovey in the *King George V* with the *Howe*, the cruiser *Bermuda*, and six destroyers put to sea to render additional support should it be necessary. Having cruised to the east of Jan Mayen Island until noon on 3 January he returned to Scapa; Hamilton and his cruisers followed the next day.

Admiral Tovey's comment on the action

The result of the engagement was admirably summed up by Admiral Tovey in his report:

> 'That an enemy force of at least one pocket battleship, one heavy cruiser, and six destroyers with all the advantage of surprise and concentration should be held off by five destroyers and driven from the field by two six-inch cruisers without any loss to the convoy is most creditable and satisfactory.'

For his gallant action in the defence of the convoy Captain R. St. V. Sherbrooke DSO, RN was awarded the Victoria Cross.

German reactions

From the German point of view the result of the operation was distinctly disappointing and it was brought home to the High Command that so long as its surface forces were obliged to operate under such crippling restrictions success would elude them. Moreover, the absence of any well-defined object was a contributory cause of failure. Captain Stänge of the *Lützow*, in particular, knowing that any damage received would prevent his ship sailing on the planned shakedown cruise must have been specially anxious on this score. The views he expressed in his report regarding the 'risk factor' were subsequently endorsed by Admiral Schniewind. However, it must be said that the destroyers failed to seize the opportunities which occurred for attacking the convoy. Except when the *Eckholdt* was detached to sink the *Bramble* they tamely followed the ships to which they were attached. Kummetz unconvincingly excused their inactivity thus: 'To make a destroyer attack was out of the question owing to possible confusion with the enemy'.

The action had far-reaching effects. Furious at the delay in rendering him a report of it, even angrier when he received it, and the expectations raised by *U 534*'s signal were not fulfilled, Hitler decreed the decommissioning of all heavy ships (battleships, battle-cruisers, and cruisers) and ordered Grand Admiral Raeder to report to him immediately. Raeder waited until 6 January before complying, and finding Hitler unwilling to listen to reason, tendered his resignation which was accepted. He was succeeded by Admiral Karl Dönitz, the brilliant chief of the U-boat arm.

Chapter 8
THE TIRPITZ IMMOBILISED

Soviet complaints

Despite Hitler's decree about paying off the big ships, on 10 January 1943 the battle-cruiser *Scharnhorst* and the cruiser *Prinz Eugen* left Götenhafen in the Baltic in an endeavour to join the other ships in north Norway. They were sighted off the Skaw by an aircraft of coastal command and, fearing interception, they turned back. It was two months before the *Scharnhorst* managed to reach Altenfiord, but the *Prinz Eugen* did not repeat the attempt and remained in the Baltic for the rest of the war.

Meanwhile the Soviet Ambassador in London, M. Maisky, was complaining to an exasperated Mr Churchill about the small size of the next two convoys programmed to sail for Murmansk. The former appeared not to be aware of Britain's still slender resources of escort vessels nor of the complicated organisation required to load ships and assemble them for convoy at the appointed place. It so happened that only fourteen freighters were ready to sail in convoy JW 52, and Admiral Tovey was anxious to make the best use of what was left of the dark period when the enemy's air reconnaissance was at a disadvantage. The Home Fleet was still without an aircraft carrier and it was believed that the German aircraft carrier *Graf Zeppelin* was about to enter service, though in fact this was not so, and this appeared to be an additional reason for not delaying the convoy's departure.

Sailing of convoy JW 52

On 17 January convoy JW 52 of 14 ships, escorted by the destroyers *Blankney*, *Middleton*, and *Ledbury*, the mine-sweeper *Britomart*, the corvettes *Lotus* and *Starwort*, and 2 trawlers left Loch Ewe, routed to pass east of the Faroe Islands. Off the east coast of Iceland the three destroyers were relieved by what became known as the Ocean Escort consisting of the destroyers *Onslaught* (Commander W. H. Selby RN Senior Officer), *Beagle*,

Musketeer, *Offa*, *Matchless*, *Bulldog*, and *Piorun* (Polish). A cruiser covering force comprising the *Kent* (flagship of Rear Admiral L. K. H. Hamilton), *Glasgow*, and *Bermuda* sailed to give cover between longitude 10°E and the Kola Inlet whilst the battleship *Anson* (flagship of Vice Admiral Sir Bruce Fraser), the cruiser *Sheffield*, and four destroyers cruised to the south-west of Bear Island during the convoy's passage between longitudes 24° and 32°E when it was thought to be most likely to be attacked by the German ships in Altenfiord. These comprised the *Tirpitz*, *Lützow*, *Hipper* (damaged), *Nürnberg*, and 8 destroyers.

The convoy's passage was favoured by fair weather and good progress was made, one ship however, the *Empire Baffin*, unable to keep up had to be sent back to Iceland. On 23 January a BV 138 flying boat of Coastal Air Wing 706 sighted and reported it and the following day four He 115 torpedo aircraft of Coastal Air Wing 406 took off to attack it, but failed to score any hits and lost two aircraft to gunfire. The U-boats ordered to the scene were equally unsuccessful due to the vigilance of the escorts, many of which were now fitted with high frequency direction finding apparatus enabling them to take bearings of the numerous signals made by U-boats to each other when operating around a convoy. This enabled evasive alterations of course to be made by the convoy and facilitated the task of the escorts in counter-attacking them. Only *U 622* (Lieutenant-Commander Queck) managed to get in an attack on the convoy but his torpedoes missed their mark. The cruiser covering force, unaware of the convoy's rapid progress, instead of being 40 miles on the port bow of the convoy as Hamilton thought, found themselves 20 miles astern of it in the area where the U-boats following it generally congregated. The *Kent* and *Bermuda* had lucky escapes when *U 625* (Lieutenant Benker) unsuccessfully attacked them. The convoy was met off the entrance to the Kola Inlet by five Soviet destroyers and all ships together with the cruisers entered harbour on 27 January.

The return convoy RA 52

Due to delays in unloading, only 11 ships out of 24 were ready to sail in the return convoy RA 52 which was scheduled to leave on 29 January and as a result the escorts outnumbered the freighters in the convoy. Besides the seven destroyers from the escort of JW 52 they included the *Forester* and *Icarus* and the damaged *Onslow* together with the mine-sweepers *Harrier* and *Seagull*, the corvettes *Rhododendron*, *Oxlip*, *Honeysuckle*, and *Hyderabad* together with four trawlers. Five Soviet destroyers accompanied the convoy for the first two days of its passage. The battleship supporting and cruiser covering forces were the same as for convoy JW 52.

On 1 February *U 625* (Lieutenant Benker) reported and unsuccessfully attacked the convoy to the south-west of Bear Island, but German air reconnaissance failed to find it. On 3 February, *U 255* (Lieutenant-Commander Reche) which five days previously had sunk the Soviet ice-breaker *Malygin* and the steamer *Ufa* during a coastal patrol, now managed to torpedo the American freighter *Greylock*, the entire crew of which was rescued by the *Harrier* and *Oxlip* assisted by the trawlers *Lady Madeleine* and *Northern Wave*. The other ten ships of the convoy reached Loch Ewe safely on 8 February.

Dönitz takes over

On the same day the new Commander-in-Chief of the German Navy, Admiral Karl Dönitz, submitted a plan to Hitler for decommissioning all the big ships in accordance with his 'irrevocable' decision. Dönitz differed from his predecessor, Raeder, in character, outlook, and experience. At the age of 51 not only was he younger, but he was more ruthless. To quote his own words he 'trusted the leadership of Adolf Hitler unreservedly' and in return Hitler listened to him with more patience than he had accorded to Raeder. Moreover, the success of the U-boat campaign commended him to his Führer. However, although hitherto he had maintained that the war at sea could be won by the U-boats, when he had had time to consider the implications of Hitler's order he reached the same conclusion as had his predecessor. Nevertheless he was too wise to attempt to cross swords with Hitler right away and so he submitted a plan for paying off the *Hipper* and *Köln* in March, the *Scharnhorst* in July, and the *Tirpitz* in the autumn.

What Dönitz particularly wanted to discuss, but time did not permit, was the relaxation of the crippling restrictions which Hitler had imposed on flag and commanding officers regarding the avoidance of damage to their ships and which had been primarily responsible for the failure to achieve decisive results against the Arctic convoys. However, he entrusted this delicate mission to his representative at Hitler's headquarters, Admiral Theodor Krancke. Much to Dönitz's surprise Hitler agreed to the suggestion that once he (Dönitz) ordered ships to sea for a particular operation, the officer in command would be left free to act as the situation demanded, even though losses might result.

Emboldened by this outcome, at his next meeting with Hitler on 26 February he revived the question of decommissioning the big ships, pointing out how useful they could be in interdicting the Arctic convoys and that, taking account of the critical situation on the Eastern front (Stalingrad had fallen on 31 January) it was the duty of the navy to support the army in every possible way. He, therefore, proposed that another attempt be made to transfer the *Scharnhorst* to north Norway where, with the *Tirpitz* and *Lützow* a 'fairly powerful' task force could be formed, the *Hipper* having returned to Germany for repairs. Hitler's reaction to the proposal was, in Dönitz's words, 'extremely immoderate', but in the end he grudgingly agreed to the transfer.

Convoy JW 53

Although every effort was being made to placate the Russians and expedite the sailing of the next convoy, it was not possible to assemble sufficient ships before 15 February, which was four days later than planned, and even so only 25 of the 30 freighters promised were ready. So on 15 February Convoy JW 53 of 25 freighters sailed from Loch Ewe escorted by the destroyers *Pytchley, Middleton*, and *Meynell*, the mine-sweepers *Jason* and *Halcyon*, the corvettes *Dianella, Poppy*, and *Bergamot*, and two trawlers. The destroyers *Musketeer, Matchless*, and the corvette *Bryony* sailed the next day with three more freighters but the weather was so bad they were obliged to return.

As by now there were approximately seven hours of daylight in the latitutde of the North Cape it was decided to provide the convoy with an Ocean Escort similar in strength to that given to PQ 18. It consisted of the cruiser *Scylla* (Captain I. A. P. Macintyre RN), the escort carrier *Dasher*, the destroyers *Milne* (Captain I. M. R. Campbell RN), *Faulknor* (Captain A. Scott-Moncrieff RN), *Boadicea, Inglefield, Orwell, Opportune, Obedient, Obdurate, Fury, Intrepid, Impulsive, Eclipse*, and (Polish) *Orkan*. The destroyers *Blankney* and *Ledbury* were attached to the *Dasher* for rescue duties and the cruiser covering force consisted of the *Belfast* (flagship of Rear Admiral R. Burnett), *Cumberland*, and *Sheffield*, whilst Admiral Tovey in the *King George V* with the *Howe* and the cruiser *Norfolk* with six destroyers provided support.

The weather which had favoured the passage of the two previous convoys now changed and as the ships of the convoy rounded the Butt of Lewis and lost the shelter of the Hebrides, they met the full force of an Atlantic gale. Many ships had deck cargoes of tanks, locomotives, and trucks, and after a few hours buffeting by tremendous seas three ships had to return to harbour to resecure cargo. The carrier *Dasher* received damage and also had to return whilst the *Sheffield* which had trained her foremost turrets on the beam to avoid damage to the canvas blast screens of their 6-inch guns, lost the roof of 'A' turret which was ripped clean off and hurled overboard. Admiral Tovey sent the *Norfolk* to take her place and the *Berwick* took hers with the battleships. The gale prevented the *Scylla* and the Ocean Escort from joining the convoy and it fell to Commander H. G. A. Lewis RN in the *Jason* as senior officer, to try to keep the convoy together, which despite the appalling conditions, he did with remarkable success.

After four days the gale blew itself out and during the night of 19/20 February the battleship support force came within radar range of it, enabling the *King George V* to plot the positions of the ships and pass the information to Captain Campbell in the *Milne*. He, with six of the destroyers, had been obliged to put in to Seidisfiord to refuel, whence he sailed on 20 February to join the convoy which by then had been re-formed and was heading up towards Bear Island.

The ice edge at this time of the year was so far south that the convoy's route lay only 250 miles north of the German base at Altenfiord and on 23 February enemy aircraft sighted and reported it. Once again high frequency direction finding apparatus proved its worth and a surprised U-boat on the surface would find herself suddenly illuminated by starshell and under attack by the escorts, and the aggressive tactics of this well trained team kept the U-boats from approaching the heavily laden freighters as they steamed steadily eastwards.

On 25 February ten Ju 88s of Bomber Group 30 carried out shallow dive attacks on the convoy but only one ship received slight damage from a near miss. A similar attack the following day was equally unsuccessful and after the convoy had been joined later that day by four Soviet destroyers, it divided, fifteen ships entering Kola Inlet on 27 February, the remaining seven proceeding to White Sea ports where they arrived safely two days later.

Disappointed by their lack of success whilst the convoy was at sea, on 27 and 28 February a number of Ju 87s of Dive-bomber Group 5 attacked the ships lying off Murmansk, damaging three of them. Further attacks by Ju 88s of the same Group on 6 and 13 March destroyed one ship and severely damaged another. As Admiral Golovko was only too well aware, the anti-aircraft defences of the port were still quite inadequate.

Convoy RA 53

The homeward convoy RA 53 of 30 ships sailed from the Kola Inlet on 1 March with the same escort as had accompanied JW 53. The day after it sailed *U 255* (Lieutenant-Commander Recke) made contact with it and continued to shadow it for several days before getting in an attack on 5 March on the freighter *Executive* which sank, and the *Richard Bland* which though damaged managed to keep up with the convoy. After an attack by twelve Ju 88s of Coastal Group 30 had been repulsed by the intensity of the convoy and escorts' anti-aircraft fire, the weather began to deteriorate as another Atlantic gale swept north-eastwards into the Barents Sea. The convoy inevitably began to straggle and the U-boats seized the chance for which they had been waiting. On 9 March *U 586* (Lieutenant-Commander Von der Esch) sank the freighter *Puerto Rican* and the following day *U 255* (Lieutenant-Commander Reche) sank the already damaged *Richard Bland*. A fourth freighter, the *J. L. M. Curry* foundered in the gale and a fifth ship the *J. H. Latrobe*, had to be towed into Seidisfiord in a sinking condition by the *Opportune*, an achievement which earned Admiral Tovey's warm approval. The 25 surviving ships reached Loch Ewe on 14 March.

The Scharnhorst joins the Battle Group

Taking advantage of the bad weather, the battle-cruiser *Scharnhorst* slipped out of the Baltic during the night of 8/9 March and after calling at Bergen reached Trondheim on 10 March. The following day in company with the *Tirpitz* and with an escort of destroyers, she joined the *Lützow* and *Nürnberg* in Bogen Bay near Narvik. Ten days later the whole force, minus the *Nürnberg* which had returned to Germany, moved north to Altenfiord.

Suspension of the Arctic convoys

When Admiral Tovey became acquainted with these movements and taking account of the increasing hours of daylight as summer approached, he informed the Admiralty that in his opinion the continuance of the Arctic convoys was no longer justifiable since the only way to ensure their safe arrival would be to give them battleship escort during their passage through the Barents Sea. This he was not prepared to do, even though the threat of air attack had diminished during the winter months for the reasons given in Chapter 4. In the event, other considerations led to a suspension of the convoys throughout the summer months. The Battle of the Atlantic was reaching its climax as Dönitz made a supreme effort to reach a decision in this vital theatre. In March the losses of merchant ships reached an alarming figure even though twelve U-boats were destroyed and the Admiralty, appreciating that a crisis was at hand, ordered all available escorts to be concentrated round the Atlantic convoys leaving Admiral Tovey with a minimum number of destroyers to escort his battleships. The battle raged fiercely throughout April and May but by the end of that month Dönitz was obliged to admit defeat.

Churchill informs Stalin of the reasons for suspending the convoys

On 30 March Mr Churchill informed Premier Stalin of the reasons for the suspension of the Arctic convoys until September and received a very churlish reply. After a further telegram in which the Prime Minister recounted the successes being achieved by the Allied armies in North Africa and with the bombing of German war centres, Stalin became more amenable.

Reorganisation of German Naval Command

As mentioned in Chapter 1 a reorganisation of the German naval command structure in the north eventually proved necessary and at the end of March Dönitz decided to combine the posts of Group North and Flag Officer Northern Waters, thus placing the Flag Officer, Battle Group, Admiral Kummetz, directly under Group North, Admiral Schniewind, at Kiel. The temporary suspension of the Arctic convoys, however, did not bring about a cessation of all maritime activity in that area. Throughout the spring and summer Soviet submarines were active in attacking German coastal convoys and laying mines with losses being incurred on both sides. There was also a small amount of air activity. On 8 July the new Commander-in-Chief of the British Home Fleet, Admiral Sir Bruce Fraser who had relieved Admiral Sir John Tovey, took his fleet supported by a United States Task Force under Rear Admiral Hustvedt USN to sea to carry out a demonstration off the coast of Norway to divert German attention from the imminent Allied landing in Sicily. Unfortunately the *demarche* went unobserved by the enemy. The operation was repeated later in the month, this time with the carriers *Illustrious* and *Unicorn* in company and five BV 138 aircraft were shot down.

German foray into the Kara Sea and attack on Spitzbergen

Between the end of July and the beginning of October U-boats were engaged laying mines in the estuary of the Pechora River and in attacking Russian coastal traffic off Port Dickson and elsewhere in the Kara Sea. On 6 September the ships in Altenfiord, which had lain idle all the summer, sailed on an operation, code-named *Zitronella*, in which the *Tirpitz* (flagship of Admiral Kummetz) accompanied by the *Scharnhorst* and the destroyers *Z 27*, *Z 29*, *Z 30*, *Z 31*, *Z 33*, *Steinbeck*, *Galster*, *Riedel*, and *Lody* were ordered to attack the installations on Spitzbergen. A battalion of the 349th Grenadier Regiment was embarked in the destroyers and the troops were landed in Grönfiord and Advent Bay early on 8 September. After the *Tirpitz* had shelled Barentsburg and destroyed the coal and supply dumps as well as the water and electricity works, the troops were re-embarked and the force returned to Altenfiord which was reached on 9 September. News of the foray reached the Admiralty whilst it was in progress and the Home Fleet put to sea, but the enemy had returned to base long before an interception could have been made.

Midget submarine attack on the Tirpitz

A long planned and carefully rehearsed operation to immobilise the *Tirpitz* using midget submarines to attack her in her heavily protected lair was now put in motion. The attack took place on 22 September and although only two of the six midgets succeeded in reaching the target, they successfully laid their charges beneath the battleship and the subsequent explosions did great damage and put her out of action until March the following year. A respite was thus gained of the threat which had hung over the Arctic convoys ever since the powerful battleship had been moved to Norway. The threat was further reduced when the *Lützow* left Altenfiord for the Baltic on 23 September. Three Beaufighters and a Fleet Air Arm squadron of torpedo-armed Tarpon aircraft were sent to intercept her but failed to make contact and she reached harbour safely. This led to a full enquiry by the Admiralty and the Air Ministry as a result of which the strength of Coastal Command's Striking Force was increased and better arrangements were made to ensure that such an opportunity was not again missed through lack of suitable aircraft.

Attack on German shipping

While preparations were being made for a resumption of the convoys to north Russia Admiral Fraser took advantage of the favourable situation resulting from the damage to the *Tirpitz* to carry out a raid on enemy

Above left Admiral Sir Harold Burrough who commanded the 10th Cruiser Squadron of the Home Fleet 1940 to 1944 (*Imperial War Museum*)

Above right Admiral Sir John Tovey Commander-in-Chief, Home Fleet 1940 to 1943. He disagreed with the First Sea Lord's handling of the PQ 17 operation (*Imperial War Museum*)

Left Grand Admiral Erich Raeder the architect of the reconstituted *Kriegsmarine* and Commander-in-Chief from 1928 to 1943 (*Imperial War Museum*)

Above Admiral Sir Robert Burnett who took part in many Arctic convoy operations and especially in those leading up to the destruction of the battle cruiser *Scharnhorst* during the action off the North Cape in December 1943. He is seen here on the bridge of the flotilla leader HMS *Faulknor* in conversation with Captain A. Scott-Moncrieff RN (*Imperial War Museum*). *Left* Captain Robert Sherbrooke VC, RN who was awarded the Victoria Cross for outstanding bravery during an action in the Barents Sea in support of convoy JW 51B against greatly superior enemy forces (*Imperial War Museum*)

A depth-charge attack by the Order of the Red Banner division of A/S craft based on Murmansk. The sailor in the foreground is using a portable rangefinder (*Novosti Press*)

Admiral of the Fleet Sir Dudley Pound, First Sea Lord and Chief of the Naval Staff from 1939 until his death in October 1943. His decision to order convoy PQ 17 to scatter remains the subject of much controversy (*Imperial War Museum*)

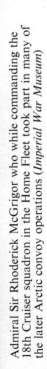

Admiral Sir Rhoderick McGrigor who while commanding the 18th Cruiser squadron in the Home Fleet took part in many of the later Arctic convoy operations (*Imperial War Museum*)

Above A Heinkel 111T torpedo bomber being armed with two F4B torpedoes with practice warheads. Flieger Gruppe 26 was the only unit of the Luftwaffe to use these aircraft with a torpedo armament, a fact which saved the Arctic convoys from more serious losses *(H. Schliephake)*. *Below* The German destroyer *Friedrich Eckholdt* off Bear Island in the Barents Sea *(Ministry of Defence)*

Above Admiral Sir Bruce Fraser, C-in-C Home Fleet seen on board his flagship HMS *Duke of York* with Admiral Arseni Golovko, C-in-C Soviet Northern Fleet during a visit to Murmansk in 1943 (*Imperial War Museum*). *Below* A Junkers 88A-4 twin-engined bomber of the type used by Flieger Gruppe 30 for attacks on the Arctic convoys. Although bombing attacks were impressive and unpleasant they were not as effective as those by torpedo aircraft (*Alfred Price Collection*)

Above The quarterdeck of the
battle cruiser *Scharnhorst*
showing the 11in gun turret
'Carl' and the after superstructure
(*Bildarchiv BfZ*). *Right* The
memorial erected at Murmansk
after the war to commemorate
the Allied victory over the
common enemy (*Novosti Press*)

В ПАМЯТЬ
О СОВМЕСТНОЙ БОРЬБЕ СТРАН
АНТИГИТЛЕРОВСКОЙ КОАЛИЦИИ
ПРОТИВ ФАШИЗМА
В ГОДЫ ВТОРОЙ МИРОВОЙ ВОЙНЫ

IN COMMEMORATION
OF THE COMMON FIGHT OF THE COUNTRY
OF THE ANTI-HITLER COALITION
AGAINST FASCISM
IN THE SECOND WORLD

Above A Soviet submarine of the 'M' class off Polyarno in the Kola Inlet (*Novosti Press*). *Left* Twice Hero of the Soviet Union Boris Safonov fraternises with British airmen on an airfield near Murmansk *(Novosti Press)*

shipping in the port of Bodo. The Home Fleet had been reinforced by the United States carrier *Ranger* and the cruiser *Tuscaloosa* and six destroyers and the US pilots were keen to undertake what would be their first operational sortie. The Home Fleet left Scapa on 2 October and two days later a force of 30 Dauntless dive bombers and Avenger torpedo-armed aircraft accompanied by 12 Hellcat fighters were launched 120 miles off the Norwegian coast. The enemy was taken by surprise and 4 freighters were sunk and 6 others damaged in Bodo harbour. Five aircraft were lost to antiaircraft fire but two enemy aircraft which subsequently attempted to shadow the force were shot down.

Admiral Golovko summoned to Moscow

On 9 October Premier Stalin summoned Admiral Golovko to Moscow. Golovko claims that the success of the German operations in the Kara Sea was the reason he was sent for, but it seems probable that a long telegram which Churchill had sent to Stalin on 1 October also had something to do with it. Besides announcing that plans had been made to sail four convoys to Russia in the months November to February, each to consist of approximately 35 British and American ships, the Prime Minister took the opportunity to bring to Stalin's personal notice, a long list of grievances about the treatment being accorded to British personnel stationed in Russia which was far from that to be expected of an ally. Stalin did not reply to the telegram until 13 October, after he had seen Golovko, and then in such offensive terms that Churchill refused to accept it. He instructed the Foreign Secretary, Mr Anthony Eden, who had arrived in Moscow on 18 October, to handle the matter. One of the points at issue was whether or not the running of the convoys was an obligation on the part of Britain and the United States or whether they were to be regarded as an operation of war to be performed to the best of their ability but without any guarantee as to the quantity of goods to be delivered in a specific time. To strengthen the Foreign Secretary's hand during his discussions with the Russian Premier, Churchill ordered a halt to be made in the arrangements being made for a resumption of the convoys. This action had the desired effect. The meeting took place on 21 October and although Stalin persisted in his view that his allies were under an obligation to run the convoys, after some plain speaking by the British Foreign Secretary and a promise by Stalin to take steps to redress some of the grievances listed by Churchill, which included permission to land a hospital unit at Vaenga, it was agreed that the convoys would be resumed in November.

Resumption of the convoys

Like his predecessor Tovey, Admiral Fraser objected to the proposed size of the resumed convoys which had now risen to 40 ships, as under winter conditions it was only too easy for ships to become separated and an easy prey to the U-boats. The Admiralty, therefore, agreed that they should be run in two sections, each of about 20 ships, a fortnight apart and each with a strong escort of destroyers. Cruisers would be used to provide close cover during the most dangerous part of the voyage, i.e. between Bear Island and the Kola Inlet, whilst a battleship covering force would cruise in an area to the south-west of Bear Island.

Convoys RA 54A and B and JW 54A and B

The first of the new series of convoys was to be a westbound one, RA 54A of 13 freighters which had been awaiting convoy in White Sea ports since the spring. An escort force consisting of the destroyers *Milne* (Captain I. M. R. Campbell RN), *Musketeer*, *Mahratta*, *Matchless*, *Savage*, *Scorpion*, *Scourge*, *Saumarez*, *Westcott*, the minesweepers *Harrier* and *Seagull* and the corvette *Eglantine* left Seidisfiord on 23 October taking with them five 'T' class minesweepers and three submarine chasers being handed over to the Russians under lend-lease. The ships reached the Kola Inlet safely on 28 October and Admiral Golovko soon inspected the latest additions to his fleet which he described as 'quite suitable for combat operations; their seaworthiness is quite reasonable and has been tested by the stormy autumn crossing of the Atlantic'.[1] On board one of the ships he was offered a tot of rum and discovering that there was a whole barrel of it onboard, he ordered that it be sent to the hospital for the use of the wounded, much to the chagrin of his hosts.

On 1 November Convoy RA 54A of 13 freighters left Archangel, having been delayed by thick fog, and reached Loch Ewe on 14 November without having been detected by the enemy. The following day convoy JW 54A of 18 freighters and a tanker escorted by the destroyers *Onslow* (Captain J. A. McCoy DSO, RN), *Onslaught*, *Orwell*, *Impulsive*, *Iroquois*, *Haida*, *Huron*, *Inconstant*, *Whitehall*, the corvette *Heather*, and the minesweeper *Hussar* sailed from Loch Ewe. It was followed a week later by convoy JW 54B of 14 freighters, a tanker and a rescue ship, with an escort consisting of the destroyers *Saumarez*, *Savage*, *Scorpion*, *Stord*, *Scourge*, *Venus*, *Vigilant*,

---

[1] Golovko, ibid, page 173

Hardy, *Beagle*, the corvettes *Rhododendron* and *Poppy*, and the mine-sweeper *Halcyon*. The cruisers *Kent* (flagship of Rear Admiral A. Palliser) *Jamaica*, and *Bermuda* went right through to Kola Inlet with JW 54A and provided cover for convoys JW 54B and RA 54B whilst in the danger zone. Battleship cover for all four convoys was provided by the *Anson* (flagship of Vice-Admiral Sir Henry Moore) with the USS *Tuscaloosa* (relieved by the *Belfast* for convoys JW 54B and RA 54B) operating from Akrureyri, Iceland. Four Soviet destroyers met the convoys as they approached and departed from the Kola Inlet and also took charge of ships proceeding to and from Archangel. Convoy RA 54B of 8 freighters sailed from Archangel on 26 November with the same escort as had arrived with JW 54A except that the minesweeper *Hussar* took the place of the *Harrier*. All ships reached Loch Ewe safely on 9 December.

Absence of German opposition

The next outward convoy JW 55A was scheduled to sail on 12 December. It consisted of 19 freighters escorted by the destroyers *Milne* (Captain I. M. R. Campbell, RN Senior Officer), *Musketeer, Meteor, Matchless, Opportune, Ashanti, Virago, Athabaskan, Westcott,* the corvette *Acanthus*, and the minesweeper *Speedwell*, and left Loch Ewe as arranged. Four U-boats were deployed east of Bear Island to intercept it, *U 277, U 387, U 354,* and *U 636*, but only the last named made contact when she sighted one of the escorts on 18 December but found herself too far away to make an attack. The convoy reached the Kola Inlet intact on 20 December and the White Sea section berthed at Archangel two days later.

The apparent lack of interest in the convoys since they were resumed surprised Admiral Fraser, but he was confident that it was due to ignorance of their movements and that once the enemy had good intelligence of a convoy operation, a determined attempt to interfere with it would be made. The battle-cruiser *Scharnhorst* and the six destroyers of the 4th Flotilla stationed in Altenfiord, were ideally situated for the purpose so that when the Commander-in-Chief heard that JW 55A had been reported he decided to take his flagship, the *Duke of York*, with the cruiser *Jamaica* right through to the Kola Inlet where they arrived on 16 December. The Germans in fact had been aware of the resumed convoy sailings since the middle of November, but the Naval Staff and Group North both considered that the superiority of British radar was such as to make the employment of the *Scharnhorst* inadvisable on an operation which at that time of the year was very likely to produce a night action. Admiral Dönitz, on the other hand, was obliged to justify the retention in commission of the heavy ships and could not, therefore, support this cautious policy. Unfortunately for him the Naval Staff was to be proved right.

Chapter 9
THE LOSS OF THE SCHARNHORST

Admirals Fraser and Golovko confer

After being very hospitably received by Admiral Golovko who confided to his diary 'I still do not grasp for what purpose the Commander-in-Chief of the British Home Fleet should have decided to visit us at the height of the polar night season' [1] and having informed himself of the situation, Admiral Fraser in the *Duke of York* with the *Jamaica* and four destroyers left the Kola Inlet on 23 December and hurried back to Akureyri to refuel and provide cover to the next two convoys JW 55B and RA 55A which were due to sail from Loch Ewe and the Kola Inlet respectively on 20 and 22 December. He already knew from most secret intelligence obtained by the German signals which had been decoded and passed to him and Admiral Burnett by the Admiralty on 20 December, that the enemy was planning to use the *Scharnhorst* for an attack on the convoys. In the event, RA 55A comprising 22 freighters, did not sail until 23 December with the same escort as had arrived with JW 55A but with the addition of the corvettes *Dianella* and *Poppy*.

Convoy JW 55B

The nineteen freighters of Convoy JW 55B sailed as scheduled from Loch Ewe on 20 December and was joined off Iceland two days later by the Ocean Escort consisting of the destroyers *Onslow* (Captain J. A. McCoy RSO, RN Senior Officer), *Onslaught*, *Orwell*, *Impulsive*, *Obdurate*, *Iroquois*, *Huron*, *Haida*, *Whitehall*, *Wrestler*, the corvettes *Oxlip* and *Honeysuckle*, and the minesweeper *Gleaner*. The cruisers *Belfast* (flagship of Vice Admiral R. Burnett), *Sheffield*, and *Norfolk* which had accompanied JW 55A to the Kola

---

[1] Golovko, ibid, page 181

Inlet sailed from there on 23 December to provide cover for the convoy east of Bear Island.

German moves

At a conference with Hitler on 18/19 December, Dönitz had secured the Führer's approval for a surface ship attack on the next convoy located carrying supplies to north Russia. He did not have long to wait because on 22 December a German meteorological flight sighted JW 55B off the Faroe Islands but reported it as 40 troop transports with an escort of cruisers. Admiral Schniewind thereupon ordered the Eisenbart Group of U-boats (*U 277*, *U 367*, *U 354*, *U 601*, *U 716*, *U 957*, and *U 314*) to concentrate off the entrance to the Vestfiord and the Battle Group to come to three hours' notice for steam. After reflection, he decided that the pilot must have been mistaken and that he had sighted an ordinary Arctic convoy, so he told the Eisenbart Group to return to its former patrol area south of Bear Island. The next day a more accurate report was received from a reconnaissance aircraft despatched to find and shadow the convoy, which reported it as comprising seventeen ships in a position 300 miles south-east of Jan Mayen Island. The following day it was reported as being 220 miles east of that island so Admiral Schniewind moved the U-boat patrol 100 miles west. Later that day *U 601* (Lieutenant Hansen) and *U 716* (Lieutenant Dunkelberg) made contact with it but were driven off by the escorts. There were no strike aircraft available and Air Group V informed Group North that continuous reconnaissance could be maintained only in the event of the Battle Group being ordered to sea, and then only to a depth of 450 miles. Contact with JW 55B was lost shortly after 16.00 hrs on 24th and all things considered Schniewind did not rate the chances of a successful sortie by the *Scharnhorst* against it very high, but he telephoned Berlin to obtain Admiral Dönitz's views.

The Commander-in-Chief was in Paris and it was decided that events must wait for his return, due the following day. To add to Group North's difficulties Admiral Kummetz had gone sick and Rear Admiral Erich Bey, Flag Officer, Destroyers, had been appointed to take his place in command of the Battle Group. Bey was an experienced destroyer officer who had taken part in the second battle of Narvik. Two weeks after being nominated to his new post he had submitted a memorandum to Admiral Schniewind in which he expressed agreement with Kummetz's views regarding the undesirability of using the *Scharnhorst* during the dark winter months to attack convoys, a task for which he considered the destroyers to be more suitable; Bey, however, ended his memorandum with a more optimistic pronouncement: 'Any prospect of success', he wrote, 'must necessarily depend mainly on chance or on some failure or major mistake by the enemy. (He was possibly thinking of PQ 17.) Yet despite our weakness, the war has given us many favourable opportunities and experience justifies the hope that luck will be on our side.'

Meanwhile Dönitz had issued a directive which modified his previously held views regarding the undesirability of using the *Scharnhorst* during the long polar nights. He now suggested that such operations might be considered, provided they were 'compatible with our strength' and that air reconnaissance could be provided, but as already explained the position regarding this last requirement was unsatisfactory.

Fraser's anxiety for the convoy's safety

Captain McCoy reported the 01.00 hrs on 24th estimated position of convoy JW 55B at 23.15 hrs to the Senior British Naval Officer North Russia, but during the night the weather deteriorated and the following morning at 07.00 hrs when the time came to alter course from 037° to 057° the ships were scattered over a wide area so he reduced speed to 7 knots in order to allow the stragglers to catch up. By noon when the main body of the convoy had reached a position 240 miles east of Jan Mayen Island and 400 miles from Altenfiord, two enemy aircraft appeared and recommenced shadowing. It was now entering on the most dangerous part of its passage but the battleship covering force, the speed of advance of which was limited by the need to conserve the fuel of the accompanying destroyers, was still some 400 miles astern. Admiral Fraser, therefore, decided to break radio silence to order Captain McCoy to reverse the course of the convoy for three hours to enable his force to catch up with it. At the same time he increased the speed of his force to 19 knots. However, after conferring with the Commodore, McCoy decided that it would be unwise to undertake the difficult manoeuvre of turning the convoy about so he maintained a speed of 8 instead of 9 knots which, while not producing the quick result which Admiral Fraser was hoping for, helped to lessen the distance between them.

Meanwhile, convoy RA 55A undetected by the enemy passed south of Bear Island early on 25 December and the Commander-in-Chief instructed Burnett to divert it to the north and since it was not actively threatened, to transfer four destroyers of its escort to reinforce that of JW 55B. At 02.00 hrs on 25th the *Musketeer*, *Matchless*, *Opportune*, and *Virago* were detached to comply. Their junction with JW 55B brought the strength of its escort to

14 destroyers, a force strong enough to give a very good account of itself in the event of a surface ship attack on the convoy.

Dönitz makes a decision

Three direction finding stations of the German radio interception service obtained accurate bearings of the two messages transmitted by the *Duke of York* but, for some unexplained reason and despite the fact that there were indications that they emanated from a British covering force, the fix was regarded as unreliable and the transmissions as possibly emanating from a straggler from the convoy. So when on the morning of 25 December Dönitz returned to Berlin the situation in the Arctic appeared to him as follows:

> 'A convoy carrying war material for Russia and protected by a cruiser escort that was no match for our battleship (*Scharnhorst*) was sailing through an area within easy reach of our Battle Group. Its position, course, and speed were known. Because of ice in the vicinity of Bear Island which prevented evasive action, and the superior speed of the German ships, it could not hope to avoid our attack.' [1]

He well knew that the Arctic convoys invariably had a battleship supporting force, but as in the past it had cruised in an area well towards the west, he says he assumed that 'it must have been a long way from the convoy'.[1] The *Duke of York*'s visit to the Kola Inlet, of which he must have been aware, evidently did not indicate to him a possible change of policy.

Having heard nothing from Naval Headquarters by noon on 25th at 12.15 hrs Schniewind brought the Battle Group to one hour's notice for steam. At 14.15 hrs Dönitz gave orders for it to sail at 17.00 hrs, later amended to 19.00 hrs to give Bey and his staff time to transfer from the *Tirpitz* to the *Scharnhorst*. A moderate gale was now blowing over the area to the north of the North Cape. A report timed 14.15 hrs on 25th from Lieutenant Hansen commanding *U 601* which had been in contact with JW 55B since 09.00 hrs stated 'Wind south force 7 (33 knots) rain, visibility two miles' and Schniewind suggested delaying the sailing of the Battle Group until conditions improved and air reconnaissance, which had ceased at 10.00 hrs, could be resumed. His suggestion was not approved and at 19.00 hrs Captain Hintze took the *Scharnhorst* accompanied by the destroyers *Z 29* (Captain Johannesson), *Z 30*, *Z 33*, *Z 34*, and *Z 38* out through the narrow entrance of Altenfiord into the stormy Barents Sea and headed northwards at 25 knots.

---

[1] Grand Admiral Karl Dönitz, *Memoirs* (George Weidenfeld & Nicolson Limited, 1959), page 375.

Admiral Bey's instructions

Group North's instructions to Admiral Bey were:

(a)   group attack on the convoy will be delivered by *Scharnhorst* and five destroyers on 26 December at first light;

(b)   concerted attack will only be delivered if conditions are favourable (weather, visibility, accurate information regarding the enemy);

(c)   if conditions do not suit *Scharnhorst*, destroyers will attack alone, battle-cruiser to stand off and observe or if decided advisable, to be in readiness in the outer fiord.

These instructions gave Bey considerable latitude, but they were supplemented by additional ones from Dönitz which, though they did not actually conflict, contained some restrictive clauses. They read:

(1)   a convoy to Russia is carrying war materials for use against our troops on the eastern front. We must come to their assistance;

(2)   the convoy is to be attacked by the *Scharnhorst* and destroyers;

(3)   the tactical situation must be skilfully and boldly exploited and the attack must not end in stalemate. Every opportunity to attack must be seized using the *Scharnhorst*'s superiority to the best advantage. The destroyers are to be used later;

(4)   you may use your judgement when to break off action. You must disengage if a superior enemy force is encountered.

(5)   inform all the crews accordingly. I have complete confidence in your offensive spirit.

The difference in emphasis in these two sets of instructions will be noted. Schniewind favoured an attack on the convoy by the destroyers whereas Dönitz gave preference to one by the battle-cruiser. Paragraph (b) of the former's orders, however, contained the most important provision of all 'accurate information regarding the enemy' and this, as will be seen, was lacking. Finally, Dönitz's order about disengaging if a superior enemy force were encountered tied Bey's hands. Many a naval action has been won by the weaker but more resolute of two opponents.

Movements of the German Battle Group

On reaching the area of operations, just before midnight Bey broke radio silence to inform Group North that the state of the weather placed severe restrictions on the operating ability of his destroyers and that he had been obliged to reduce speed. With their five 5.9-inch (150mm) guns these ships were inclined to roll heavily in a seaway. In reply Schniewind suggested what he called 'cruiser action' by the *Scharnhorst* alone, but he left it to his discretion how to act.

Fraser's dispositions

In the early hours of 26th Admirals Fraser and Burnett had received from the Admiralty the decoded versions of two intercepted German signals, one reporting that air reconnaissance had relocated convoy JW 55B the previous afternoon and the second giving the executive order for the *Scharnhorst* and four destroyers to sail at 17.00 hrs on 25th. The Admiralty followed this up with a general signal timed 03.19 hrs on 26th to all the forces taking part which, without in any way disclosing the source of the information, stated that the Admiralty appreciated that the *Scharnhorst* was at sea. Admiral Fraser thereupon increased the speed of his force to 24 knots.

At 04.01 hrs on 26th the British Commander-in-Chief ordered Admiral Burnett and Captain McCoy to indicate the positions of the cruiser force and convoy JW 55B respectively, at the same time giving them that of his force (71° 07'N, 10° 48'E, course 080° 24 knots). He also ordered the convoy to turn to a northerly course. In his view it was most desirable under the prevailing conditions of darkness and poor visibility that the three groups of ships should be aware of their relative positions to each other. He considered this more important than the possible disclosure of the *Duke of York*'s position. These signals were detected by the German direction finding stations but once again no use appears to have been made of the information. At 06.28 hrs he sent a further message to the convoy telling it to steer north-east and to the cruisers to close it. The message was received by Captain McCoy at 07.05 hrs just as he had finished altering the convoy's course to 035° to comply with the Commander-in-Chief's previous signal; the cruisers turned to a course of 270° at 07.12 hrs.

Bey's problems

A number of delayed aircraft reports had reached Bey during the night and one of them timed 15.10 hrs on 25th informed him that a radar sweep round the convoy had not detected any other enemy force within 50 miles of it. At 07.00 hrs, having reached the area in which he expected to find the convoy, he told Captain Hintze to steer 250° and he spread his destroyers ten miles ahead, five miles apart on this course. As they were now steaming head on to the wind and sea he was obliged to reduce the speed of his force to 12 and eventually to 10 knots. At 07.55 hrs he signalled a new course of 230° then at

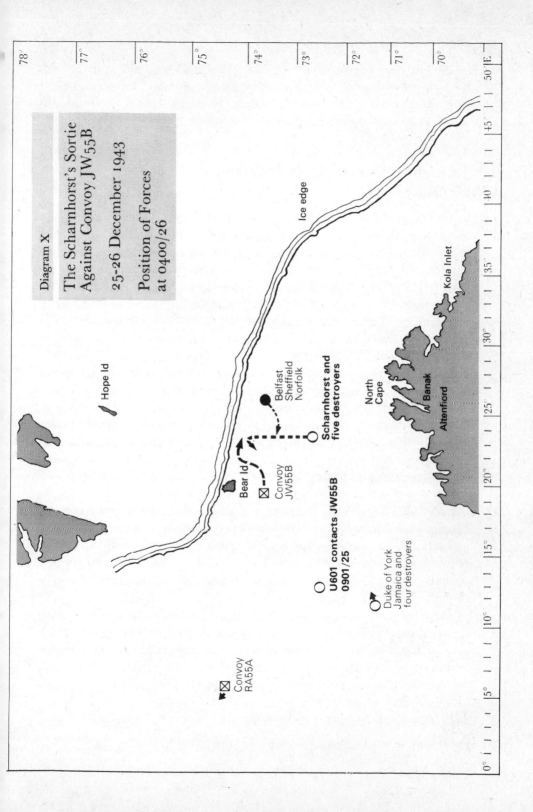

Diagram X

The Scharnhorst's Sortie
Against Convoy JW55B

25-26 December 1943

Position of Forces
at 0400/26

Hope Id

Ice edge

Kola Inlet

Bear Id

North
Cape

Banak

Altenfjord

Belfast
Sheffield
Norfolk

Scharnhorst and
five destroyers

Convoy
JW55B

U601 contacts JW55B
0901/25

Duke of York
Jamaica and
four destroyers

Convoy
RA55A

08.20 hrs, doubtless considering that this speed was too slow for the *Scharnhorst's* safety from submarine attack, he ordered Captain Hintze to increase speed and alter course towards the north, possibly intending to carry out a broad zig-zag astern of the destroyers, though he did not make any signal to that effect.

The first brush with Burnett's cruisers
(see Diagram X)

In turning to the northward Bey had put the *Scharnhorst* on a converging course with Burnett's cruisers approaching from the eastward. These last had gone to action stations at 08.30 hrs in accordance with normal practice and ten minutes later Burnett led round to a course of about 315°. Meanwhile at 08.34 hrs the *Norfolk*'s radar picked up a ship bearing 280° 16½ miles and a few minutes later the *Belfast* radar registered a similar echo bearing 295° 17 miles. According to the plot the unknown ship which at first appeared to be steering north subsequently altered round to a southerly course. Then at 09.21 hrs the *Scharnhorst* was sighted by the *Sheffield* bearing 222° 6½ miles on the southerly leg of her zig-zag. Three minutes later the *Belfast* unsuccessfully tried to illuminate her with starshell and so did the other two ships but the bursts were all short. At 09.29 hrs Burnett, unwilling to wait any longer, gave the order to open fire and ordered all ships to turn to port together to close the range. This move had the effect of blanking the 'A' arcs of the *Belfast*'s and *Sheffield*'s after guns, but the *Norfolk* had all guns bearing and at 09.30 hrs she fired six broadsides at a range of 9800 yards and scored three hits on the battle-cruiser destroying her port high angle director and the radar aerial as well as causing minor damage inside the ship. Taken by surprise, the *Scharnhorst* increased speed and set off on a south-easterly course until clear of the cruisers when she began to work round to the north in order to get at the convoy which Bey probably guessed was to the west of the cruisers. Burnett rightly refused to be enticed away from the convoy which it was his primary duty to protect, so as the *Scharnhorst* streaked away from him at 10.00 hrs he turned back to the north-west to close it. He fully appreciated that the enemy ship could make a better speed against the wind and sea than could his much smaller cruisers so he hoped to reach a position from which he would be able to head her off should she approach the convoy from the east.

British force movements

On receipt of the *Sheffield*'s enemy report, Admiral Fraser ordered convoy

JW 55B to turn to a northerly course in order to keep clear of the battle area and he told McCoy to detach four destroyers to join the cruisers. His signal crossed one from McCoy to Burnett asking if he wanted any assistance, but on receipt of the Commander-in-Chief's message he detached the same four destroyers which had joined him from the escort of convoy RA 55A and they reached the cruisers at 10.25 hrs, just after radar touch with the *Scharnhorst* had been lost.

Meanwhile, at 10.12 hrs one of three BV 138 reconnaissance aircraft sent to assist the *Scharnhorst* to find the convoy, made radar contact with the *Duke of York*, *Jamaica*, and four destroyers which were reported as one large ship and several small ones, but the position given was 49 miles east of their true one. If Admiral Bey received this report direct, which is not known, it might have set him wondering who were these unidentified ships 107 miles south-west from him, but all we know is that at that time he was concerned as to the position of his destroyers with which he had been out of contact since 08.00 hrs. At 10.09 hrs, however, he managed to get a message to Captain Johannessen telling him to report on the situation. The latter replied that he was steering 230° at 12 knots as last ordered and gave his estimated position. To this Bey replied at 10.30 hrs 'Steer 070° at 25 knots and advance into the immediate vicinity of the convoy' from which it can be presumed that he now had a fairly clear idea of where it was. An hour later he amended his destroyers' course to 030°.

The second brush with the Scharnhorst

Burnett's cruisers had taken up a position some ten miles ahead of the convoy with the four destroyers forming an anti-submarine screen ahead whilst the cruisers zig-zagged behind them on a mean course of 045° at 28 knots. However, the destroyers had some difficulty in steering with the wind and sea on the quarter, so at 11.08 hrs he reduced speed to 18 knots, altered round to north, and told the destroyers to re-form the anti-submarine screen. When they had done so, at 11.21 hrs he resumed a course of 045°, the convoy being at that time eight miles on his port quarter. At 11.22 hrs the Commander-in-Chief gave McCoy discretion to alter the course of the convoy which was heading up towards the ice edge, so at 11.55 hrs he changed course to 125°. Whilst the turn was in progress at 12.05 hrs the *Belfast*'s radar picked up an echo bearing 072° 15 miles, which Burnett suspected might be the *Scharnhorst* and fifteen minutes later he was proved right when she came into sight steering towards him on a mean course of about 240°. Meanwhile, he had ordered his four destroyers to concentrate a mile ahead of the *Belfast*, then two miles on a bearing 090° whilst he led the cruisers round to a course of 100°. At 12.20 hrs he ordered the destroyers to attack the enemy with torpedoes and a minute later the *Belfast* illuminated the battle-cruiser with starshell and all three cruisers opened broadside fire at a range of 10,500 yards.

Captain Hintze's immediate reaction to this second encounter was to turn away so preventing the destroyers from being able to fire their torpedoes, but this time he was not taken by surprise and the German ship opened fire as she steadied on a course of about 040°. Then after a feint to the north-west, he swung his ship round through 180° turn to port and steadied on a heading of 110°. The *Norfolk*, the only one of the three cruisers not supplied with flashless cordite, was singled out by the enemy as target and received two hits from his 11-inch guns, one of which put X turret out of action; another exploded amidships putting her Type 273 and 284 radars out of action. One officer and six men were killed and five severely wounded. The *Sheffield* was slightly damaged by splinters from near misses. It is probable that the *Scharnhorst* was hit during this engagement but not seriously enough to impair her fighting efficiency. The range, which had fallen at one time to 8000 yards, now began to open rapidly as the enemy ship sped south-eastwards at high speed and at 12.41 hrs she disappeared from view and fire was checked. Burnett was determined that the battle-cruiser should not escape and he led his cruisers in pursuit at a speed of 28 knots keeping in touch by radar. So long as she continued on her present course she could not endanger the convoy, so his task now was to shadow and report her position, course, and speed to Admiral Fraser hastening eastwards with his force to cut her off. At 13.06 hrs the Air Commander, Lofoten, re-transmitted the aircraft sighting report of Fraser's force timed 10.12 hrs, referred to above, but he omitted the reference to 'one large ship'. This message would almost certainly have been seen by Admiral Bey but in its mutilated form it probably did not convey a warning of immediate danger.

Fraser's problem

Just prior to the engagement described above, Admiral Fraser had been seriously concerned about the fuel consumption of his destroyers and whether or not to go on to the Kola Inlet or to return to Iceland. When, however, he received Burnett's enemy report timed 12.05 hrs he knew, as he wrote in his report, 'there was every chance of catching the enemy'.[1]

---

[1] *London Gazette*, 5 August 1947, paragraph 33

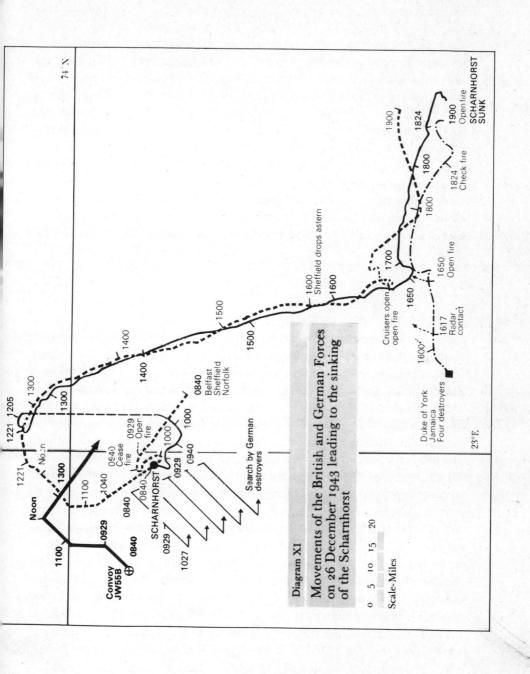

Diagram XI

**Movements of the British and German Forces
on 26 December 1943 leading to the sinking
of the Scharnhorst**

Scale-Miles

0 5 10 15 20

74° N.

23° E.

Convoy
JW55B

0840

0929

Noon

1100

1300

SCHARNHORST

0929

1027

0929

0840

0840

1040

1100

1221

1205

1221

1300

1300

1400

1400

1500

1500

1600

1600

1700

1800

1800

1824

1824
Check fire

1900

1900
Open fire

SCHARNHORST
SUNK

0940
Cease
fire

0929
Open
fire

0929

0940

1000

1000

0840
Belfast
Sheffield
Norfolk

Search by German
destroyers

Sheffield drops astern

Cruisers open
open fire

1650

1650
Open fire

1617
Radar
contact

1600

Duke of York
Jamaica
Four destroyers

JW 55B's narrow escape

Captain McCoy had observed the starshell and gunflashes of the short action between the cruisers and the *Scharnhorst* and had formed his destroyers in divisions on the port side of the convoy in readiness to attack the enemy ship should she appear, but when it became evident that she was heading away from the convoy at high speed he re-formed the screen as he was aware that U-boats were still in touch. Little did he know that, acting on a delayed U-boat report, at 12.18 hrs Bey had ordered his destroyers to operate in an area further to the west and that at 13.00 hrs, whilst carrying out this order, they had passed only eight miles south of the convoy. At 14.18 hrs they were ordered by Bey to return to base, an order which Captain Johannessen queried, but on receiving confirmation, he set course for Altenfiord at a speed of 12 knots and the German destroyers took no further part in the proceedings.

The long chase
(see Diagram XI)

Throughout the dark afternoon Burnett maintained radar contact with the *Scharnhorst* from a position seven and a half miles astern of her. The enemy gradually worked round to a mean course of 160° and at 15.25 hrs Bey informed Group North of his expected time of arrival off Altenfiord. The continuous flow of reports from the *Belfast* enabled the *Duke of York* (Captain The Hon. G. H. E. Russell RN) to determine that action with the *Scharnhorst* would be joined about 17.15 hrs and all preparations were made to this end. At 16.17 hrs her search radar recorded an echo bearing 020° 22 miles and closing rapidly, and there was no doubt that this was the enemy ship. By 16.32 hrs the range had dropped to 14 miles and twelve minutes later the *Duke of York* altered course to 080° to open her 'A' arcs. At 16.47 hrs the *Belfast* fired starshell to illuminate the target and the *Duke of York* did likewise. In the pale light of the flares the *Scharnhorst* could be seen plainly with her guns fore and aft, speeding south towards the Norwegian coast. She was taken completely by surprise. At 16.50 hrs the ten 14-inch guns of the *Duke of York* thundered out a salvo at a range of 12,000 yards, being joined soon after by the *Jamaica*'s 6-inch guns. The *Scharnhorst* was not long in replying at the same time turning away to port only to come under fire from the cruisers. Realising he was caught in a trap, Cap. Hintze steadied on an easterly course, relying on his superior speed to escape.

A long chase ensued with the range gradually opening and both the heavy ships pounding each other at intervals. By 18.20 hrs the distance between them was 20,000 yards and they both checked fire and it looked for a moment as if the enemy ship was going to escape, then her speed suddenly began to drop as the result of a hit aft by the *Duke of York*. At last the four destroyers which Fraser had ordered to attack her with torpedoes began to gain bearing and at 18.50 hrs from positions on either bow they fired their torpedoes scoring, it was estimated, three hits and further reducing the battle-cruiser's speed. When the range had fallen to 10,400 yards the *Duke of York* and *Jamaica* re-opened fire, being joined soon afterwards by the *Belfast* and *Norfolk*, the *Sheffield* having dropped astern with shaft trouble. In a matter of twenty minutes the *Scharnhorst* was brought to a standstill with her guns silenced and she was despatched by torpedo fire from the cruisers and destroyers. At 19.45 hrs she rolled over to starboard and sank, taking with her all but 36 of her ship's company of just on 2000 who were rescued by the cruisers and destroyers.

Fraser returns to the Kola Inlet

Admiral Fraser in the *Duke of York* with the *Jamaica*, Burnett's three cruisers, and four destroyers reached Kola Inlet on 27 December and Admiral Golovko went onboard the flagship to congratulate the British Commander-in-Chief on his success. He had done his best to co-operate with the limited forces at his disposal, sending three of his submarines to watch the approaches to Altenfiord in case the *Scharnhorst* should return and ordering his destroyers to raise steam, as well as alerting his bombers and torpedo-armed aircraft. He was disappointed, nevertheless, at not being allowed to interrogate the 36 survivors from the German ship.

The U-boats remained in contact with convoy JW 55B until the morning of 27 December when they were ordered to search for survivors of the *Scharnhorst*. The Murmansk section of the convoy of ten ships and a tanker entered the Kola Inlet two days later while the Archangel section reached the White Sea on 29 December.

Effect of the sinking of the Scharnhorst

The running of the Arctic convoys was much simplified by the sinking of the *Scharnhorst* as, with the *Tirpitz* out of action, the surface threat was now reduced to that of a few destroyers. The U-boats still constituted the main threat and the enemy had an ally in the weather at this time of the year.

Convoys JW 56A and B

Convoy JW 56A of 20 ships sailed from Loch Ewe on 12 January 1944 with a strong destroyer escort similar to that provided for its predecessor. It was covered by the cruisers *Kent* (flagship of Vice Admiral Arthur Palliser), *Berwick*, and *Bermuda*. A heavy gale was encountered off the Faroes and the convoy was obliged to put into Akureyri to repair damage, where five ships had to remain. It set sail again on 21 January escorted by 9 destroyers and 2 corvettes. The following day convoy JW 56B of 16 ships sailed from Loch Ewe with an escort of 13 destroyers and corvettes. An enemy agent in Iceland reported the departure of JW 56A and the Isegrim group of 10 U-boats was stationed south of Bear Island to intercept it. Air reconnaissance failed to locate it but at noon on 26 January *U 739* sighted it and summoned 8 more boats of the Group. As a result, during the darkness of the afternoon and night of 26/27 January they delivered a series of attacks torpedoing the freighters *Penelope Barker*, *Fort Bellingham*, and *Andrew Curtin* all of which eventually sank. The *Fort Bellingham* was in fact given her *coup de grâce* by *U 957* (Lieutenant Schaar) who rescued some of her crew and took them prisoner. These successes were attributed to the lack of experience of some of the escort commanders.

Introduction of the Gnat

In September 1943 the Germans had introduced a homing torpedo designated T5 but given the code-name of Gnat by the Allies and the Arctic U-boats were equipped with them towards the end of the year. It contained a listening device in the head which enabled it to home on to the noise made by an escort vessel's propellers and had been introduced especially to enable the U-boats to counter-attack these ships. During the course of the attack mentioned above *U 360* (Lieutenant-Commander Becker) fired one of them at the destroyer *Obdurate*, but although hit, she managed to reach port. On 27 January the escort was reinforced by the Russian destroyers *Razumy*, *Gremyashchi*, and *Grozny* and the twelve remaining ships of the convoy and its escort entered the Kola Inlet the following day.

In view of the U-boat's success in sinking three ships of JW 56A, Admiral Fraser postponed the sailing of the homeward convoy RA 56A and ordered its intended escort comprising the ships which had escorted JW 56A to reinforce the escort of JW 56B. It was in charge of that veteran of Arctic convoys, Captain I. M. R. Campbell RN and had been diverted to the north. Campbell had been anxiously watching the situation ever since his convoy had been reported by aircraft when five days out from Loch Ewe. He has recorded how it was 'with infinite relief Captain Robson in the *Hardy* with six other destroyers arrived from Kola in support'.[1] The U-boats had been re-formed as the Werwolf Group and brought up to a strength of 15 boats so the Commander-in-Chief's decision had been most timely.

At 09.34 hrs on 29th *U 956* (Lieutenant Mohs) obtained a first sighting of JW 56B and was driven off on three occasions by the escorts at which he fired Gnat torpedoes but without success. All during the night of 29/30 January the U-boats attempted to penetrate the powerful screen, replying to successive counter-attacks with Gnat torpedoes. Eventually one of these weapons fired by *U 278* (Lieutenant Franze) homed on the *Hardy*'s propellers and blew off her stern. There could be no question of taking her in tow in the middle of such an intensive battle with the U-boats and after the *Venus* had rescued her ship's company she sank her with a torpedo. The *Milne* herself was narrowly missed by Gnats fired by *U 737* and *U 957* but later that day after a hunt lasting four hours the *Meteor* and *Whitehall* destroyed *U 314*, though at the time they were not aware of their success. The skill and determination with which the convoy was defended prevented the U-boats from making an attack and the 16 freighters entered Kola Inlet safely on 1 February.

Convoy RA 56

The delayed convoy RA 56 of 37 freighters sailed from the Kola Inlet on 3 February with an escort of 23 destroyers and corvettes, and successfully avoiding the 8 remaining boats of the Werwolf Group which had been misled by an incorrect aircraft report as to its course, reached Loch Ewe intact on 11 February.

Convoy policy changed

With the increasing hours of daylight and the possibility that the enemy might strengthen his air forces in north Norway, Admiral Fraser decided to change the policy of splitting the convoys in two, to one of sailing one large convoy heavily escorted. He arranged with the Commander-in-Chief, Western Approaches, to borrow some of his escort carriers which, now that the Battle of the Atlantic had been won, and very long range aircraft were available, were no longer in such great demand in that area. The next convoy

---

[1] Campbell and Macintyre, ibid, page 209

JW 57 of 52 freighters and a tanker was, therefore, given an escort comprising the anti-aircraft cruiser *Black Prince* (flagship of Vice Admiral I. G. Glennie), the escort carrier *Chaser* (Captain H. V. P. McClintock RN), 13 destroyers under Captain I. M. R. Campbell RN, and a Western Approaches Support Group of 4 ships under Commander Tyson RN in the *Keppel*. The cruisers *Kent* (flagship of Vice Admiral A. Palliser), *Jamaica*, and (Polish) *Dragon* provided cover. The convoy left Loch Ewe on 20 February and three days later was located by a Ju 88 aircraft and was subsequently shadowed by it and a FW 200 aircraft, for ten hours. After the disappointing results achieved with the previous convoys the U-boats were deployed in an all-out effort and two Groups *Werwolf* and *Hartmut*, totalling 14 U-boats were stationed to intercept JW 57.

Convoy JW 57 attacked

On 24 February a FW 200 aircraft regained contact with JW 57 and having survived attacks by Wildcat and Martlet fighters from the *Chaser*, managed to home four U-boats on to the convoy, one of which, *U 713*, was sunk by the *Keppel*. Throughout that day and the next the escorts assisted by a Catalina flying boat of No. 210 Squadron RAF and Swordfish aircraft from the *Chaser* fought off the U-boats which by the evening of 26th were no longer in touch. They had lost another of their number during the battle, *U 601* to the Catalina, but in return *U 990* homed a Gnat on to the destroyer *Mahratta* which capsized before the crew could be taken off and only 17 of them were saved by the *Impulsive*. During the next two days the convoy was persistently shadowed by aircraft but although five boats of the Werwolf Group managed to regain contact, they were never allowed to get near enough to the convoy to deliver an attack, nor were their efforts to counter-attack the escorts successful and the convoy reached the Kola Inlet safely on 28 February.

Convoy RA 57

The return Convoy RA 57 of 31 ships sailed from the Kola Inlet on 2 March with the same escort as JW 57 except for the Support Group which had returned to base after reaching Bear Island. In order to deceive the U-boats which it was expected would be lying in wait for it and which we now know numbered 4 boats of the Boreas Group, later reinforced by 8 more, on leaving harbour the convoy made a wide detour to the east whilst Soviet ships and aircraft carried out an intensive search off the entrance. However, on 4 March the convoy was located by enemy aircraft and the U-boats quickly gained touch with it. Once again they found themselves faced with an active and skilful defence. *U 472* (Lieutenant Freiherr von Forstner), after being damaged by one of the *Chaser*'s aircraft and under fire from the *Onslaught*, scuttled herself but both the *Swift* and the *Milne* had narrow escapes from Gnat torpedoes fired at them by *U 739* and *U 703* respectively. This new weapon, as Captain Campbell has recorded, placed a considerable strain on Asdic (Sonar) operators and on bridge personnel as instant action was needed to avoid one of these menacing weapons, such as dropping a depth charge and increasing speed the moment one was detected approaching.

On 4 March when the convoy was 70 miles east-south-east of Bear Island, *U 703* (Lieutenant Brünner) managed to get within range of it and fired a salvo of pattern running torpedoes, one of which struck the freighter *Empire Tourist* which sank soon after. The bad weather which had made the operation of the *Chaser*'s aircraft very hazardous, now showed signs of improvement and on 5 March *U 336* succumbed to a rocket attack by a Swordfish aircraft. The following day *U 973* shared a similar fate. The U-boats found great difficulty in operating their anti-aircraft guns on account of the ice which formed on them. As the convoy steamed south the U-boats fell away and it reached Loch Ewe on 10 March without further loss.

Attacks on the Tirpitz renewed

There were now indications that the *Tirpitz* might be seaworthy once again, so while the next convoy operation was in progress under the code name of Tungsten a heavy attack on her was mounted by a force under Vice Admiral Sir Henry Moore with his flag in the battleship *Anson*, accompanied by the fleet carriers *Victorious* and *Furious* and the escort carriers *Emperor*, *Searcher*, and *Pursuer* supported by the *Duke of York* (flagship of Admiral Fraser), with the cruisers *Belfast*, *Sheffield*, and *Jamaica* with a screen of destroyers. The attack took place on 3 April and was delivered by two strikes each of 21 Baracuda aircraft escorted by 21 Corsairs and 20 Hellcat fighters and was completely successful, the *Tirpitz* being struck by 14 bombs which damaged her severely and caused 318 casualties of which 122 were killed. She was put out of action for a further three months. Four aircraft were lost.

Convoy JW 58

Meanwhile Convoy JW 58 of 49 freighters had sailed from Loch Ewe on 27

March and it was given the most powerful escort of any Arctic convoy yet. It was under the overall command of Vice Admiral F. H. G. Dalrymple-Hamilton with his flag in the cruiser *Diadem* accompanied by the escort carriers *Tracker* and *Activity*, reinforced by Support Groups Nos. 2 and 8 from the Western Approaches Command, making a total of 20 destroyers, 5 sloops, and 5 corvettes. The US cruiser *Milwaukee* being transferred to the Soviet Navy in lieu of ships of the surrendered Italian fleet, accompanied the convoy. One freighter had to put into Iceland with engine defects. A chance encounter with *U 961* on passage to the Atlantic led to her being sunk by that ace of U-boat killers, Captain Walker RN in his sloop *Starling*, leader of the 2nd Support Group.

The convoy was located by aircraft on 30 March, but Martlet fighters shot down a Ju 88 aircraft of Long Range Reconnaissance Group 22 and the next day three FW 200s of Coastal Group 40 shared a similar fate. On 1 April a BV 138 of sea Patrol Wing 130 was destroyed and the following day another Ju 88 of Long Range Reconnaissance Group 124 was shot down. Three U-boat Groups, Thor (*U 278*, *U 312*, *U 313*, and *U 674*), Blitz (*U 277*, *U 355*, *U 711*, and *U 956*), and Hammer (*U 288*, *U 315*, *U 354*, and *U 968*) together with *U 716*, U 739, *U 360*, *U 361*, and *U 990* on passage, 17 in all, were deployed against the convoy, but despite repeated Gnat attacks on the escorts they achieved no success. On 1 April *U 355* (Lieutenant La Baume) after being damaged by aircraft rocket attack was sunk by the *Beagle* and the next day *U 360* (Lieutenant Commander Becker) was sunk by the *Keppel*. On 3 April aircraft sank *U 288* (Lieutenant Meyer) after she had shot down a Swordfish aircraft. The escorts had scored an undoubted victory shooting down 6 aircraft and sinking 4 U-boats for the loss of 1 aircraft. The convoy was joined by 4 Soviet destroyers, 4 minesweepers, and 4 submarine chasers as it approached the Kola Inlet which it reached safely on 5 April.

Convoy RA 58

The return convoy RA 58 of 36 ships with the same escort as JW 58 sailed from the Kola Inlet on 7 April. After the heavy losses incurred with the previous eastbound convoy, the Luftwaffe decided to abandon attempts at daylight reconnaissance and to restrict their efforts to night radar searches. The convoy was located by this means on 9 April. Two Groups of U-boats were deployed against it, Donner and Keil (*U 313*, *U 636*, *U 703*, *U 277*, *U 361*, *U 362*, *U 711*, *U 716*, *U 347*, and *U 990*) but they failed to achieve any success and the convoy reached Loch Ewe safely on 14 April.

Interruption of the Arctic Convoys

The extensive preparations being made for the invasion of Normandy once again brought about a suspension of the Arctic convoys since every available escort vessel was needed for this great enterprise. There were, however, a large number of empty ships in north Russian ports which the Ministry of War Transport was anxious to retrieve. In addition 2300 Soviet officers and men assigned to commission the ships allocated to the Soviet Navy in compensation for its share of the Italian fleet, were awaiting passage to the United Kingdom. A force under Rear Admiral R. McGrigor with his flag in the cruiser *Diadem* accompanied by the escort carriers *Activity* and *Fencer*, 8 destroyers, the 6th (Canadian) and 8th Support Groups, with 1 corvette sailed for the Kola Inlet where it arrived undetected on 23 April. On 27 April 16 freighters from the White Sea with an escort of Soviet ships joined the 29 freighters in the Kola Inlet and the following day Convoy RA 59 of 45 ships sailed. It was located by enemy aircraft at about midnight on 28/29 April and the Donner and Keil Groups of U-boats were ordered to operate against it. Galled by their lack of success against recent convoys the U-boats engaged in a series of determined attacks on both the escorts and the freighters and their intrepidity was rewarded with the sinking of the freighter *William S. Thayer* by *U 711* (Lieutenant Lange) during the night of 30 April/1 May. The following day *U 277* was sunk by aircraft from the carriers and on 2 May *U 959* and *U 674* were similarly accounted for. These successes were witnessed by Admiral Levchenko of the Soviet Navy who was taking passage to the United Kingdom in the *Fencer*. Nothing daunted, the U-boats continued their assault and on 3 May *U 278* successfully defended herself against attacks by two Swordfish and a Martlet aircraft, the last named of which she shot down while she herself escaped without damage. There were no further incidents and RA 59 reached Loch Ewe on 6 May with 44 ships.

Review of the winter season of convoys

Summing up the result of the 1943/44 winter series of Arctic convoys the Commander-in-Chief, Home Fleet wrote in his despatch:

'Taken as a whole the campaign can be claimed as a success. A large volume of valuable supplies has reached Russia almost intact and the enemy has sustained far greater losses in attempting to hinder them than he has inflicted on our forces.'

The enemy, nevertheless, could not afford to give up the struggle and he still had a surprise in store when the convoys were resumed in the autumn.

Chapter 10
THE LAST CONVOYS

By the time the Arctic convoys were resumed in the autumn of 1944 Admiral Sir Henry Moore had relieved Admiral Sir Bruce Fraser as Commander-in-Chief, Home Fleet. Although the situation had changed very little since the spring there was one new factor to be reckoned with. This was the gradual introduction of 'schnorkels' or breathing tubes in the U-boats which enabled them to charge their batteries whilst remaining submerged and use their main engines whilst travelling at periscope depth. Dönitz saw in this development an opportunity for the U-boats to regain the initiative they had lost.

Attacks on the Tirpitz renewed

During the summer several attempts were made to cripple the *Tirpitz* permanently, but improved methods of making smoke and unfavourable weather had robbed the Fleet Air Arm pilots who made the attacks of success and it was obvious that better types of aircraft were needed. After the first of these attacks in April Dönitz proposed to Hitler that the battleship should be repaired and kept in north Norway as her presence obliged the British to maintain forces capable of dealing with her which might otherwise be sent out to the Far East. At the same time he did not foresee further opportunity for action unless Britain and Russia fell out and, Göring being present, he emphasised the need for fighter protection if the ship did go to sea and he also pointed out how successful the British carrier-borne aircraft were in preventing the U-boats from attacking the Arctic convoys and what easy targets the carriers themselves presented to the Luftwaffe. Somewhat reluctantly, Göring promised to transfer some more aircraft to north Norway from time to time, but he reminded the Commander-in-Chief of the Navy that the bulk of the Luftwaffe was fully occupied in support of the German armies now fighting on three fronts.

Convoys JW 59 and RA 59A

The first of the new series of convoys, JW 59 with 33 freighters, a rescue ship, and 11 submarine chasers being transferred to Russia under lend-lease, left Loch Ewe on 15 August. The escort consisted of the escort carriers *Vindex* (flagship of Vice Admiral F. H. G. Dalrymple-Hamilton) and *Striker*, the cruiser *Jamaica*, and 7 destroyers, 4 sloops, 2 frigates, and 5 corvettes. It was a new departure for the Admiral to fly his flag in a carrier, but it provided him with better 'action information' and enabled him more readily to assess the risk and control the air operations under the varying conditions of weather to be expected.

At 08.20 hrs on 20th when the convoy was to the east of Jan Mayen Island it was sighted by a Ju 88 aircraft of the 5th Air Fleet and the following day it crossed the patrol line of the Trutz Group of five U-boats. At 06.00 hrs on 21st one of these, *U 344* (Lieutenant-Commander Pietsch), unsuccessfully attacked the escorts with Gnat torpedoes but with a salvo of pattern-running torpedoes he hit the sloop *Kite* (Lieutenant-Commander A. N. G. Campbell RN) which sank with heavy loss of life, only nine survivors being rescued. A Soviet Catalina from the 118th Reconnaissance Regiment and aircraft from the carriers obliged the U-boats to submerge and by 23 August only three of them had been able to get ahead of the convoy and establish a new patrol line further east. Three more coming up astern fired Gnat torpedoes at the escorts, all of which missed, but *U 344* was detected and hunted by the *Keppel*, *Mermaid*, *Peacock*, and *Lord Dunvegan* for twelve hours and finally destroyed. The convoy reached the Kola Inlet without loss on 25 August.

The return convoy RA 59A, of 9 freighters escorted by the escort of JW 59, set sail on 28 August and had an almost uneventful passage. On 28 August an aircraft from the *Vindex* damaged *U 394* of the Trutz Group which was ultimately sunk after a hunt lasting six hours by the combined efforts of the *Keppel*, *Peacock*, *Mermaid*, and *Whitehall*. All ships of the convoy reached Loch Ewe on 6 September.

Further attacks on the Tirpitz

Whilst the convoy movements were in progress Admiral Moore, with a larger force of carriers than before, mounted another attack on the *Tirpitz*. After a delay caused by unfavourable weather, the attack went in on 22 August and two hits were obtained, but one forward of the bridge which could have caused severe damage failed to explode. During the evening, whilst the escort carriers *Trumpeter* and *Nabob* were refuelling some of the

127

escorts of JW 59, they encountered *U 354* (Lieutenant St∴amer) on passage which fired a salvo of pattern running torpedoes at the *Nabob*, one of which hit, and with a Gnat torpedo she hit and sank the sloop *Bickerton*. The carrier, however, remained afloat and reached port. Another attack on the *Tirpitz* was made on 29 August but without success and the fleet returned to Scapa Flow on 1/2 September.

Transfer of the battleship Royal Sovereign to Russia

Also synchronised with the convoy operations was the transfer of the battle-ship HMS *Royal Sovereign* (renamed *Arkhangelsk*) and eight former US 'Town' class destroyers to the Northern Fleet. The force was commanded by Admiral Levchenko with his flag in the *Arkhangelsk* and on 23 August it encountered *U 711* (Lieutenant-Commander Lange) who fired a salvo of pattern-running torpedoes at the battleship and a Gnat at one of the destroyers, all of which detonated prematurely and the ships reached the Kola Inlet safely. Admiral Golovko was not over enthusiastic about the additions to his fleet.

> 'The main thing is not, of course, these two "steamers", as northern sailors sarcastically dub the English battleship and the American cruiser. The latter is in truth obsolete. . . . The important thing is that we now possess twice the number of light forces . . . than we did last year.' [1]

Convoys JW 60 and RA 60

The next pair of convoys, JW 60 and RA 60 also had comparatively uneventful voyages. They were escorted by a force composed of the escort carriers *Campania* (flagship of Rear Admiral R. McGrigor) and *Striker*, the cruiser *Diadem* and 12 escort vessels. The battleship *Rodney* and 11 destroyers acted as a covering force in case the *Tirpitz* should put to sea. Convoy JW 60 of 30 freighters left Loch Ewe on 15 September and the Grimm Group of 6 U-boats was deployed to intercept it but failed to do so and it arrived intact at the Kola Inlet on 23 September.

Convoy RA 60 also of 30 freighters left the Kola Inlet on 28 September. Two Groups of U-boats, Grimm and Zorn totalling 12 boats were deployed against it. On the day after sailing the convoy overran *U 310* (Lieutenant Ley) who seized the opportunity to torpedo the freighters *Samsuva* and

---

[1] Golovko, ibid, page 191

Edward H. Crockett both of which sank. Gnat torpedoes were fired at the escorts without success. Swordfish aircraft from the *Campania* attacked and sank *U 921* of the Grimm Group, but that was the end of the attacks and the 28 surviving ships of the convoy reached Loch Ewe on 5 October.

Tirpitz severely damaged

On 15 September RAF heavy bombers operating from the north Russian airfield at Yagodnik made a successful attack on the *Tirpitz*, hitting her forward with a 12,000lb bomb which caused such severe damage that it was decided not to repair her, but to employ her as a fixed battery in case of an attack on Norway. To this end a month later on the night of 15/16 October she was moved from her berth in Altenfiord to a shallow anchorage west of Tromso which was to prove her final resting place.

The enemy employs new tactics

The meagre results achieved by the U-boats during the recent convoy operations disturbed the German Naval Staff, so as more 'schnorkel' fitted boats came into service it was decided to station them outside the entrance to the Kola Inlet where they could not fail to intercept the convoys passing in and out and might get an opportunity to attack ships whilst the latter were in an unformed state. Admiral Moore had been expecting such action and appropriate counter-measures were devised. Convoy JW 61 of 29 freighters and 6 lend-lease submarine chasers for the Northern Fleet sailed from Loch Ewe on 20 October. The ocean escort consisted of the carriers *Vindex* (flagship of Vice Admiral F. H. G. Dalrymple-Hamilton), *Nairana*, and *Tracker*, the cruiser *Dido* and 24 escort vessels. The Panther Group of 19 U-boats was deployed off the entrance to the Kola Inlet so the convoy encountered no opposition during its passage and when it reached a position east of Bear Island the 21st and 24th Escort Groups were sent on ahead to search the approaches to the port. Despite the large number of U-boats in the area, Asdic conditions were so bad that no contacts were made. For their part the U-boats made a number of attacks on the escorts but equally without success. However, the counter-measures to the enemy's tactics proved successful and after being met on 28 October by Soviet destroyers, minesweepers, and submarine chasers, the ships of JW 61 passed safely into the Kola Inlet.

Similar tactics were adopted prior to the sailing of the return convoy RA 61 of 33 freighters on 2 November. This time the U-boats hit back, the frigate *Mounsey* being damaged by a Gnat fired by *U 295*, and being obliged to return to port. Although the boats of the Panther Group tried hard to get at the convoy as it emerged the escort forces proved too strong and well drilled and the convoy reached Loch Ewe without loss on 9 November.

The end of the Tirpitz

In her new anchorage the *Tirpitz* was now 200 miles nearer and just within range of heavy bombers operating from Britain. On 29 October, 38 Lancaster bombers of Numbers 9 and 617 squadrons of the Royal Air Force took off from Lossiemouth (Scotland) armed with 12,000lb bombs but on reaching the target they encountered low cloud which prevented accurate aiming and the only damage done resulted from a near miss which flooded the after steering compartment and damaged a shaft. After the attack Göring felt obliged to strengthen the air force in Norway and he transferred three torpedo-bomber squadrons from the Mediterranean to the airfields at Banak and Bardufoss, but fighters were needed to protect the battleship from attack by shore-based aircraft.

For his part, Dönitz ordered two former Norwegian cruisers which had been converted to anti-aircraft ships to be stationed in the fiord where the *Tirpitz* lay and steps to be taken to improve the smoke-making facilities. These added precautions, however, proved of no avail when on 12 November Numbers 9 and 617 squadrons totalling 21 Lancaster bombers repeated the attack. Although warning was received of their approach and the fighters at Bardufoss were alerted, by some mischance the order was cancelled and the bombers had a clear run over the target. Using the new Mark XIV bomb sight they scored several hits and the great ship, engulfed in smoke and flame, and rent by explosions turned over on her side and came to rest bottom upwards. Only 880 members of her ship's company were rescued while 28 officers and 874 men perished. All the bombers returned safely to base having finally removed the greatest menace to the Arctic convoys on the destruction of which so much effort had been expended.

Convoys JW 61A, JW 62, and RA 62

There were 11,000 Russian ex-prisoners of war in Britain awaiting repatriation and a token force of Norwegian troops to accompany the Russian army about to advance into north Norway. A special fast convoy of two troopships escorted by the cruiser *Berwick*, the carrier *Campania*, the 3rd Escort Group, and 6 destroyers, designated JW 61A left the Clyde on 29 October and reached the Kola Inlet on 6 November without being attacked.

Convoy JW 62 of 30 freighters escorted by the carriers *Campania* (flagship of Rear Admiral R. McGrigor) and *Nairana* and 21 escort vessels, and covered by the cruiser *Bellona* with 10 destroyers, sailed from Loch Ewe on 29 November. Although its passage was barred by the Stock and Grübe Groups totalling 17 U-boats deployed off the approaches to the Kola Inlet, similar tactics to those used during the two previous convoys were successfully employed and no ships were lost.

Convoy RA 62 of 28 freighters with the escort of JW 62 sailed from Kola Inlet on 10 December. Hunting Groups of British and Russian escorts sailed the previous day to harass the U-boats and, whilst they were so employed, *U 997* unsuccessfully attacked the Soviet destroyers *Razumny* and *Zhivachi*, while the frigate *Bamborough Castle* attacked and sank *U 387* with depth charges. The day after the convoy sailed *U 365*, the only one still in touch, torpedoed the destroyer *Cassandra*, blowing off her bows and she had to be escorted back to the Kola Inlet. The Luftwaffe now took a hand and on 12 December, when the convoy was south-west of Bear Island, nine torpedo-armed aircraft of Coastal Group 26 made an attack without scoring any hits and two Ju 88s were shot down. The following day *U 365*, which had tenaciously clung on to the convoy, was sunk by a Swordfish aircraft from the *Campania*. The convoy reached Loch Ewe safely on 19 December.

Convoys JW 63 and RA 63

Convoy JW 63 of 35 freighters escorted by the carriers *Vindex* (flagship of Vice Admiral Sir Frederick Dalrymple-Hamilton), the cruiser *Diadem* and 20 escort vessels left Loch Ewe on 30 December. It was the last convoy to do so it having been decided to close down the base as an economy measure and transfer the facilities to the Clyde. Only the Stier Group of U-boats was deployed to intercept JW 63, four boats being stationed south of Bear Island and three off the entrance to the Kola Inlet, but none of them made contact and the convoy had an uneventful passage, arriving safely on 8 January. The return convoy RA 63 of 30 freighters with the same escort sailed on 11 January and had an equally uneventful passage, reaching Loch Ewe on 21 January and the Clyde two days later.

Convoys JW 64 and RA 64

Unlike the two previous ones the next pair of convoys were to meet with opposition both from the enemy and the weather. Convoy JW 64 of 26

131

freighters and an ocean escort comprising the carriers *Campania* (flagship of Rear Admiral R. McGrigor) and *Nairana*, the cruiser *Bellona* and 17 escort vessels, sailed from the Clyde on 3 February. It was sighted by an enemy aircraft on a weather flight from Trondheim on 4 February when north-east of the Faroes and later that afternoon the first shadowing aircraft, a Ju 88, appeared and was promptly shot down by two Wildcats from the *Campania*, one of which was also lost. The Rasmus Group of 12 U-boats had been detailed to intercept it, 8 of which were stationed south of Bear Island and 4 off the Kola Inlet. On 7 February 48 Ju 88s of Coastal Group 26 were sent to find and attack the convoy but failed to do so and 7 aircraft did not return. During the next two days shadowing aircraft were much in evidence and appeared to be homing the U-boats on to the convoy; then on 9 February the weather began to deteriorate and by the evening the carriers were obliged to cease operating aircraft. On 10 February, when the convoy was south of Bear Island, 30 Ju 88s of Coastal Group 26 made another attempt to attack it. The weather at the time was ten-tenths cloud, rain squalls, and a maximum visibility of five miles. The first wave of aircraft appeared on the radar screens of the escorts at 10.19 hrs and their well-directed fire, coupled with emergency turns by the merchant ships, prevented the aircraft from scoring any hits with their torpedoes and several of them were shot down. Unfortunately, some of the fighters which had been scrambled from the carriers to meet the attack were damaged by ship's gunfire whilst returning to land on. After a brief lull, a second wave of the attack came in and this was also broken up and once again the convoy was unharmed. In these two attacks the enemy lost seven aircraft while one British fighter was lost, but the pilot was recovered.

The U-boats stationed to the south of Bear Island, finding themselves unable to penetrate the screen, moved on to join the rest of their Group off the Kola Inlet. The convoy's escort was reinforced on 12 February when rendezvous was made with a Soviet escort which took charge of the ships destined for the White Sea and that night the remainder of the ships entered the Kola Inlet in snow squalls and short visibility. Soon after midnight as the last freighter passed safely through the entrance, the corvette *Denbigh Castle* which had been covering her, was torpedoed by *U 992* (Lieutenant Falke). By the strenuous efforts of her ship's company she remained afloat and was towed into harbour by the *Bluebell* but she had to be beached to prevent her from sinking, and later became a total loss.

The U-boats, disappointed by their lack of success, went in search of easier targets and on 14 February they encountered a small Soviet convoy Bk3 from the White Sea to the Kola Inlet. It was attacked by *U 968*

(Lieutenant Westphalen), *U 711* (Lieutenant Commander Lange), and *U 992*, which between them succeeded in torpedoing the tanker *Nordfjell*, and the freighter *Horace Gray* both of which sank.

Before the return convoy RA 64 got under way 500 Norwegian patriots on the island of Söroy off the entrance to Altenfiord, which had appealed for help, were evacuated by the destroyers *Zambesi*, *Sioux*, and *Zest* and distributed amongst the ships of the convoy. Despite a thorough search off the entrance on the previous day, soon after RA 64 put to sea on 17 February it ran into trouble. The search had resulted in the sinking of *U 425* by the sloop *Lark* and the corvette *Alnwick Castle*, but there were nine more U-boats lying in wait for the convoy which took a long time to clear the harbour. The *Lark* was sweeping ahead of the convoy when, at 10.24 hrs *U 968* hit her with a Gnat which blew off her stern. She remained afloat and was towed back to harbour. About an hour and a half later *U 711* managed to torpedo the freighter *Thomas Scott* which was abandoned and sank whilst being towed back to harbour by the Soviet destroyer *Zhestiki*. Lange then went on to cap his success later that day when at 15.23 hrs he torpedoed the corvette *Bluebell* which blew up; there was only one survivor.

During the afternoon of 18 February the wind rose and the barometer fell, indicating the approach of a gale. All flying soon had to be abandoned and during the night with the wind, now gusting at 60 knots, a steep sea, and a big swell, the ships of the convoy scattered. It was 23.00 hrs on 19th before the weather began to moderate and the following morning, like sheep dogs rounding up a flock, the escorts set about collecting ships and re-forming the convoy. Urgency was lent to the task by knowledge that it had been sighted and reported by enemy aircraft at 04.20 hrs that morning. By 09.00 hrs, 29 ships had been collected, leaving only 4 still missing, and the convoy re-formed which was just as well as 40 Ju 88s of Coastal Group 26 had taken off to attack it. They appeared over the horizon at 10.00 hrs and the *Nairana* launched her fighters to break them up, while McGrigor manoeuvred the convoy to put the approaching aircraft on its quarter. The aircraft succeeded in dropping a large number of torpedoes, many of which exploded prematurely in the rough sea, and no hits were obtained; 6 Ju 88s were lost.

About noon 3 destroyers which the Commander-in-Chief had sent to replace the casualties suffered off the Kola Inlet joined the escort of RA 64 and by the evening there were only 2 freighters still straggling. One of these rejoined the next day but the other, the *Crosby Noyes* was not heard of for a week when she reported her position 300 miles astern of the convoy! During 21 and 22 February enemy aircraft shadowed the convoy off and on and the U-boats maintained touch without being able to get in an attack. Then another and even fiercer gale blew up and again the convoy was scattered. Some ships were obliged to heave to with engine trouble, steering gear defects, shifting cargoes, and even splitting deck seams. The *Campania* was at one time rolling 45° each way and she too hove to. At 05.15 hrs on 23rd whilst the gale was still raging, an enemy reconnaissance aircraft sighted and reported the convoy, but torpedo bombers of Coastal Group 26 sent out to attack it, only found one of the stragglers, the *Henry Bacon*, 50 miles astern of the convoy which they sank. Despite the considerable movement of the ship the *Nairana* flew off her fighters on receipt of the *Henry Bacon*'s enemy report, an operation which Admiral McGrigor mentioned in his report as deserving the highest credit. An incident of great courage and self-sacrifice followed on the torpedoing of the freighter. She had on board as passengers some of the Norwegians evacuated from Söroy, including women and children, and the crew insisted that the passengers have priority in the boats, thereby many of these brave men went down with their ship whilst all those in the boats were rescued. This was the last ship in the Second World War to be sunk by German aircraft.

The gale continued for another two days with gusts of 70 knots and in consequence the convoy's speed of advance was a mere 3½ knots. To add to the Admiral's anxieties the cruiser *Bellona* and many of the destroyers were running short of fuel and he was obliged to detach a few ships at a time to refuel in the Faroes. During the evening of 23 February, 3 more destroyers from Scapa joined, 2 of which were ordered to escort 2 of the stragglers into the Faroes. A shift of wind to the north-west during the night of 25/26 February enabled speed to be increased to 7 knots, but only for a short time. Gradually the tribulations of the sorely tried convoy came to an end and it reached the Clyde on 1 March.

These were the last two convoys to meet with serious opoosition. In his report Admiral McGrigor commented on 'the continuous heavy seas and adverse gales which persisted during the easterly run of JW 64 and for practically the whole passage of RA 64' and on the renewed activity of enemy aircraft. He also drew attention to the need for night fighters to shoot down night shadowers and on the important part played by radar Type 277 in detecting the approach of enemy low-flying torpedo bombers. The problem of dealing with the concentration of U-boats off the Kola Inlet pointed to the need for some escorts with long endurance to carry out intensive harrassment of the U-boats during the whole period between the arrival of one convoy and the departure of the next one.

Above Swordfish IIIs of 813 Squadron (HMS *Campania*) at Murmansk early in 1945, with snow and slush on the flight deck. The aircraft nearest the camera is a Grumman FM-1 Wildcat of the same squadron (*Imperial War Museum*). *Below* Swordfish aircraft on the flight deck of the Merchant Aircraft Carrier (MAC-ship) *Ancylus* in the Arctic (*Imperial War Museum*)

The escort carrier HMS *Trumpeter* edges through the pack ice as a Russian tug helps her to take up her moorings in the Kola Inlet, April 1944 (*Admiralty*)

Above Sweeping the decks of snow for the Swordfish of 842 Squadron aboard HMS *Fencer* in May 1944. During this voyage the squadron sank three U-boats *(Imperial War Museum)*. *Below* The escort carrier *Nairana* seen from the *Fencer*, while covering convoy RA 59A in April or May 1944 *(J. D. Brown)*

A Swordfish of HMS *Activity* in April 1944 covering Arctic convoys JW 58 and RA 59. Note the ASV radar dome between the legs of the undercarriage (*Imperial War Museum*)

Above The German heavy cruiser *Admiral Hipper* (left) and a destroyer in northern waters in July 1942, seen from the battleship *Tirpitz* (*J. D. Brown*). *Below* The Canadian corvette HMCS *Cobalt*, seen here in Iceland, was typical of the small warships which escorted the Arctic convoys. Capable of 16 knots, they were armed with a 4in gun, a single pom-pom, and depth-charges (*Imperial War Museum*)

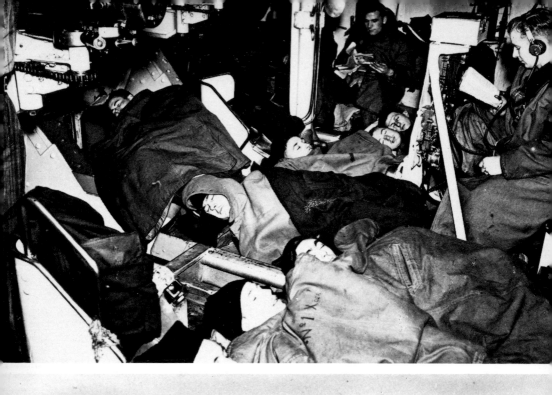

Above The crew of a cruiser's 6in gun turret try to snatch some sleep or read to pass the time. Gun-crews were often closed up for long periods, and if the mounting was open to the weather the conditions were grim (*National Maritime Museum*). *Below* Merchant ships of an Arctic convoy skirt the pack ice as they near the Kola Inlet (*National Maritime Museum*)

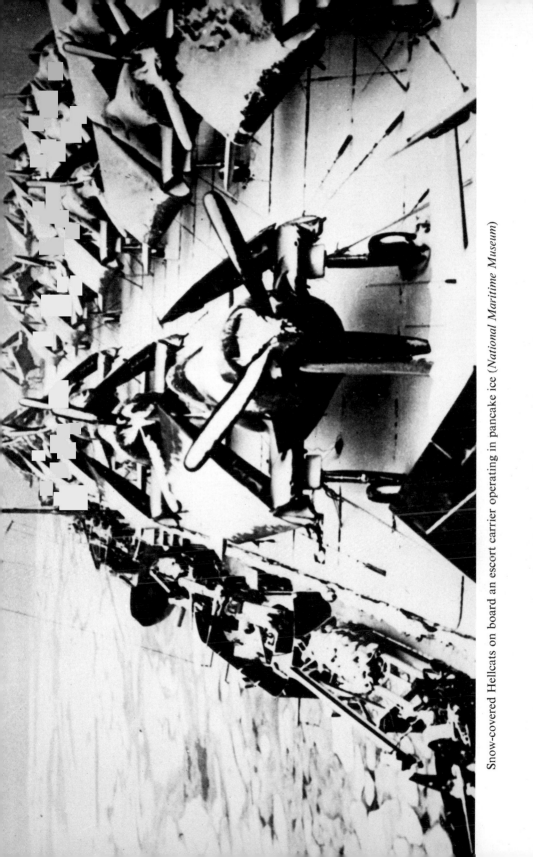

Snow-covered Hellcats on board an escort carrier operating in pancake ice (*National Maritime Museum*)

Above The German destroyer *Z 28* was fitted out as a flotilla leader with extra accommodation in place of one 15cm gun on the after superstructure. She accompanied the *Tirpitz* on her sortie against convoy PQ 17 in 1942 (*Foto Drüppel*). *Below* HMS *Anchusa*, another example of the 'Flower' Class corvette. She has had her forecastle extended to improve seaworthiness and to extend accommodation (*Admiralty*)

Convoys JW 65, 66, 67 and RA 65, 66, 67

The story of the last six Arctic convoys can be told in a few words since none of them had to compete with action by the enemy or the contrariness of the elements similar to that endured by JW 64 and RA 64. The delayed arrival of RA 64 and the weather damage suffered by many of the escorts delayed the departure of JW 65 until 11 March. It comprised 24 freighters and the ocean escort consisted of the carriers *Campania* (flagship of Vice Admiral Sir Frederick Dalrymple-Hamilton) and *Trumpeter*, the cruiser *Diadem* and 19 escort vessels. Initially 6 U-boats of the Hagen Group were stationed south of Bear Island and 4 off the Kola Inlet, but on 17 March the entire Group was deployed in two lines off the entrance to the harbour. Aircraft from the carriers supported by Russian aircraft, patrolled the area as the convoy approached, but during a snowstorm which stopped flying for one and a half hours, *U 995* (Lieutenant Hess) at 09.00 hrs on 20 March, succeeded in torpedoing the freighter *Horace Bushnell* which sank. Towards midday the convoy passed over the second line of U-boats and *U 716* (Lieutenant Thimme) torpedoed the sloop *Lapwing* and *U968* (Lieutenant Westphalen) the freighter *Thomas Donaldson*, both of which sank. The convoy reached port the following day.

Convoy RA 65 of 25 freighters with the same escort as JW 65, made use of a new swept channel into Kola when it sailed on 23 March. There were only two U-boats off the entrance and an attempt to establish a line of nine boats across its path was unsuccessful on account of the change in route. Similarly an attempt by the Luftwaffe to make contact with it was equally unsuccessful and all ships reached the Clyde safely on 1 April.

Convoy JW 66 of 22 freighters, a rescue ship, a tanker, and 2 Norwegian relief vessels had as ocean escort the carriers *Vindex* (flagship of Rear Admiral A. Cunningham-Graham), and *Premier*, the cruiser *Bellona*, and 22 escort vessels. Six U-boats of the Faust Group were deployed west of Bear Island to intercept it but due to the failure of air reconnaissance they were moved to positions off the Kola Inlet where they were joined by 10 more boats. Despite this formidable concentration the escorts prevented any attacks from being made and all ships reached port safely on 25 April.

The return convoy RA 66 of 24 freighters with the escort of JW 66 was equally fortunate. Sixteen U-boats were deployed off the entrance to the Kola Inlet when it sailed on 29 April but an intensive search of the area prior to sailing by the 7th and 9th Escort Groups coupled with a simulated sailing 24 hours in advance, proved effective. *U 286* (Lieutenant Dietrich) was sunk by the frigates *Loch Insh*, *Loch Shin*, and *Cotton* of the 19th Escort Group, but *U 968* (Lieutenant Westphalen), after an unsuccessful attack on the *Alnwick Castle*, torpedoed the frigate *Goodall* which sank with heavy loss of life. *U 427* (Lieutenant Gudenus) unsuccessfully attacked the Canadian destroyers *Haida* and *Iroquois* which hunted her for several hours during which 678 depth charges were dropped but the U-boat managed to make good her escape. Apart from these incidents, all of which took place on 29 April, the remainder of the voyage was uneventful, the convoy reaching the Clyde on 8 May, three days after the war in Europe can to an end.

Two more Arctic convoys, JW 67 and RA 67 made the voyage to and from north Russia after hostilities had ceased. They were given a token escort in case any of the U-boats at sea had not received the cease fire order. Both were without incident. With the arrival in the Clyde on 31 May of the 23 ships of RA 67 the Arctic convoys came to and end.

Retrospect

It is not easy to evaluate the assistance given to Russia by her Allies in achieving victory over the common enemy due to the absence of any reliable information from Soviet sources. However, Mr Alexander Werth who spent most of the war years in that country is well qualified to give an opinion on the matter. In his book *Russia at War* he says,

> 'A substantial number of tanks were received from Britain and the USA in 1942 and 1943 but Soviet historians are even more critical about them than about the British planes. Fifty-five per cent of the tanks received in 1942 were light tanks; in 1943 the proportion of light tanks was even higher – 70 per cent. The quantities received were described as mediocre and the quality left much to be desired.'

A little further on he writes,

> 'From my personal observation I can say that from 1943 on, the Red Army unquestionably appreciated the help from the West. . . . And the fact remains that the Allied raw materials enormously helped the Soviet war industries.' [1]

The late Sir Basil Liddell Hart has also written how when the Soviet Army went over to the offensive 'The exploiting bounds became longer and faster as the war advanced. That was due not only to growing skill and diminishing opposition but even more to the inflowing supplies of American trucks and also of canned food.' [2] On the German side Herr Wolfgang Schlauch in his study of American aid to the Allies in the Second World War says,

---

[1] Alexander Werth, *Russia at War* (Barrie, Rockliff, 1964), pages 623 and 627
[2] Edited by B. H. Liddell Hart, *The Soviet Army*, page 5

'The real strategic importance of American weapons for the Red Army's struggle against the Germans in the summer of 1942 cannot be estimated or valued because almost no information has been released by the Soviets. . . . It is, however, a fact that the delivery of American goods up to the beginning of the year 1942 was of the greatest importance to the Russian Army. The American trucks, the delivery of telephone equipment, the boots, met the critical needs of the Soviet troops.'[1]

So the available evidence points to the important part played by much of the equipment and raw materials supplied to Russia during the war. In addition to that carried by the Arctic convoys there was a steady stream of supplies flowing across the Pacific and later through the Persian Gulf. As can be seen from the figures in Appendix X the Arctic route carried about one quarter of the total and although by far the shortest route it was also the most vulnerable, the loss rate being 7½ per cent, a figure far higher than on any other convoy route. A total of 18 warships, including 2 cruisers, 6 destroyers, 2 sloops, a frigate, 2 corvettes, and 4 minesweepers were lost in operations with the Arctic convoys and naval personnel casualties amounted to 1944 killed or drowned. Of the ships convoyed 87 were lost, 6 sailing independently and 5 as a result of bombing in Russian ports. Casualties of Merchant Navy personnel were 829 killed or drowned.

German attempts to interdict the Arctic convoys cost them 1 battleship, 1 battle-cruiser, 3 destroyers, 32 U-boats, and an unspecified number of aircraft.

Soviet appreciation

Although, as we have seen, the Russians were difficult allies, it is satisfactory to be able to end this history of the Arctic Convoys by quoting the tribute paid by M. Ivan Maisky, Soviet Ambassador in London during the war, to all those who took part in that perilous adventure:

'The Russian convoys are a northern saga of heroism, bravery, and endurance. This saga will live for ever, not only in the hearts of your people, but also in the hearts of the Soviet people, who rightly see in it one of the most striking expressions of collaboration between Allied governments without which our common victory would have been impossible.'

---

[1] Schlauch, ibid, page 118

Select Bibliography

BEESLY, Patrick, *Very Special Intelligence,* Hamish Hamilton Limited, 1977
BRENNECKE, Jochen, *The Tirpitz,* Robert Hale & Company, 1963
BROOME, J. (Captain, RN, retired), *Convoy is to Scatter,* William Kimber and Company Ltd, 1972
CAMPBELL, Sir Ian (Vice Admiral) and MACINTYRE, Donald (Captain, RN), *The Kola Run,* Frederick Muller Ltd, 1958
CHURCHILL, Winston S., *The Second World War,* Volumes I-IV, Cassell & Co Ltd, 1948-53
DÖNITZ, Karl (Grand Admiral), *Memoirs,* George Weidenfeld & Nicolson Limited, 1959
GEMSELL, Carl Axel, *Raeder, Hitler, und Skandinavien,* Bernard und Graefe, 1965
GOLOVKO, Arseni (Admiral), *With the Red Fleet,* Putnam & Co Ltd, 1965
IRVING, *The Destruction of PQ 17,* Cassell & Co Ltd, 1968
ISAKOV, I.S. (Admiral of the Fleet). *The Red Fleet in the Second World War,* The Hutchinson Publishing Group Ltd, 1947
LEACH, Barry, *German Strategy against Russia,* Oxford University Press, 1973
LEWIS, Michael, *History of the British Navy,* George Allen & Unwin Ltd, 1957
LIDDELL HART, Basil H., *The Soviet Army*
MITCHELL, Donald W., *A History of Russian and Soviet Sea Power,* Macmillan Publishing Co., New York, 1974
MORISON, S. E. (Rear Admiral), *History of US Naval Operation in World War II,* Little, Brown & Co, 1963
OGDEN, Graeme, *My Sea Lady,* The Hutchinson Publishing Group Ltd, 1963
RAEDER, E. (Grand Admiral), *Struggle for the Sea,* William Kimber and Company Limited, 1959
ROSKILL, S. W. (Captain, RN, retired), *The War At Sea,* Volumes I-III, Her Majesty's Stationery Office, 1954-61
RUGE, Friedrich (Vice Admiral), *Sea Warfare,* Cassell & Co Ltd, 1962
SCHLAUCH, Wolfgang, *Rustungshilfe der USA an die Verbundeten in Zweiten Weltkrieg,* Darmstadt, 1967
SCHOFIELD, B. B. (Vice Admiral), *The Russian Convoys,* B. T. Batsford Ltd, 1964
The Führer Naval Conferences, Her Majesty's Stationery Office, 1948
TIPPELSKIRCH, Kurt von, *Geschichte des Zweiten Weltkrieges,* Athenäum Verlag, 1951
WALLIS, Ransome, *Two Red Stripes,* Ian Allan Ltd, 1973
WERTH, Alexander, *Russia at War,* Barrie, Rockcliff, 1964
WERTH, Alexander, *The Year of Stalingrad,* Hamish Hamilton, 1946
ZIEMKE, E. F., 'The German Northern Theatre of Operations', Department of Army Pamphlet No 20-271, Washington, 1959

Appendixes

Appendix I

SCHEDULE OF CONVOYS TO AND FROM NORTH RUSSIA
1941 – 45

Convoy	Commodore	Port of Departure & Date	No of Ships Sailed	Returned	Lost	Arrived	Port of Arrival & Date
Dervish	Capt J.C.K. Dowding, DSO, RD, RNR	Hvalfiord 21.8.41	7	–	–	7	Archangel 31.8.41
PQ 1	Capt D. Ridley	Hvalfiord 29.9.41	10	–	–	10	Archangel 11.10.41
PQ 2		Scapa Flow 17.10.41	6	–	–	6	Archangel 31.10.41
PQ 3		Hvalfiord 9.11.41	8	1	–	7	Archangel 28.11.41
PQ 4		Hvalfiord 17.11.41	8	–	–	8	Archangel 28.11.41
PQ 5		Hvalfiord 27.11.41	7	–	–	7	Archangel 12.12.41
PQ 6		Hvalfiord 8.12.41	7	–	–	2	Murmansk 20.12.41
						5	Molotovsk 23.12.41
PQ 7		Hvalfiord 26.12.41	2	–	1	1	Murmansk 12.1.42
PQ 7B		Hvalfiord 31.12.41	9	–	–	9	Murmansk 11.1.42
PQ 8	Capt R.W. Brundle	Hvalfiord 8.1.42	7	–	–	7	Murmansk 17.1.42

Convoy	Commodore	Port of Departure & Date	No of Ships	Returned	Lost	Arrived	Port of Arrival & Date	Remarks
PQ 9 & 10		Hvalfiord 1.2.42	10	–	–	10	Murmansk	
PQ 11		Loch Ewe 6.2.42	13	–	–	13	Murmansk 23.2.42	
PQ 12	Capt H.T. Hudson, RD, RNR	Reykjavik 1.3.42	16	–	–	16	Murmansk 12.3.42	
PQ 13	Capt D.A. Casey, CBE, DSO, RD, RNR	Reykjavik 20.3.42	19	–	5	14	Murmansk 31.3.42	HMS *Trinidad* torpedoed Z26 sunk
PQ 14	Capt E. Rees DSC, RD, RNR	Reykjavik 8.4.42	24	16	1	7	Murmansk 19.4.42	16 ships forced to return due to ice and weather damage
PQ 15	Capt H.J. Anchor, OBE, RD, RNR	Reykjavik 26.4.42	25*	–	3	22	Murmansk 5.5.42	*including 2 ice-breakers
PQ 16	Capt N.H. Gale DSO, RD, RNR	Reykjavik 21.5.42	35	1	7	27	Murmansk 30.5.42 Archangel 1.6.42	
PQ 17	Capt J.C.K. Dowding, DSO, RD, RNR	Reykjavik 27.6.42	36	2	23	11	4 Archangel 11.7.42 6 Archangel 25.7.42 1 Molotvsk 28.7.42	Figures do not include 3 rescue ships 1 of which was lost
PQ 18	RADM E.K. Boddam-Whetham, DSO	Loch Ewe 2.9.42	40	–	13	27	Archangel 17.9.42	
JW 51A	RADM C.E. Turle, DSO	Loch Ewe 15.12.42	16	–	–	16	Kola Inlet 25.12.42 Molotovsk 27.12.42	

Convoy	Commodore	Port of Departure & Date	No of Ships Sailed	Returned	Lost	Arrived	Port of Arrival & Date	Remarks
JW 51B	Capt R.A. Melhuish, RIN (Ret'd)	Loch Ewe 20.12.42	14	–	–	14	Kola Inlet 3.1.43	Attacked by German surface forces
JW 52	VADM Sir Malcolm Goldsmith, KBE, DSO	Loch Ewe 17.1.43	14	1	–	13	Kola Inlet 27.1.43	
JW 53	RADM E.W. Leir, DSO	Loch Ewe 15.2.43	28	6	–	22	Kola Inlet 27.2.43 White Sea 2.3.43	
JW54A	Capt B.B. Grant, RD, RNR	Loch Ewe 15.11.43	18	–	–	18	Kola Inlet 24.11.43 White Sea 28.11.43	
JW 54B	Capt E.C. Denison, MVO, RN (Ret'd)	Loch Ewe 22.11.43	14	–	–	14	Kola Inlet 2.12.43 White Sea 4.12.43	
JW 55A	Capt W.J. Mills, RD, RNR	Loch Ewe 12.12.43	19	–	–	19	Kola Inlet 20.12.43 White Sea 22.12.43	
JW 55B	RADM M.W.S. Boucher, DSO	Loch Ewe 20.12.43	19	–	–	19	Kola Inlet 29.12.43 White Sea 31.12.43	*Scharnhorst* sunk
JW 56A	Capt I.W. Whitehorn, RN (Ret'd)	Loch Ewe 12.1.44	20	5	3	12	Kola Inlet 28.1.44	HMS *Hardy* sunk
JW 56B	Capt M.J.D. Mayall, RD, RNR	Loch Ewe 22.1.44	16	–	–	16	Kola Inlet 1.2.44	

Convoy	Commodore	Port of Departure & Date	No of Ships Sailed	Returned	Lost	Arrived	Port of Arrival & Date	Remarks
JW 57	Capt R.D. Binks, OBE, RD, RNR	Loch Ewe 20.2.44	42	–	–	42	Kola Inlet 28.2.44	HMS *Mahratta* sunk
JW 58	Capt J.O. Dunn, RD, RNR	Loch Ewe 27.3.44	49	1	–	48	Kola Inlet 5.4.44	
JW 59	Capt G.H. Creswell, CB, DSO, DSC, RN (Ret'd)	Loch Ewe 15.8.44	33	–	–	33	Kola Inlet 25.8.44 White Sea 27.8.44	HMS *Kite* sunk
JW 60	Capt J. Smith RD, RNR	Loch Ewe 15.9.44	30	–	–	30	Kola Inlet 23.9.44 White Sea 25.9.44	
JW 61	RADM M.W.S. Boucher, DSO	Loch Ewe 20.10.44	29	–	–	29	Kola Inlet 28.10.44 White Sea 30.10.44	
JW 62	Capt E. Ullring, R NorN	Loch Ewe 29.11.44	30	–	–	30	Kola Inlet 7.12.44 White Sea 9.12.44	
JW 63	RADM M.W.S. Boucher, DSO	Loch Ewe 30.12.44	35	–	–	35	Kola Inlet 8.1.45 White Sea 9.1.45	
JW 64	Capt E. Ullring, R NorN	Clyde 3.2.45	26	–	–	26	Kola Inlet 13.2.45 White Sea 15.2.45	

Convoy	Commodore	Port of Departure & Date	No of Ships Sailed	Returned	Lost	Arrived	Port of Arrival & Date	Remarks
JW 65	Capt W.C. Meek, RD, RNR	Clyde 11.3.45	24	–	2	22	Kola Inlet 21.3.45	HMS *Lapwing* sunk
JW 66	Capt Sir Roy K. Gill, KBE, RD, RNR	Clyde 16.4.45	22	–	–	22	Kola Inlet 25.4.45 White Sea 28.4.45	
JW 67	Capt G.E. Sutcliffe, RN (Ret'd)	Clyde 12.5.45	23	–	–	23	Kola Inlet 20.5.45 White Sea 22.5.45	
Total 40			811	33	58*	720		*In addition 5 ships were sunk after arrival in the Kola Inlet
QP 1	Capt J.C.K. Dowding, DSO, RD, RNR	Archangel 28.9.41	14	–	–	14	Scapa Flow 9.10.41	
QP 2		Archangel 2.11.41	12	–	–	12	Kirkwall 17.11.41	
QP 3		Archangel 27.11.41	10	2	–	8	Seidisfiord 7.12.41	
QP 4		Archangel 20.12.41	13	2	–	11	Seidisfiord 16.1.42	
QP 5		Murmansk 13.1.42	4	–	–	4	Reykjavik 24.1.42	
QP 6	Capt Davitt	Murmansk 24.1.42	6	–	–	6	Clyde 2.2.42	
QP 7		Murmansk 12.2.42	8	–	–	8	Seidisfiord 22.2.42	

Convoy	Commodore	Port of Departure & Date	No of Ships Sailed	Returned	Lost	Arrived	Port of Arrival & Date	Remarks
QP 8		Murmansk 1.3.42	15	–	1	14	Reykjavik 11.3.42	
QP 9	Capt H.T. Hudson, RD, RNR	Murmansk 21.3.42	19	–	–	19	Reykjavik 3.4.42	
QP 10	Capt D.A. Casey, CBE, DSO, DSC, RD, RNR	Murmansk 10.4.42	16	1	4	11	Reykjavik 21.4.42	
QP 11	Capt W.H. Lawrence	Murmansk 28.4.42	13	–	1	12	Reykjavik 7.5.42	
QP 12		Murmansk 21.5.42	15	1	–	14	Reykjavik 29.5.42	
QP 13	Capt N.H. Gale, DSO, RD, RNR	Archangel 26.6.42 Murmansk 27.6.42	12 } 35 23	–	5	30	14 Reykjavik 7.7.42 16 Loch Ewe	
QP 14	Capt J.C.K. Dowding, DSO, RD, RNR	Archangel 13.9.42	15	–	3	12	Loch Ewe 26.9.42	HMS *Somali, Leda,* & RFA *Gray Ranger* lost
QP 15	Capt W.C. Meek, RD, RNR	Archangel 17.11.42	28	–	2	26	Loch Ewe 30.11 to 3.12.42	Convoy scattered by gales
RA 51	RADM C.E. Turle, DSO	Kola Inlet 30.12.42	14	–	–	14	Loch Ewe 11.1.43	
RA 52	Capt R.A. Melhuish, RIN (Ret'd)	Kola Inlet 29.1.43	11	–	1	10	Loch Ewe 8.2.43	
RA 53	VADM Sir M.L. Goldsmith, KBE, DSO	Kola Inlet 1.3.43	30	–	4	26	Loch Ewe 14.3.43	

Convoy	Commodore	Port of Departure & Date	No of Ships Sailed	Returned	Lost	Arrived	Port of Arrival & Date	Remarks
RA 54A	Capt W.L.P. Cox, RNR	Archangel 1.11.43	13	–	–	13	Loch Ewe 14.11.43	
RA 54B		Archangel 26.11.43	9	–	–	9	Loch Ewe 9.12.43	
RA 55A	Capt B.B. Grant, RD, RNR	Kola Inlet 23.12.43	22	1	–	21	Loch Ewe 1.1.44	
RA 55B	Capt E.C. Denison, MVO, RN (Ret'd)	Kola Inlet 31.12.43	8	–	–	8	Loch Ewe 8.1.44	
RA 56	RADM M.W.S. Boucher, DSO	Kola Inlet 3.2.44	37	–	–	37	Loch Ewe 11.2.44	
RA 57	Capt M.J.D. Mayall, RD, RNR	Kola Inlet 2.3.44	31	–	1	30	Loch Ewe 10.3.44	
RA 58	Capt R.D. Binks, OBE, RD, RNR	Kola Inlet 7.4.44	36	–	–	36	Loch Ewe 14.4.44	
RA 59	Capt J.O. Dunn, RD, RNR	Kola Inlet 28.4.44	45	–	1	44	Loch Ewe 6.5.44	
RA 59A		Kola Inlet 28.8.44	9	–	–	9	Loch Ewe 6.9.44	
RA 60	Capt G.H. Creswell, CB, DSO, DSC, RN (Ret'd)	Kola Inlet 28.9.44	30	–	2	28	Loch Ewe 5.10.44	
RA 61	RADM M.W.S. Boucher, DSO	White Sea 30.10.44 / Kola Inlet 2.11.44	33	–	–	33	Loch Ewe 9.11.44 / Clyde 10.11.44	
RA 62	Capt E. Ullring, RNorN	Kola Inlet 10.12.44	28	–	–	28	Loch Ewe 19.12.44 / Clyde 20.12.44	

147

Convoy	Commodore	Port of Departure & Date	No of Ships Sailed	Returned	Lost	Arrived	Port of Arrival & Date	Remarks
RA 63	RADM M.W.S. Boucher, DSO	Kola Inlet 11.1.45	30	–	–	30	Loch Ewe 21.1.45 Clyde 23.1.45	
RA 64	Capt E. Ullring, RNorN	Kola Inlet 17.2.45	34*	1	2	31	Loch Ewe 28.2.45 Clyde 1.3.45	*2 ships sunk off Kola Inlet prior to joining convoy
RA 65	Capt W.C. Meek, RD, RNR	Kola Inlet 23.3.45	25	–	–	25	Kirkwall 31.3.45 Clyde & Belfast 1.4.45	
RA 66	Capt Sir Roy K. Gill, KBE, RD, RNR	Kola Inlet 29.4.45	24	–	–	24	Clyde 8.5.45	
RA 67	Capt G.E. Sutcliffe, RN (Ret'd)	Kola Inlet 23.5.45	23	–	–	23	Clyde 31.5.45	
Total 35			715	8	27	680		

INDEPENDENT SAILINGS

	Port of Departure & Date	No of Ships Sailed	Returned	Lost	Arrived	Port of Arrival & Date
Eastbound Between 29.10.42 & 2.11.42	Reykjavik	13	3	5	5	
Westbound Between 29.10.42 & 24.1.43	Russian ports	28	–	1	27	Akureyri

Appendix II
ABSTRACT OF ALLIED MERCHANT SHIP LOSSES

Category	British	USA	Panamanian	Russian	Dutch	Norwegian	Total	Gross Tons
Convoys to north Russia	21	29	5	2	1	–	58	353,366
Convoys from north Russia	6	15	2	5	–	1	29	178,317
Independents	3	1	–	2	–	–	6	42,004
In Russian ports	3	2	–	–	–	–	5	27,278
In other ways	2	–	–	–	–	–	2	4,872
Grand Total	35	47	7	9	1	1	100	604,837

Appendix III
ANALYSIS OF ALLIED MERCHANT SHIP LOSSES BY CAUSE

Cause	Ships sailing in Convoy				Ships sailing Independently	
	E-going PQ – JW	QP – RA	Under Escort	Straggling	E-going	W-going
Surface Attack	1	2	–	3	–	1
Submarine	23	18[1]	24	17[1]	4	–
Aircraft bombing	17	2	9	10	–	–
Aircraft torpedoes[2]	17	1	17	1	–	
Mined	–	5[3]	5[3]	–	–	–
Foundered	–	1	1	–	–	–
Wrecked	–	–	–	–	1	–
Total	58	29	56	31	5	1
Grand Total		87		87		6

[1] Including two ships lost off Kola before joining Convoy RA 64
[2] Torpedo-armed aircraft operated in force from May to September 1942, and again from December 1944 to February 1945 but on a reduced scale
[3] In British minefield off Iceland

Appendix IV
ANALYSIS OF ALLIED WARSHIPS LOST ESCORTING ARCTIC CONVOYS

Ship	Type	Cause
Trinidad	Cruiser	Damaged by her own torpedo supporting PQ 13 on 29.3.42. Sunk by dive-bombing 14.5.42
Edinburgh	Cruiser	Torpedoed by U 456 30.4.42 and by Z 24 on 2.5.42 abandoned and sunk
Matabele	Destroyer	Torpedoed and sunk by U 454 off Kola Inlet 17.1.42
Punjabi	Destroyer	Sunk after collision with King George V 1.5.42
Somali	Destroyer	Sunk by U 703 20.9.42 escorting QP 14
Achates	Destroyer	Sunk by gunfire from Hipper 31.12.42 (JW 51B)
Hardy	Destroyer	Sunk by U 278 30.1.44 (JW 56A)
Mahratta	Destroyer	Sunk by U 990 25.2.44 (JW 57)
Kite	Sloop	Sunk by U 344 21.8.44 (JW 59)
Lapwing	Sloop	Sunk by U 716 20.3.45 (JW 65)
Goodall	Frigate	Sunk by U 968 29.4.45 (RA 66)
Denbigh Castle	Corvette	Sunk by U 992 13.2.45 (JW 64)
Bluebell	Corvette	Sunk by U 711 16.2.45 (RA 64)
Gossamer	Minesweeper	Sunk by bombing in Kola Inlet 24.6.42
Niger	Minesweeper	Mined and sunk 5.7.42 (QP 13)
Leda	Minesweeper	Sunk by U 435 20.9.42 (QP 14)
Bramble	Minesweeper	Sunk by Hipper and destroyers 31.12.42 (JW 51B)
Shera	Armed Whaler	Capsized and sank 9.3.42 (PQ 12)
P 551	Submarine	Sunk by escorts of PQ 15 2.5.42
Sokrushitelny[1]	Destroyer	Broke in half and sank escorting QP 15 22.11.42
Deyatelny[1,2]	Destroyer	Sunk by U 997 16.1.45

[1] Russian. The Northern fleet also lost some 20 submarines in operations along the coast
[2] ex HMS Churchill ex USS Herndon

Appendix V

GERMAN WARSHIPS SUNK DURING ARCTIC CONVOY OPERATIONS

Ship	How Lost	Date	Remarks
Tirpitz – battleship	Bombing	29.10.44	After 22 attacks
Scharnhorst – battle-cruiser	In action	26.12.43	JW 55B HMS *Duke of York* and others
Z 26 – destroyer	In action	29.3.42	PQ 13
Hermann Schoemann – destroyer	In action	1.5.42	QP 11
Friedrich Eckholdt – destroyer	In action	31.12.42	JW 51B

SUBMARINES

Ship	How Lost	Date	Remarks
U 655	Rammed	24.3.42	QP 9 HMS *Sharpshooter*
U 585	Depth charge	29.3.42	PQ 13 HMS *Fury*
U 589	Depth charge	12.9.42	PQ 18 HMS *Faulknor*
U 88	Depth charge	14.9.42	PQ 18 HMS *Onslow*
U 457	Depth charge	16.9.42	PQ 18 HMS *Impulsive*
U 253	Depth charge	28.9.42	QP 14 Catalina aircraft
U 644	Torpedoed	7.4.43	HMS/M *Tuna* on patrol
U 314	Depth charge	30.1.44	JW 51B HMS *Whitehall* and *Meteor*
U 713	Depth charge	24.2.44	JW 57 HMS *Keppel*
U 601	Depth charge	25.2.44	JW 57 Catalina aircraft
U 472	Rocket and gunfire	4.3.44	RA 57 Swordfish aircraft and HMS *Onslaught*
U 366	Rocket and gunfire	5.3.44	RA 57 Swordfish aircraft
U 973	Rocket and gunfire	6.3.44	RA 57 Swordfish aircraft
U 961	Depth charge	29.3.44	JW 58 HMS *Starling*
U 355	Depth charge	1.4.44	JW 58 HMS *Beagle* and *Avenger* aircraft
U 360	Hedgehog	2.4.44	JW 58 HMS *Keppel*
U 288	Depth charge	3.4.44	JW 58 Aircraft from HMS *Tracker* and *Activity*
U 277	Depth charge	1.5.44	RA 59 Swordfish aircraft
U 674	Depth charge	2.5.44	RA 59 Swordfish aircraft
U 959	Depth charge	2.5.44	RA 59 Swordfish aircraft
U 361	Depth charge	17.7.44	Liberator aircraft
U 347	Depth charge	17.7.44	Catalina aircraft
U 742	Depth charge	18.7.44	Catalina aircraft
U 354	Depth charge	22.8.44	JW 59 Swordfish aircraft
U 344	Depth charge	23.8.44	JW 59 HMS *Keppel, Mermaid, Peacock* and *Loch Dunvegan*
U 394	Depth charge and rocket	2.9.44	RA 59A Swordfish aircraft and HMS *Keppel. Whitehall, Mermaid,* and *Peacock*
U 921	Depth charge	30.9.44	Swordfish aircraft
U 387	Depth charge	9.12.44	RA 62 HMS *Bamborough Castle*
U 365	Depth charge	13.12.44	RA 62 Swordfish aircraft
U 425	Squid	17.2.45	Off Kola Inlet HMS *Lark* and *Alnwick Castle*
U 307	Gunfire	29.4.45	RA 66 HMS *Loch Ingh*
U 286	Gunfire	29.4.45	RA 66 HMS *Loch Shin, Anguilla,* and *Cotton*

Note: In January 1942 only four U-boats were deployed in north Norway but by April 1942 the number had risen to 20 and from then on to the end of 1943 the average was 21. During 1944 the number rose to a maximum of 32 in July, but by January 1945 it had decreased again to 20.

Appendix VI
DETAILS OF ALLIED WARSHIPS OPERATING WITH THE
ARCTIC CONVOYS

HMS *King George V*, *Duke of York*, *Anson*, and *Howe* – battleships

---

Standard displacement: 35,000 tons
Dimensions: 745 × 103 × 27¾ft (226¾ × 31½ × 8½m)
Propulsion: Geared turbines, four shafts; 110,000shp
Speed: 30 knots
Armament: 10 14in (35.6cm) guns (2 × 4 and 1 × 2)
    16 5.25in (13.3cm) anti-aircraft guns (8 × 2)
    48 2-pounder anti-aircraft guns (6 × 8)
    32 20mm Oerlikon anti-aircraft guns (*Anson* 40, *Duke of York* 56)
    Four aircraft
'rotection:
    Main belt: 5½ to 4½in (14 to 11.4cm), amidships 14 to 15in (35.5 to
    38cm)
    Deck: 1in (2.5cm) to 5.6in (14.2cm)
    Turrets: 9 to 16in (23 to 40cm)
    DCT: 16in (40cm)
Complement: 1555

USS *Washington* – battleship of the 'South Dakota' class

Standard displacement: 35,000 tons
Dimensions: 750 × 108 × 36ft (228 × 33 × 11m)
Propulsion: Geared turbines; four shafts; 115,000shp
Speed: 28 knots
Armament: Nine 16in (40.6cm) guns (3 × 3)
    20 5in (12.7cm) DP guns (10 × 2)
    16 20mm Oerlikon anti-aircraft guns
    Four aircraft
Protection:
    Main belt: 16in (40.6cm)
    Upper deck: 6in (15.2cm)
    Lower deck: 4in (10.2cm)

HMS *Renown* – battle-cruiser

Standard displacement: 32,000 tons
Dimensions: 794 × 103¹ × 27ft (242 × 31¹ × 8.2m)
Propulsion: Geared turbines; four shafts; 120,000shp
Speed: 29 knots
Armament: Six 15in (38cm) guns (3 × 2)
    20 4.5 (11.4cm) DP guns (10 × 2)
    24 2-pounder anti-aircraft guns (3 × 8)
    Four aircraft
Protection:
    Main belt: 6.9 to 3in (17.5 to 7.6cm)
    Deck: 2½ to 3in (6.3 to 7.6cm)
Complement: 1181

HMS *Furious* – aircraft carrier

Standard displacement: 22,450 tons
Dimensions: 786¼ × 90 × 24ft (239.6 × 27.4 × 7.3m)
Propulsion: Geared turbines; four shafts; 90,000shp
Speed: 30½ knots
Armament: Twelve 4in (10cm) anti-aircraft guns (6 × 2)
    24 2-pounder anti-aircraft guns (3 × 8)
Protection:
    Main belt: 2in (5cm) forward, 3in (7.6cm) amidships
    Deck: 1 to 3in (2.5 to 7.6cm)
Aircraft: 15 Swordfish, 18 fighters
Complement: 748 excluding air crew

---

¹ Outside bulges

HMS *Victorious* – fleet aircraft carrier of the 'Illustrious' class

---

Standard displacement: 23,000 tons
Dimensions: 753½ × 95¾ × 24ft (229¾ × 29 × 7¼m)
Propulsion: Geared turbines; three shafts; 110,000shp
Speed: 31 knots
Armament: 16 4.5in (11.4cm) DP guns (8 × 2)
   48 2-pounder anti-aircraft guns (6 × 8)
   46 20mm Oerlikon anti-aircraft guns (12 × 1 and 17 × 2)
Aircraft: 12 Albacores, 12 Fulmars
Protection:
   Main belt: 4½in (11.4cm)
   Hangar side: 4½in (11.4cm)
   Deck: 2½ to 3in (6.3 to 7.6cm)
Complement: 1392

HMS *Campania* – converted aircraft carrier

Standard displacement: 12,450 tons
Dimensions: 540 × 70 × 19ft (164.6 × 21 × 5.7m)
Propulsion: Diesel engines; two shafts; 11,000bhp
Speed: 17 knots
Armament: 2 4in (10cm) anti-aircraft guns (1 × 2)
   16 2-pounder anti-aircraft guns (4 × 4)
   16 20mm anti-aircraft guns (8 × 2)
Aircraft: 12 Swordfish, 4 Wildcats, 3 Fulmars (convoys JW 60 and 62)
   An extra Fulmar was embarked for convoy JW 64 and three additional
   Wildcats for JW 65.
Complement: 700

HMS *Avenger* and *Dasher* – escort carriers of the 'Archer' class

Standard displacement: 8200 tons
Dimensions: 492½ × 66¼ × 23¼ft (150 × 20 × 7m)
Propulsion: Two diesel engines; one shaft; 8500bhp
Speed: 16½ knots
Armament: Three 4in (10cm) anti-circraft guns (3 × 1)
  15 20mm anti-aircraft guns (4 × 2 and 7 × 1)
Aircraft: 12 Hurricanes, 3 Swordfish
Complement: 555

HMS *Activity* – escort carrier formerly MS *Breconshire*

Standard displacement: 11,800 tons
Dimensions: 513 × 66½ × 26ft (156 × 20 × 7.6m)
Armament: Two 4in (10cm) anti-aircraft guns (1 × 2)
  20 20mm anti-aircraft guns (10 × 2)
Aircraft: 3 Swordfish and 7 Wildcats

HMS *Nabob*, *Premier*, *Queen*, *Trumpeter*, and *Tracker* – escort carriers of
  the 'Ruler' class

Standard displacement: 11,420 tons
Dimensions: 492 × 69½ × 23¼ft (160 × 30½ × 7m)
Propulsion: Geared turbines; one shaft; 9350shp
Speed: 17 knots
Armament: Two 4in (10cm) anti-aircraft guns (2 × 1)
  Eight 40mm anti-aircraft guns (4 × 2) and 15 20mm anti-aircraft guns
  (15 × 1)
Aircraft: *Nabob* – 14 Swordfish, 6 Wildcats
  Premier – 12 Avengers
  Queen – 8 Avengers, 8 Wildcats
  Trumpeter – 8 Avengers, 8 Wildcats
  Tracker – 10/12 Avengers, 6/7 Wildcats

HMS *Chaser*, *Fencer*, *Striker* – escort carriers of the 'Attacker' class

---

Details similar to those of the 'Ruler' class above.

Aircraft: Chaser – 11 Swordfish, 11 Wildcats
  Fencer – 11 Swordfish, 9 Wildcats
  Striker – 12 Swordfish, 10 Wildcats
Complement: 646

HMS *Vindex* and *Nairana* – escort carriers

Standard displacement: Vindex 13,455 tons; *Nairana* 14,050 tons
Dimensions: Vindex: 524 × 68½ × 21ft (161 × 21 × 6.4m)
  Nairana: 528½ × 68½ × 21ft (161 × 21 × 6.4m)
Propulsion: Two diesel engines; two shafts; 11,000bhp
Speed: 17 knots
Armament: 2 4in (10cm) anti-aircraft guns (1 × 2)
  16 2-pounder anti-aircraft guns (4 × 4)
  16 20m anti-aircraft guns (8 × 2)
Aircraft: Vindex – 12 Swordfish, 6 Hurricanes, or 7 to 12 Wildcats
  Nairana – 14 Swordfish, 6 Wildcats
Complement: Vindex 700 – *Nairana* 728

HMS *Belfast* – cruiser

Standard displacement: 10,000 tons
Dimensions: 613½ × 63¼ × 17¼ft (187 × 19.5 × 5.2m)
Propulsion: Geared turbines; four shafts; 80,000shp
Speed: 32 knots
Armament: 12 6in (15cm) guns (4 × 3)
  12 4in (10cm) anti-aircraft guns (6 × 2)
  16 2-pounder anti-aircraft guns (2 × 8)
  Six 21in (533mm) torpedo tubes (2 × 3)
  Three aircraft
Protection:
  Main belt: 4½in (11.4cm)
  Deck: 2in (5cm)
  Turrets: 1 to 2½in (2.5 to 6.3cm)
Complement: 850

HMS *Kent*, *Cumberland*, *Berwick*, and *Suffolk* – cruisers of the 'County' class

---

Standard displacement: 9750 tons (*Kent* 9850 tons)
Dimensions: 630 × 68¼ × 16¼ft (192 × 20.7 × 4.9m)
Propulsion: Geared turbines; four shafts; 80,000shp
Speed: 31½ knots
Armament: Eight 8in (20cm) guns (4 × 2)
   Eight 4in (10cm) anti-aircraft guns (4 × 2)
   Eight 2-pounder anti-aircraft guns (2 × 4)
   Eight 21in (533mm) torpedo tubes in *Kent* only
Protection:
   Main belt: 3½in (9cm)
   Deck: 1½in (3.8cm)
   Turrets: 1½ to 2in (3.8 to 5cm)
   DCT: 3in (7.6cm)
Complement: 679, as flagship 710

HMS *Bermuda*, *Nigeria*, *Trinidad*, *Jamaica*, and *Kenya* – 'Colony' class cruisers

---

Standard displacement: 8000 tons
Dimensions: 555½ × 62 × 16½ft (169 × 19 × 5m)
Propulsion: Geared turbines; four shafts; 72,500shp
Speed: 33 knots
Armament: 12 6in (15cm) guns (4 × 3)
   Eight 4in (10cm) anti-aircraft guns (4 × 2)
   Nine 2-pounder anti-aircraft guns (2 × 4 and 1 × 1)
   Six 21in (533mm) torpedo tubes (2 × 3)
   Three aircraft
Protection:
   Main belt: 3¼in (8.2cm)
   Deck: 2in (5cm)
   Turrets: 2in (5cm)
   DCT: 4in (10cm)
Complement: 730

HMS *Devonshire*, *London*, and *Norfolk*

Standard displacement: 9850 tons (*Norfolk:* 9925 tons)
Dimensions: 633 × 66 × 17ft (192 × 20 × 6m)
Propulsion: Geared turbines; four shafts; 80,000shp
Speed: 32 knots
Armament: Eight 8in (20cm) guns (4 × 2)
  Eight 4in (10cm) anti-aircraft guns (*London* and *Norfolk*: 4 × 2;
  Devonshire: 8 × 1)
  Eight (*Devonshire*), 16 (*London* and *Norfolk*) 2-pounder anti-aircraft
  guns (2 × 4) and (2 × 8)
  Eight 21in (533mm) torpedo tubes (2 × 4)
  One to three aircraft
Protection:
  Main belt: 3.5in (9cm)
  Deck: (*London* only) 1½ to 4in (3.8 to 10cm)
  Turrets: 1½ to 2in (3.8 to 5cm)
  DCT: 3in (7.6cm)
Complement: 650

HMS *Glasgow*, *Liverpool*, *Manchester*, and *Sheffield* – 'Town' class cruisers

---

Displacement: Glasgow and *Sheffield*: 9100 tons; *Liverpool* and *Manchester*: 9400 tons
Dimensions: Glasgow and *Sheffield* – 591½ × 61¾ × 17ft (162 × 18.8 × 5.2m)
   Liverpool and *Manchester* – 591½ × 62¼ × 17½ft (162 × 19 × 5.3m)
Propulsion: Geared turbines; four shafts
   Glasgow and *Sheffield* 75,000shp
   Liverpool and *Manchester* 82,500shp
Speed: 32 and 32½ knots respectively
Armament: 12 6in (15cm) guns (4 × 3)
   Eight 4in (10cm) anti-aircraft guns (4 × 2)
   Eight 2-pounder anti-aircraft guns (2 × 4)
   Six 21in (533mm) torpedo tubes (2 × 3)
   Three aircraft
Protection:
   Main belt: 3 to 4in (7.6 to 10cm)
   Deck: 2in (5cm)
   Turrets: 1 to 2in (2.5 to 5cm)
Complement: 700

HMS *Bellona*, *Black Prince*, *Diadem*, and *Scylla* – 'Dido' class cruisers

---

Standard displacement: 5770 tons, except *Scylla* 5450 tons
Dimensions: 512 × 50½ × 14¾ (*Scylla* 14)ft (247 × 15 × 4.4 (4.2)m)
Propulsion: Geared turbines; four shafts; 62,000shp
Speed: 33 knots
Armament: Eight (*Scylla* ten) 5.25in (13.3cm) DP guns (4 × 2) *Scylla* (5 × 2)
   Twelve (*Scylla* eight) 2-pounder anti-aircraft guns (3 × 4) and (2 × 4)
   Twelve 20mm anti-aircraft guns (6 × 2) except *Scylla*
   Six 21in (533mm) torpedo tubes (2 × 3)
Protection:
   Main belt: 2 to 3in (5 to 7.6cm)
   Deck: ½ to 2in (1.2 to 5cm)
   Turrets: 1 to 2in (2.5 to 5cm)
   DCT: 1in (2.5cm)
Complement: 535

USS *Tuscaloosa* – heavy cruiser

Standard displacement: 9975 tons
Dimensions: 588 × 61¾ × 19½ft (178.8 × 18.8 × 5.8m)
Propulsion: Parsons geared turbines; four shafts; 107,000shp
Speed: 32.7 knots
Armament: Nine 8in (20.3cm) guns (3 × 3)
    Twelve 5in (12.7cm) anti-aircraft guns (6 × 1 and 3 × 2)
    Numerous 40mm and 20mm anti-aircraft guns
Protection: 1½in (3.7cm) sides forward and aft
    5in (12.7cm) sides amidships
    5 to 6in (12.7 to 15.2 cm) on turret faces
    3in (7.6cm) on turret sides
    8in (20cm) conning tower
Complement: 1200

USS *Wichita* – heavy cruiser

Standard displacement: 9324 tons
Dimensions: 614 × 61¾ × 20ft (187.2 × 18.8 × 6.1m)
Propulsion: Geared turbines; four shafts; 100,000shp
Speed: 32½ knots
Armament: Nine 8in (20cm) guns (3 × 3)
    Twelve 5in (12.7cm) DP guns (4 × 2 and 4 × 1)
    Numerous 40mm and 20mm anti-aircraft guns
Protection: 1½in (3.8cm) sides forward and aft
    5in (12.7cm) sides amidships
    5 to 6in (12.7 to 15.2cm) on turret faces
    3in (7.6cm) on turret sides
    8in (20.3cm) conning tower
Complement: 1250

HMS *Alynbank* – anti-aircraft ship

Displacement: 5150 tons
Dimensions: 434 × 54 × 25¾ft (135 × 16.5 × 7.8m)
Propulsion: Diesel engines; two shafts; 2500bhp
Speed: 12 knots
Armament: Eight 4in (10cm) anti-aircraft guns (4 × 2)
  Eight 2-pounder anti-aircraft guns (2 × 4)
  Six 20mm anti-aircraft guns (6 × 1)

HMS *Palomares* and *Pozarica* – anti-aircraft ships

Displacement: 1895 tons
Dimensions: 306½ × 45 × 17½ft (93 × 3.7 × 5.2m)
Propulsion: Diesel engine; one shaft; 2640bhp
Speed: 16¾ knots
Armament: Six 4in (10cm) anti-aircraft guns (3 × 2)
  Eight 2-pounder anti-aircraft guns (2 × 4)
  Eight 20mm anti-aircraft guns (8 × 1)

HMS *Ulster Queen* – anti-aircraft ship

Displacement: 3791 tons
Dimensions: 359 × 46¼ × 15¼ft (109 × 14 × 4.6m)
Propulsion: Diesel engines; two shafts; 4155bhp
Speed: 18 knots
Armament: Six 4in (10cm) anti-aircraft guns (3 × 2)
  Eight 2-pounder anti-aircraft guns (2 × 4)
  Ten 20mm anti-aircraft guns (10 × 1)

Note: In *Palomares* and *Ulster Queen* the three twin 4in mountings were replaced by three 6in anti-aircraft guns (3 × 1)

ORP *Dragon* – Polish light cruiser

Standard displacement: 4850 tons
Dimensions: 472½ × 46½ × 14½ft (144 × 14 × 4.4m)
Propulsion: Geared turbines; two shafts; 40,000shp
Speed: 29 knots
Armament: Six 6in (15cm) guns (6 × 1)
   Three 4in (10cm) anti-aircraft guns (3 × 1)
   Two 2-pounder anti-aircraft guns (2 × 1)
   Twelve 21in (533mm) torpedo tubes (4 × 3)
Protection:
   Main belt: 1½ to 3in (3.8 to 7.6cm)
   Deck: 1in (2.5cm)
   Gunshields: 1in (2.5cm)
Complement: 450

USSRS *Baku* – Flotilla leader of the 'Leningrad' class

Standard displacement: 2225 tons
Dimensions: 418½ × 38½ × 13¼ft (128 × 12 × 4m)
Propulsion: Geared turbines; three shafts; 66,000shp
Speed: 36 knots
Armament: Five 5in (12.5cm) guns (5 × 1)
   Two 3in (7.6cm) anti-aircraft guns (2 × 1)
   Two 45mm anti-aircraft guns
   Eight 21in (533mm) torpedo tubes (2 × 4)
   32 depth charges. Fitted to carry 84 mines
Complement: 250

USSRS *Gremyaschi*, *Razumny*, *Sokrushitelny*, and *Razyaryenny* – Type VII destroyers

Standard displacement: 1660 tons
Dimensions: 370¾ × 33½ × 12¼ft (112.6 × 10 × 4m)
Propulsion: Geared turbines; two shafts; 48,000bhp
Speed: 38 knots
Armament: Four 5.1in (13cm) guns (4 × 1)
   Two 3in (7.6cm) anti-aircraft guns (2 × 1)
   Four 37mm anti-aircraft guns and one 20mm anti-aircraft gun
   Six 21in (533mm) torpedo tubes (2 × 3)
   15 depth charges or 60 mines
Complement: 197

Note: The seakeeping qualities of this type left much to be desired. The *Razumny* and *Razyaryenny* together with the *Baku* reached Kola Inlet by the Northern Sea Route from Vladivostok on 14 October 1942.

USSRS *Uritzky* – There were five destroyers of this class known as Type V

Displacement: 1440 tons
Dimensions: 321½ × 30½ × 10½ft (98 × 10 × 3.2m)
Propulsion: Four Thornycroft boilers; Parsons turbines; two shafts; 32,000shp
Speed: 24 knots
Armament: Four 4in (10.2cm) guns (4 × 1)
   Two 45mm anti-aircraft guns (2 × 1)
   Two 37mm anti-aircraft guns (2 × 1)
   Three 13mm anti-aircraft guns (3 × 1)
   Nine machine guns
   Six 17.7in (450mm) TT
   60 mines
Complement: 160

USSRS *Kuibyshev – Karl Liebknecht* – There were four destroyers of this class known as Type IV

Displacement: 1260 tons
Dimensions: 321½ × 30¾ × 12¾ft (98 × 10 × 3.8m)
Propulsion: Four Norman boilers; turbines; two shafts; 31,500shp
Speed: 24 knots
Armament: Four 4.1in (10.2cm) guns (4 × 1)
   One 3in (76mm) anti-aircraft gun
   Two 45mm anti-aircraft guns (2 × 1)
   Two 37mm anti-aircraft guns (2 × 1)
   Three 13mm anti-aircraft guns (3 × 1)
   Nine machine guns
   Nine 17.7in (450mm) TT (3 × 3)
   70 mines, 15 depth charges
Complement: 168

Doblestny ex HMS *Roxborough* ex USS *Foote*
Dostoiny ex HMS *St Albans* ex USS *Thomas*
Dyerzki ex HMS *Chelsea* ex USS *Crowninshield*
Dyeyatelni ex HMS *Churchill* ex USS *Herndon*
Druzhny ex HMS *Lincoln* ex USS *Yarnall*
Zharki ex HMS *Brighton* ex USS *Cowell*
Zhguchi ex HMS *Leamington* ex USS *Twiggs*
Zhivuchi ex HMS *Richmond* ex USS *Fairfax*
Zhyostki ex HMS *Georgetown* ex USS *Maddox*

These nine 'Flush Deck' or 'Four Pipe' destroyers formed part of the 50 transferred from the United States Navy to the Royal Navy in 1940. They were transferred to the Soviet Navy in 1944.
Standard displacement: 1090 tons
Dimensions: 314⅓ × 30½ × 12ft (95.7 × 9.2 × 3.6m)
Propulsion: Geared turbines; two shafts; 25,200shp
Speed: 35 knots
Armament: Four 4in (10cm) guns (4 × 1)
   One 3in (76mm) anti-aircraft gun
   Six 21in (533mm) TT (3 × 2)
Complement: 153

Note: The armament of these ships was altered during the course of the war in various ways.

WHALERS

The undermentioned requisitioned whalers were transferred to the Soviet Navy's Northern Fleet in 1942 and used as minesweepers.

Name	Gross Tonnage
Shera	253
Shusa	251
Silja ·	251
Stefa	253
Sulla	251
Sumba	251
Svega	253 ·

DESTROYERS

Name	Class	Displacement Tons	SHP	Speed Knots	Guns						Torpedo Tubes	Hedgehog	Complement
					4.7in	4.0in	3.0in	2-pdr	40mm	20mm			
Ashanti													
Bedouin													
Eskimo													
Matabele	Tribal	1870	44,000	36	8	–	–	4	–	–	4 – 21in	–	190/219
Punjabi													
Somali													
Tartar													
Athabaskan													
Haida	RCN	1927											240
Huron													
Iroquois													
Worcester	Mod W	1120	27,000	34	4	–	–	2	–	–	6 – 21in	–	134
Woolston	W (T)	1120	30,000	35	–	4	–	2	–	4	–	–	125
Verdun	Escort	1090	27,000	34	–	4	–	2	–	4	–	–	125
Windsor	SR Escort	1100	27,000	35	3	–	–	2	–	4	3 – 21in	1	125
Keppel													
Broke	Shakespeare	1480	43,500	36½	2	–	1	–	–	4	6 – 21in	1	164
Amazon	Prototype	1352	39,500	37	4	–	–	2	–	–	6 – 21in	–	138
Campbell					3	1	–	–	–	4	6 – 21in	–	
Mackay					–	3	1	–	–	4	6 – 21in	–	
Douglas	Scott	1530	40,000	36	2	–	1	2	–	2	3 – 21in	1	164

DESTROYERS

Name	Class	Displacement Tons	SHP	Speed Knots	Guns 4.7in	4.0in	3.0in	2-pdr	40mm	20mm	Torpedo Tubes	Hedgehog	Complement
Malcolm	Scott	1530	40,000	36	2	1		2 6 pdr – 2		2	6 – 21in		
Montrose													
Westcott	LR Escort	1100											
Wrestler					–	2	1	2	–	2	–	1	
Venomous		1090	18,000	25	2	–	1	2	–	2/4	–	1	125
Volunteer													
Whitehall		1120											
Newmarket	Town												
Lancaster													
St Albans		1090	25,200	35	–	3	1	–	–	–	3 – 21in	1	146
Leamington													
Beverley													
Wells													
Achates	A	1350	34,000	35	4	–	–	2	–	–	8 – 21in	–	138
Beagle	B												
Boadicea		1360	34,000	35	4	–	–	2	–	–	8 – 21in	–	138
Bulldog													
Echo	E												
Eclipse		1375	36,000	35½	4	–	–	–	–	–	8 – 21 in	–	145
Escapade													

DESTROYERS

Name	Class	Displacement Tons	SHP	Speed Knots	Guns 4.7in	4.0in	3.0in	2-pdr	40mm	20mm	Torpedo Tubes	A/S	Complement
Fury													
Forester	F												
Foresight		1350	36,000	36	4	–	–	–	–	–	8 – 21in	–	145
Faulknor	(Leader)		38,000										
Garland	G	1335	34,000	35½	4	–	–	–	–	–	8 – 21in	–	145
Inglefield	(Leader)	1530	38,000	36	5	–	–	–	–	–	10 – 21in	–	175
Icarus													
Impulsive	I	1370	34,000	36	4	–	–	–	–	–	10 – 21in	–	145
Intrepid													
Javelin	J	1690	40,000	36	6	–	–	4	–	–	10 – 21in	–	183
Lookout	L	1920											
Milne	(Leader)	1935											
Maharatta													
Marne													
Matchless			48,000	36	6 DP	–	–	4	–	–	8 – 21in	–	221
Meteor	M	1920											
Musketeer													
Myrmidon													
Martin													
Onslow	(Leader)	1550	40,000	36¾	4	–	–	4	–	8	8 – 21 in	–	217

Name	Class	Displacement Tons	SHP	Speed Knots	Guns 4.7in	4.0in	3.0in	2-pdr	40mm	20mm	Torpedo Tubes	A/S	Complement
DESTROYERS													
Obdurate		1550											217
Obedient	O												
Offa													
Onslaught		1540	40,000	36¾	4	–	–	4	–	8	8 – 21 in		175
Opportune													
Oribi													
Orwell													
Nerissa	N	1690	40,000	36	6	–	–	4	–	2	10 – 21in	–	183
Quadrant	Q	1705											
Queenborough			40,000	36¾	4	–	–	4	–	8	8 – 21in	–	175
Raider	R												
Saumarez	(Leader)	1730											225
Savage													
Scorpion					4	–	–	–	2 or	8 / 12			
Scourge	S	1710	40,000	36¾							8 – 21in	–	180
Serapis													
Stord	(RNorN)												
Hardy	(Leader)	1730											225
Vebus													
Vigilant	V	1710	40,000	36¾	4	–	–	–	2 or	8 / 12	8 – 21in	–	180
Virago													

DESTROYERS

Name	Class	Displacement Tons	SHP	Speed Knots	Guns 4.7in	4.0in	3.0in	2-pdr	40mm	20mm	Torpedo Tubes	A/S	Complement
Sioux	V(RCN)	1710	40,000	36¾	4	–	–	–	2 or	8 / 12	8 – 12in	–	180
Myngs	(Leader)	1730											222
Zambesi													
Zealous	Z	1710	40,000	36¾	4 (4.5in DP)	–	–	–	2 or 4 or 6	8 / 4 / –	8 – 21in	–	186
Zebra													
Zest													
Cassandra													
Cavalier	C	1710	40,000	36¾	4 (4.5in DP)	–	–	–	4	–	8 – 21in	–	186
Meynell													
Pytchley	Hunt	907			–	4	–	5	–	2	–	–	
Badsworth													
Blankney													
Bramham													
Cowdray													
Grove													
Lamerton	Hunt	1050	19,000	26	–	4	–	4	–	2	–	–	146
Ledbury													
Middleton													
Oakley													
Wheatland													
Wilton													

DESTROYERS

Name	Class	Displacement Tons	SHP	Speed Knots	Guns 4.7in	4.0in	3.0in	2-pdr	40mm	20mm	Torpedo Tubes	A/S	Complement
Inconstant (ex Turkish)		1360	34,000	35½	4	–	–	–	–	–	8 – 21in	–	145
Emmons	USS	1700							4	4	5 – 21in		210
Mayrant	USS ⎫												
Rhind	USS	1500	42,800	36½	4 (5.0in)				4	8	8 – 21in		200
Rowan	USS ⎭												
Wainwright	USS	1570	50,000	37	4 (5.0in)	–	–	–	–	–	8 – 21in		

FRIGATES

Name	Class	Displacement Tons	Propulsion SHP	Speed Knots	Guns 4.0in	3.0in	40mm	20mm	A/S	Complement
Monnow	RCN ⎫									
Nene	RCN	1370	5500	20	2	–	10	20	1H	140
Matane	RCN									
St Pierre	RCN ⎭									

FRIGATES

Name	Class	Displacement Tons	Propulsion SHP	Speed Knots	Guns				A/S	Complement
					4.0in	3.0in	40mm	20mm		
Loch Dunvegan ⎫ Loch Alvie ⎭	Loch	1435	4 cyl recip 5500	20	1	4 2 pdr		6	2 SQ	114
Bazely Drury Goodall Maunsey Pasley	Captain ex US DE	1085	Diesel/Electric 6000	20	–	3	2	10	–	200
Bentinck		1300	Turbo Electric 12,000	26	–	3	2 or	8 10	–	200
Byard	Captain ex US DE									

CORVETTES

Name	Class	Displacement Tons	Propulsion HP	Speed Knots	Guns			A/S	Complement
					4.0in	2-pdr	20mm		
Acanthus Bergamot Bluebell Bryony Camelia Campanula Dianella Eglantire Heather	Flower	925	4 cyl recip 2750	16	1	1 2pdr or 4 MG		–	85

Name	Class	Displacement Tons	Propulsion HP	Speed Knots	Guns 4.0in	2-pdr	20mm	A/S	Complement
CORVETTES									
Honeysuckle									
Lotus									
Oxlip									
Poppy									
Rhododendron	Flower	925	4 cyl recip 2750	16	1	1 2pdr or 4 MG		–	85
Saxifrage									
Starwort									
Sundew									
Sweetbriar									
Snowflake									
La Malouine	FFS								
Alnwick Castle	Castle	1010	4 cyl recip 2880	16½	1	–	10	1SQ	120
Bamborough Castle									
Denbigh Castle									

173

Name	No	Displacement Tons Surface/Submerged	Propulsion	Speed	Armament Guns	Torpedo Tubes	Complement
SUBMARINES							
Unison	P43	} 545/740	Diesel/Electric 615/825	11¼/9	1 – 3in	4 21in (bow)	31
Unrivalled	P45						
Unshaken	P54						
Sahib	P21	} 715/990	Diesel/Electric 1900/1300	14¾/9	1 – 3in	7 – 21in (6 bow, 1 stern)	44
Shakespeare	P221						
Jastrzab (Polish)	P551	854/1062	Diesel/Electric 1200/1500	14/11	1 – 4in	4 – 21in (bow)	42
—	P614	} 683/856	Diesel/Electric 1550/1300	13¾/10	1 – 3in	5 – 21in (4 bow, 1 stern)	–
—	P615						
Seadog	P216	} 715/990	Diesel/Electric 1900/1300	14¾/9	1 – 3in	7 – 21in (6 bow, 1 stern)	44
Sea Nymph	P223						
Seawolf	N47	} 670/960	Diesel/Electric 1550	15/10	1 – 3in	6 – 21in (bow)	38
Sealion	N72						
Sturgeon	N73	640/927	Diesel/Electric 1550	15/10	1 – 3in	6 – 21in (bow)	38
Taurus	P339	} 1090/1575	Diesel/Electric 2500/1450	15/9	1 – 4in 1 – 20mm	11 – 21in (8 bow, 3 stern)	65
Trespasser	P312						
Tigris	N63	} 1090/1575	Diesel/Electric 2500/1450	15¼/9	1 – 4in	10 – 21in (8 bow, 2 stern)	59
Torbay	N79						
Tribune	N76						
Trident	N52						
Tuna	N94						

SUBMARINES

Name	No	Displacement Tons Surface/Submerged	Propulsion	Speed	Armament Guns	Torpedo Tubes	Complement
Ursula	N59	540/730	Diesel/Electric 615/825	11¾/9	1 – 3in	6 – 21in (bow)	27
Unique	N95						
Unruly	P49	545/740	Diesel Electric 615/825	11¼/9	1 – 3in	4 – 21in (bow)	31
Junon	FFS	597/825	Diesel/Electric 1800/1000	14/9	1 – 3in	7 – 21.7in 2 – 15.7in	–
Minerve	FFS						
Rubis		669/925	Diesel/Electric 1300/1000	12/9	1 – 3in	5 – 21.7in	32 mines
0.14	R Neth N	546/704	Diesel/Electric 1800/600	15/8	2 – 40mm	5 – 21in (4 bow, 1 stern)	38
Unredd RNorN	P41	545/740	Diesel/Electric 615/825	11¼/9	1 – 3in	4 – 21in (bow)	31
Graph ex U 570	N46	769/871	Diesel/Electric 2800/750	17/7½	1 – 3.5in 1 – 37mm 2 – 20mm	5 – 21in (4 bow, 1 stern)	44

SLOOPS

Name	Class	Displacement Tons	Propulsion HP	Speed Knots	Guns				A/S	Complement
					4.0in	3.0in	2 pdr	20mm		
Cygnet	Modified Black Swan	1350	Geared turbines 4300	20	6 A/A	–	–	12	–	192
Kite										
Lapwing										
Lark										

Name	Class	Displacement Tons	Propulsion HP	Speed Knots	Guns 4.0in	3.0in	2 pdr	20mm	A/S	Complement
SLOOPS										
Mermaid *Peacock*	Modified Black Swan	1350	Geared turbines 4300	20	6 A/A	–	–	12	–	192
MINESWEEPERS										
Halcyon *Harrier* *Hussar* *Speedwell* *Niger* *Salamander*		815	Reciprocating 1770	16½	1 A/A	–	–	–	–	
Gleaner *Hazard* *Hebe* *Sharpshooter* *Gossamer* *Jason* *Leda* *Seagull*	Halcyon	835	Reciprocating 2000	17	2 A/A	–	–	–	–	80
Bramble *Britomart* *Speedy*		875	Geared turbines 1750	17	2 A/A	–	–	–	–	

Name	Tons	Remarks
TRAWLERS		
Ayrshire	540	Requisitioned trawlers, armed with a single 4in gun when employed on A/S duties and with a single 12-pounder gun on minesweeping duty. Originally supplied with Lewis guns as A/A armament but these were gradually replaced by 20mm Oerlikon guns. All ships were fitted with Scotch boilers and reciprocating engines.
Blackfly	482	
Cape Argona	494	
Cape Mariato	497	
Daneman	516	
Lady Madeleine	464	
Lord Austin	473	
Lord Middleton	464	
Northern Gem	655	
Northern Pride	655	
Northern Spray	655	
Northern Wave	655	
Paynter	472	
Retriever	869	
St Elstan	564	
St Kenan	565	
Vizalma	608	

Appendix VII
DETAILS OF GERMAN WARSHIPS OPERATING
AGAINST THE ARCTIC CONVOYS

Tirpitz – battleship

Standard displacement: 42,900 tons
Dimensions: 792 × 118 × 26ft (241 × 36 × 8m)
Propulsion: Geared turbines; three shafts; 138,000shp
Speed: 30 knots
Armament: Eight 15in (38cm) guns (4 × 2)
   12 5.9in (15cm) DP guns (6 × 2)
   16 4.1in (10.4cm) anti-aircraft guns (8 × 2)
   16 37mm anti-aircraft guns (8 × 2) .
   16 increased to 58 20mm anti-aircraft guns
   Eight 21in (533mm) torpedo tubes (2 × 4)
   Six Arado aircraft
Protection: Main belt: 12.6in (32cm)
   Turrets: 14in (35.5cm)
   Deck: 8in (20.3cm)
Complement: 2400

Scharnhorst – battle-cruiser

Standard displacement: 32,000 tons
Dimensions: 741½ × 98½ × 24½ft (226 × 30 × 7.5m)
Propulsion: Geared turbines; three shafts; 160,000shp
Speed: 31½ knots
Armament: Nine 11in (28cm) guns
   12 5.9 (15cm) DP guns (6 × 2)
   14 4.1in (10.4cm) anti-aircraft guns (7 × 2)
   16 37mm anti-aircraft guns (8 × 2)
   10 increased to 20mm anti-aircraft guns
   Six 21in (533mm) torpedo tubes
   Four aircraft
Protection: Main belt: 12 to 13in (30.5 to 33cm)
   Turrets: 12in (30.5cm)
   Deck: 6in (15.2cm)
Complement: 1800

Admiral Scheer, Lützow – pocket battleships (*Panzerschiffe*)

Standard displacement: 12,100 tons
Dimensions: 609 × 70 × 21½ft (185.6 × 23 × 6.5m)
Propulsion: Diesel engines; two shafts; 56,000shp
Speed: 26 knots
Armament: Six 11in (28cm) guns (2 × 3)
 Eight 5.9in (15cm) guns (8 × 1)
 Six 4.1in (10.4cm) anti-aircraft guns
 Eight 37mm anti-aircraft guns
 10 increased to 28 20mm anti-aircraft guns (14 × 2)
 Eight 21in (533mm) torpedo tubes (2 × 4)
 Two aircraft
Protection: Sides: 4in (10cm)
 Turrets: 2 to 5½in (5 to 13cm)
 Deck: 1½ to 3 in (3.7 to 7.6cm)
 Conning tower: 2 to 5in (5 to 12.7cm)
Complement: 1150

Admiral Hipper – heavy cruiser

Standard displacement: 13,900 tons
Dimensions: 640 × 70 × 15ft (195 × 21 × 4.6m)
Propulsion: Geared turbines; three shafts; 132,000shp
Speed: 32 knots
Armament: Eight 8in (20cm) guns (4 × 2)
 12 4.1in (10.4cm) anti-aircraft guns (6 × 2)
 12 37mm anti-aircraft guns (6 × 2)
 Eight increased to 28 20mm anti-aircraft guns (14 × 2)
 12 21in (533mm) torpedo tubes (4 × 3)
 Three aircraft
Protection: Sides: 5in (12.7cm)
 Deck: 4in (10cm)
 Turrets: 5in (12.7cm)
Complement: 1600

Note: The *Prinz Eugen* was a sister ship of the *Hipper* but took no part in operations against the Arctic Convoys after being torpedoed by HMS *Trident* whilst on passage to Trondheim.

Friedrich Eckholdt, Friedrich Ihn, Hans Lody, Herman Schoemann, Paul Jacobi, Richard Beitzen, Theodor Riedel – destroyers of the 'Leberecht Mass' class

---

Standard displacement: 2200 tons
Dimensions: 374 × 37 × 9½ft (114 × 11 × 3m)
Propulsion: Geared turbines; two shafts; 70,000shp
Speed: 30 knots
Armament: Five 5in (12.7cm) DP guns (5 × 1)
   Four 37mm anti-aircraft guns (2 × 2)
   Six increased to eight 20mm anti-aircraft guns
   Eight 21in (533mm) torpedo tubes (2 × 4)
   60 mines (optional)
Complement: 315

Karl Galster – destroyer of the 'Von Roeder' class

Standard displacement: 2400 tons
Dimensions: 384 × 38½ × 9½ft (117 × 11.5 × 3m)
Propulsion: Geared turbines; two shafts; 70,000shp
Speed: 38 knots
Armament: Five 5in (12.7 cm) DP guns (5 × 1)
   Six 37mm anti-aircraft guns (2 × 2 and 2 × 1)
   Twelve 20mm anti-aircraft guns (5 × 2 and 2 × 1)
   Eight 21in (533mm) torpedo tubes (2 × 4)
   60 mines (optional)
Complement: 313

Z24 to 31 – destroyers

Standard displacement: 2600 tons
Dimensions: 390 × 40 × 10ft (119 × 12 × 3m)
Propulsion: Geared turbines; two shafts; 70,000shp
Speed: 38½ knots
Armament: Four 5.9in (15cm) DP guns
   Four 37mm anti-aircraft guns (2 × 2)
   14 20mm anti-aircraft guns (6 × 2 and 2 × 1)
   Eight 21in (533mm) torpedo tubes (2 × 4)
Complement: 321

T1 to 12 – torpedo boats

Standard displacement:
   T1 to 8: 844 tons
   T9 to 12: 839 tons
Propulsion: Geared turbines; two shafts; 31,000shp
Speed: 35½ knots
Armament: One 4.1in (10.4cm) anti-aircraft gun
   Eight 20mm anti-aircraft guns (4 × 2)
   Six 21in (533mm) torpedo tubes
   30 mines (optional)
Complement: 119

Note: In some ships the armament was modified to include one 37mm anti-aircraft gun in lieu of one 20mm anti-aircraft gun.

U-BOATS

The Germans employed some 20 different types of U-boats during the war, but those allocated to operations against the Arctic convoys were mainly Type VII of which there were seven variants. Type VIIA had a displacement of 626/745 tons and speeds of 16/8 knots while Type VIIF displaced 1084/1181 tons with speeds of 17/8 knots. The normal complement of torpedoes was 11 in the smaller craft and 14 in the larger ones.

Appendix VIII
GERMAN AIR FORCES EMPLOYED IN OPERATIONS AGAINST
THE ARCTIC CONVOYS

It was not until March 1942 after representations by Admiral Raeder that *Reichsmarschall* Göring ordered the Luftwaffe units stationed in northern Norway to co-operate with the Navy in attacks against the Arctic convoys. At the time these amounted to 120 aircraft comprising 60 Ju 88 long range bombers, 30 Ju 87 dive-bombers, and 30 fighters. The Navy also had 15 He 115 torpedo-armed floatplanes.

The increased defensive armament of the merchant ships caused the Luftwaffe to look more favourably on the torpedo as opposed to the bomb and on 1 May 1942 the first 12 crews trained in torpedo attack arrived at Bardufoss airfield. A month later the Luftwaffe reached its peak strength of 264 aircraft in this area. As a result of the Allied landings in North Africa in November 1942 most of the Luftwaffe units were withdrawn leaving only a long range reconnaissance force to locate the convoys in co-operation with the U-boats, and a few dive bombers together with the naval floatplanes.

Appendix IX
ORDERS FOR OPERATION RÖSSELSPRUNG

1 Task – Attack on Convoy PQ 17

2 Task Forces
Trondheim Group
Tirpitz with the Fleet Commander onboard. *Hipper*, six destroyers (*Ihn*, *Lody*, *Galster*, *Riedel*, *Eckholdt*, and *Steinbrink*).
Narvik Group
Lützow, six destroyers (*Z 24, Z 27, Z 28, Z 29, Z 30*, and *Beitzen*).
Submarines
Three submarines will be stationed north-east of Iceland beginning 10 June. They have the task of locating the convoy. Other available submarines, probably three or four, will be in attack positions between Jan Mayen and Bear Island. Submarines becoming available at a later date will be stationed off Bear Island in attack position.

Note: There are at this time only two destroyers in Trondheim (*Ihn* and *Lody*). The other four destroyers will be transferred from Germany to Norway within the next few days. Besides these, there are two or three torpedo-boats in Trondheim, which are to serve as escorts to the Trondheim Group.

3 Command
Operational command for the entire mission: Group North with Headquarters at Kiel.
Tactical Command
Trondheim Group and all other forces: Fleet Commander onboard *Tirpitz*
Narvik Group Admiral Commanding Cruisers onboard *Lützow*. The submarines will be under the command of Group North through Admiral, Arctic Ocean at Narvik by means of radio relaying station. It is not intended to place submarines directly under the command of the Fleet Commander.

4 Execution
As soon as Convoy PQ 17 has been located, the task forces will take their stations. This is to be done as late as possible. The Trondheim Group will proceed to the northern exit of Alta Fiord. There they will refuel. They will depart for the operation on receipt of the code word from Group North. The Fleet Commander will head for the convoy at full speed. The Admiral commanding cruisers is to join forces with the Fleet Commander.

Main Task

Rapid destruction of enemy merchant ships. If necessary these should only be crippled and the sinking left to the submarines and Air Force. The escort forces should be engaged only if this is indispensable for accomplishing the main task. In such an event it is primarily the task of the *Tirpitz* and *Hipper* to fight the escort forces, while the *Lützow* and *Scheer* dispose of the convoy during that time.

An engagement with superior enemy forces is to be avoided. The operation itself should be executed quickly; and should be completed before an enemy security unit composed of battleships and carriers – presumably stationed in the Faroes-Iceland area – has a chance to intervene. The operation can be cancelled by the Fleet Commander or by the order of Group North.

5 Aerial Reconnaissance

Extensive aerial reconnaissance is a prerequisite for the execution of the operation and especially for the participation of the *Tirpitz* and *Hipper*. The Air Force has the following assignment:

(a) An attempt should be made to locate a heavy naval force in the Shetland-Faroes-Iceland-Jan Mayen area, scouting Reykjavik, Scapa, Firth of Forth, and Moray Firth in the process. Once the enemy has been located, continuous contact should be maintained.

(b) After the convoy has been located, continuous contact should be maintained. The composition of the convoy and the strength of the escort forces should be reported as quickly as possible.

(c) As long as the heavy enemy force has not been located, the area within a 250-mile radius of the convoy is to be carefully patrolled and all enemy forces sighted are to be reported.

6 Battle operations of the Air Force

The Air Force has been requested to order aircraft to attack only aircraft carriers and merchant ships once our forces have engaged the enemy, unless the identity of the ships is unmistakable, or Group North has issued special orders.

Remarks

(1) This once we shall probably have 12 destroyers available for the operation.

(2) The fuel situation permits an operation of this scope at this time.

(3)   The weather is especially favourable in June.The period of the spring storms is over. Heavy summer fogs do not occur until July.

(4)   The ice situation likewise is especially favourable in June. The ice has receded very little to the north, so that it will be impossible for a convoy to evade us to the north. As a matter of fact, beginning about 150 nautical miles west of Bear Island, the enemy convoy has to sail east within 200 to 250 nautical miles off the Norwegian coast. This area is completely dominated by our Air Forces. Therefore no heavy enemy vessels have sailed into this area so far.

(5)   The operation will be executed only if reconnaissance has established with certainty that there is no risk of becoming involved with superior enemy forces.

(6)   It is particularly important that the Air Force fulfil the request of the Navy in regard to aerial reconnaissance, if necessary at the expense of participating in battle. The Navy's request would appear to be justified in view of the total success it seems possible to achieve with the aid of our heavy naval forces.

Appendix X

DELIVERIES OF WAR MATERIAL BY THE UNITED STATES TO
THE USSR VIA PERSIA, PACIFIC, AND ARCTIC BETWEEN 22
JUNE 1941 AND 20 SEPTEMBER 1945

Year	Persian Gulf Tons	%	Pacific Tons	%	Arctic Tons	Total %	Tons
1941[1]	13,502	3.7	193,299	53.6	153,977	42.7	360,778
1942	705,259	29.5	734,020	30.7	949,711	39.7	2388,990
1943	1606,979	34.4	2388,579	51.1	681,043	14.6	4676,601
1944	1788,864	29.4	2848,181	46.8	1452,775	23.8	6089,820
1945[2]	44,513	1.5	2079,320	73.0	726,725	25.5	2850,558
Totals	4159,117	25.5	8243,399	50.3	3964,231	24.2	16366,747

[1] June to September   [2] January to September

(Source: Wolfgang Schlauch, *Rüstungshilfe der USA an die Verbündeten im Zweiten Weltkrieg*)

Appendix XI

DELIVERIES OF WAR MATERIAL BY GREAT BRITAIN TO THE USSR VIA THE ARCTIC ROUTE BETWEEN 10 OCTOBER 1941 AND 31 MARCH 1946

By Britain

3830 tanks + 1388 from Canada

7411 aircraft (of which 3129 from the USA)

4932 anti-tank guns

4005 rifles and machine guns

1805 sets of radar equipment

4338 sets of radio equipment

2000 telephone sets

743 million projectiles

9 motor torpedo boats

4 submarines

14 minesweepers

In addition raw materials, foodstuffs, machinery, industrial plant, medical supplies, and hospital equipment to the value of £120 million.

(Source: Statement by the Prime Minister in the House of Commons 16th April 1946 and *3rd Report on Mutual Aid.*)

Note: According to Soviet sources Canada delivered some 710,000 tons of weapons, war materials, and foodstuffs to the Soviet Union.

Index